Born Pissed

-Essays and other ramblings
by Thomas Waters

AmErica House
Baltimore

First printing

ISBN: 1-58851-964-3
PUBLISHED BY AMERICA HOUSE BOOK PUBLISHERS
www.publishamerica.com
Baltimore

Printed in the United States of America

Table Of Contents

Barbs and Bad Jokes

Projects, Collaborations, and other miscellany

1. Disembodied Anecdotal Tiddlywinks (1/13/98)
2. Relentless Logic (revised, 11/18/99)
3. Ars Longas, Vita Brevis (Art is Long, Life Is Short) (6/23/00)
4. The Sting Of Local Satire (with Ken Barnes)
5. Appendixitis (12/21/00)
6. The Stigmata of Exorcist 3 (12/30/00)

Poems

1. Gem (11/4/97)
2. Burst (11/10/97)
3. gray (2/12/98)
4. paper swans (11/9/98)
5. wind-fall (12/1/98)
6. activity (10/19/99)
7. Kismet (11/7/99)
8. blonde obsession (11/26/99)
9. trinket (12/17/99)
10. critical (1/14/00)
11. miracle girl (8/2/00)
12. reverie (8/7/00)
13. a hidden smile (8/17/00)
14. Marzipan (9/3/77)
15. Erosion (9/8/00)
16. linoleum lust (10/10/00)
17. Queen City Checkers (10/19/00)
18. Valerie (11/26/00)
19. tell me (2/28/01)

Santa Relief

I don't operate in metaphors very often, but here's a pretty astute one for my family's Christmas progression through the years: the candy house. We have this sort of glucose diorama that's been with the family for eons. The entire scene is made of sugar, or at least I hope it is, but we'll get to that later. It's a cute little white house, with flowers for gutters and a perky little red sleigh on the top with an adorable white picket fence around the lot. Three generations of brothers (who had no appreciation of artistic beauty in their youth) have chipped away and made a slow snack out of this decoration. Each year a few more flowers would mysteriously disappear. Every time Christmas rolled around it looked like the owners of the house were more than due to call a saccharine roofing company to have their candy house reshingled. I realize now (as do my brothers, I'm sure) that treating a twenty year old semi-heirloom like an hors d'oeuvres is not the wisest (or healthiest) thing under the sun to be doing. We're probably all incredibly lucky not to have come down with food poisoning or toxic shock or hair balls.

Like I said, I don't do metaphors often as they tend to give off the impression of being smug, but this one is accurate. Our Christmas', although our family is still intact, have slowly eroded in intensity and presentation. Like that sugarcane cottage, a little bit more has been chipped away with age, and it doesn't quite sparkle like it used to. This can be partially attributed to two of the perpetrators. My big brother and I are both work whores (punching in enough overtime to make Chris Cringle look like a temp.), me actually more than him. He still puts a bit of priority on holidays and spending time with the folks, but I don't mind working. Selling my soul to retail almost a decade ago, I came to understand that if you don't work like a mule during peak season, your employers don't have much use for you. That, and it's exciting and fun and exhilarating to work in retail during Christmas. People pouring into a store like rats out of a sinking ship, buying in bulk, melting their credit cards from the sheer volume of purchases; there's a certain seize the day quality to it all, don't you think? And every once in a great while, I'll help out one genuinely pleasant, charitable person with good manners who makes the remainder of the job all worth it. The rest of the time, working during Christmas, scoping out hot broads suffices. 'Tis the season!

Our decorations leave something to be desired. I don't feel one-upped or anything when I pass the testaments to GE outside some people's abodes, it's just a statement of fact. We get our tree about fifteen minutes before Christmas day, and then we throw tinsel around it sometime before January. There's a poinsettia on the table right now, but other than that, if it weren't for the snow, it could be any other given holiday. Even a worthless one, like Canada's Boxing Day, whatever that is. We don't have any bona fide depressing reasons for not putting up spangles and bangles and dangling yule tide mobiles, we're just lazy. To coin another metaphor, imagine how rambunctious Barbara Walters is when she's shooting for her 50,000th special interview on tv. She knows the routine, she's done it one or two times before, so the energy level isn't going to be quite at the maximum capacity it used to be.

Part of it has to do with just getting older (a good random excuse as of late in my essays). When there's a kid in the house, every little event is exciting to the point of heart murmurs, up to and including the holidays. And that kind of excitement is electric, it rockets through the whole family. I've seen it happen before, even read about group electrocutions caused by adolescent static electricity. Well, nobody in our family is pre-puberty, and we all know that Santa Claus doesn't exist (or if he does, he's hiding out due to tax evasion). The only fat and jolly participants of the holiday are three quarters of the family (present party grudgingly included), and we're not too jolly all year round. To make a confession, during the rest of the year, I enjoy drop kicking children when no one's looking and then squealing in delight. Come to think of it, maybe Santa does exist, and he's just never dropped anything off at our house since I'm such a miserable bastard. Anything's possible.

The general routine at the house is that we all get together on Christmas Eve, drool expectantly on the bounty of gifts (none of the Water's siblings have the patience to wait until the morning), open gifts, snap pictures, round up all of the wrapping debris into a garbage bag, and then split off to play with our toys. To my knowledge, everything I've asked for the last, oh, let's say, ten years, has required at least one electrical outlet. Games, stereos, VCR's, you name it, and it's plugged into my hydroelectric generator in the basement. After we've cooed over our presents sufficiently, we all meet back up at the dinner table where my dad takes a montage of pictures around food. I think he missed his calling as a professional photographer for Martha Stewart or Wolfgang Puck. Rarely does the family schedule deviate from this.

Let's level with each other, too, shall we? No one likes a Christmas church service, whether you're Catholic, Protestant, Baptist, Jehovah's Witness, or any other militant fringe group of faith. No matter how exciting they try to gear the spectacular religious bonanza, the general pulse in the audience is akin to a transcendental mountain monk. Everyone's checking their watch so they can get home and eat, sleep, whatever (more so than during usual church services), and most fanfare (although I've never gone to a service in Taiwan) is missing a fireworks display, so why bother? If some higher being wanted to give mankind a gift for Christmas, he could free the priest of a boring-ass monotone for once.

Now if I was a snowballing liberal, I'd go off on a tangent about how none of us have the right to enjoy the holidays because of all the crime and poverty and injustice in the world, but I'm not. I know that this occasion is about charity, but let me ask you this: why would you send canned goods to a starving country that doesn't celebrate Christmas? Maybe that came out the wrong way. All these donated toys and canned goods and crap are fantastic for needy families, but why use Christmas as a platform for a culture that doesn't even celebrate Christmas? Maybe that makes more sense, but probably not. Most non-profit organizations make a pretty damned good profit off of the charitable spirit of people (PBS has been in the black for over five years now, despite their whining and begging and tearing of clothes during pledge weeks), and even though it's no reason not to give, it makes me weary. On the same train of thought, I also wonder if there's such a thing as genuine Charity anymore. Most of the time it's a degree of bravado that's very conspicuous and faux-humble, ala' Ted Turner (but not on quite the same scale). True, get-out-of-purgatory-free charity is supposed to be performed privately, for the good of the community. Not so your friends or your conscience or your tax consultant will give you a pat on the back to make you feel good about yourself. What's that under my feet, you say? A soapbox? Well dammit, I don't know how it got there, and I'm too old and set in my ways to change now, so live with it. Oh, and I almost forgot! Bah humbug.

If you give a moose a muffin, then maybe you
should grab some lax-caps while you're still
in the store,
Tom "egg-noggin" Waters

Eulogy

My grandfather, Francis Cable, passed away today at 5:00 A.M. He turned 84 this December, and was supposed to be recovering from a fall he took about a month back until the doctors discovered that he had some sort of degenerative muscle disease. I loved the man dearly, and no one will ever replace him in my heart. If I'm lucky, I'll live long enough to make him proud and be half the man that he was. He was a faithful husband, a patient , loving father, a generous, benevolent grandfather, and a caring friend to everyone in Andover, NY. Not one day went by while visiting him that a person passing by on the street wouldn't say hello and crack a smile when they spotted 'Fran'. Close friends of his quipped that he was a saint, half-jokingly, half-sincerely. Well, I can tell you this with all conviction: he was the closest thing to a saint that anyone could ever have the pleasure and the privilege of having known.

If I could describe his character to someone who never knew him, Jimmy Stewart's character George Bailey in *It's A Wonderful Life* immediately comes to mind. A wholesome, decent man who always had a kind word for anyone. Another similarity to the movie is that he saved two drowning boys during the winter when he was in his twenties. Saw them going under the ice coming home from a night out and dove in to rescue them. He got a letter from Ronald Reagan commending him on his bravery, but I don't think that that kind of heroism can be properly rewarded. Over the last decade, he's faithfully gone around town to visit and look after his old friends who were alone and couldn't quite get around as well as they used to, bringing them the brief pleasure of his company, a daily newspaper, and winding their clocks. He went to see his wife every single day in a nursing home for three years when she was wasting away with Alzheimer's. I can't even fathom how much it must've torn him apart inside to see the love of his life disappear a little more each day, and he went to see her daily anyway, without fail.

He and my mom would write back and forth and talk on the phone every week. He 'helped out' with finances, even when we didn't need it, more than I'll ever know. He never held grudges with family to my knowledge, and if he had a bee in his bonnet, he'd say so. If you disagreed, or resisted, he'd just let it pass. When I was 17 and ran away from home to live with a girlfriend, he wrote and talked to me even when I wasn't speaking to my parents. Sent checks to cover rent when we were short, asking for nothing in return. Fran cared after his daughter (my aunt) for her entire life up to this point, even when he could hardly lift a finger to help himself. She has some sort of illness, most likely schizophrenia, and he just assumed responsibility, 'cause that's what people did from his day and age. Waited on her hand and foot, without cease, for almost fifty years. If I or my brothers came to visit, he always welcomed us with open arms, racing around to prepare a special meal or taking time out from his routines to sit down and get reacquainted.

He made us all feel like the center of the universe when we were children, keeping a trunk full of toys for when we were in the neighborhood. It makes me smile to think of all the afternoons spent during holiday vacations making building block houses and watching television with the sound blaring while he dozed on the couch. He called it 'resting his eyes'. One year, I played with the thermostat before we all went out to dinner. By the time we got back, the heat was up to about 90 degrees, and this was in the summer, so we had to wait outside until it was below sweltering in the house.

And maybe you think that I'm canonizing my grandfather when I say that he had a way with pets, but it's true. Any animal was instantly meek when he was around, no matter what their disposition was. It's almost as if they could recognize on some level that he was a pure and kind man. Through the years, three different cats from other families in the neighborhood would get gold-carpet treatment at the Cable residence. One cat (Ozzie was his name I think) spent more time at that house than the family that owned him. A man-eating tiger probably would have rolled over to get his belly scratched if he was next to my grandfather.

Good weather seemed to follow him wherever he went. I'm reminded of a famous Irish proverb: "May the sun always shine upon you, and may the wind always be at your back". Nine times out of ten when there was a family meal outdoors, the sun would smile on the get-together. He prayed for a lot of things, and he'd always say a prayer before a day together at our summer-home for the weather.

A devout Catholic, Fran went to church every day, right 'til the end. He'd say the rosary, three times a day, like clockwork. He had a degree of belief and faith that I've never seen in anyone, from any denomination. Please don't take this lightly when I say that he *had* faith. I never saw the man go through a period of doubt, or disbelief; he firmly believed in his religion, praying for every close friend and relative diligently.

A second generation Irishman, he grew up next to poverty. He told me a story once about how happy he was to get an orange for Christmas, and how great home-made root beer tasted. During the Depression, he took odd jobs and chauffeured for a short while. Later, he joined the Service to fight in World War II. As far as I know, he always took an interest in American history, even before he enlisted. He was a lexicon of Civil War information, and could name any battle, location, and the generals involved. My uncle Mike tells me that I get my gift for writing and my proclivities for humor from him, and that his letters home during the war were very funny. I believe that.

Fran had a great sense of humor. We called him "The Cruncher" when we were kids because he had these big, slender, Bela Lugosi-type hands that he would pretend to strangle you with, tickling the heck out of you more than anything. In letters and birthday cards, he'd draw cartoons just for me, doodling Mortimer Snerd from the Edgar Bergen days for a brief delight. It must've been ironically amusing to him when he saw me butcher the heydays of ventriloquism giving one man shows with Charlie McCarthy in the fifth grade. There was an ongoing joke in the family with the butter dish during meals. He'd offer it to you with a hand under the dish and then pull a quick rope-a-dope maneuver so that you ended up with a hand in the butter. He's gotten everyone in the family with this trick.

Over the last 20 years he was in and out of the hospital for heart troubles. Around 1980 he had a triple bypass. I don't think any of this can be explained away as an organ difficulty or a mere malfunction of the body, though. My grandfather had a kind, sensitive heart, and he gave love unselfishly to anyone willing to accept it. It's so easy even at my age to be hardened and embittered by the world and it's inhabitants, to get trapped by our motives and perceived limitations, and he never gave in in this sense. That alone is hope enough for anyone. The one million kindnesses he left us with are almost enough to ease the hurting inside from his departure. God bless you, Grandpa, and don't slip any butter under the thumb of St. Peter while you're up there, either.

Fetal Spray Fad

It's been said (by me, and frequently, at that) that you have to be a bit of a masochist to work in retail. On that same train of thought (a few cars down), you pretty much have to have a death wish to seek seasonal employment in retail. You're never guaranteed a job after the holidays, most of the permanent co-workers despise you for the first, oh, month or so (because they assume that you're just as cranially deficient as the other gimps they drag off the street to fill the store for quick help), the influx of customers is comparable to a tsunami ridden by Rupaul, and by the time you know what you're doing, it's January, and you're staring at the exit door while a foot is being planted into your back, a couple bucks richer. Well brother, I am that masochist. For all the miscellaneous head and heartaches,

I've taken a shine to fourth quarter temp work. I may be sick (well, I know I'm sick), but there's a lot of fun and excitement and a very 'seize the day' thrill to a three month job. Now that it's coming to a close, I thought I'd look back and reflect on the good times, the bad times, and, well, the rest of it.

Rather than sit back and enjoy the managerial promotion at my other job, I threw caution, reason, and whatever leftover energy I may have had to the wind and went back to the superstore that I worked at last Christmas. As always, for legal reasons, I won't give you the name of the company, but it kind of rhymes with 'fetal spray' and they cater to all forms of media, be it music, books, movies, or computer software. After having a psychotic break the previous year from operating the microfiche in the book department, I shot for the movie department and got it (figuring that it was one of the last unchartered frontiers of retail for our narrator). Luckily, and rather to my delight, the video department is one of the least busy sections of the store, and I had a history with the manager from a previous job, so butt-kissing wouldn't be a problem.

Going into the job, I thought to myself, "There's an incredible discount on anything, I'll only have to work one or two days a week, and I'll earn some more trivial knowledge that has no practical use in society about obscure movies!" Yippie Ki Yay. Like a deal with the devil, I got what I wanted, but it wasn't exactly what I expected. No complaints with the discount, which I exploited for my ongoing materialistic crusade to stuff the Water's batcave with every advent of information, technology, and entertainment. I did only work one or two days a week, but after managing at my other job. So by the time I got to the video job, my varicose veins were pulsing like spastic green beans under my legs and I had to take frequent naps under a pile of laser discs (since no one buys, let alone browses them anymore) just to keep going. As for trivial knowledge, replace the word 'trivial', and insert the word 'banal' with much inflection. I assumed, since leaving books, that I wouldn't be assaulted with non-stop questions about child-type entertainment, and I thought wrong. After two months, I can name every live action Disney movie since "The Parent Trap", in alphabetical order. I phoned a professional deprogrammer yesterday, so I should be all right in a week or two. Of the entire time that I worked there (and I'm rounding up here, in the interest of optimism), I've received half a dozen semi-intelligent movie requests out of five billion. If only the store stocked taste and tact. I'd suggestive-sell the crap out of that.

My co-workers were all warped, twisted, and demented, so we got along famously. That's one of the reasons why I came back. In one department, they put a santa hat and an employee name tag on a cardboard standup of

Han Solo, in the music department, we made self-deprecating jokes about our pony tails, and video, well, that's almost a telephone directory of anecdotes. We had a stuffed animal at the central kiosk that someone thought was cute and cuddly, so I taped his ears on the top of his head and we put sunglasses on him. We've all watched "The Merry Mishaps Of Mr. Bean" on the cube of tv screens 200 times, I raced around the carpet on the push vacuum so fast that I sheared off someone's leg, and hours were spent by all watching a wind-up toy dog scuttle across the desk out of some sick fascination. Rising to the spirit of everyone else's dementia, I'd use a mock-baritone, silk-throated d.j. voice when paging anyone over the loudspeakers: "Kelly, dial 22, Kelly....twenty two pleeeaase."

Managing at my other job, I've been lovingly referred to as a "tyrant". To be taken with the utmost affection. My manager at the superstore was a polar opposite, almost a mildly maternal figure. Benevolent, patient (even during nervous breakdowns), and fond of Sesame Street ballads in her leisure time, Kelly and I knew each other since our days at Cavages (a music store) back in the early '90s, so we were hardly shocked with each others' respective sense of humor. Small world, small town. I vowed to her during the interview in November that, upon hiring, I would take a touring trip with her to Niagara Falls. Haven't quite gotten around to it.

You don't really realize just how *many* movies are in circulation on how many formats until you're completely entrenched in the product. There's VHS, 8mm, Super 8, Laserdisc, DVD, and Viewmaster gift crates of "Forrest Gump". It's exciting to see when you're shopping, but you feel like plunging your skull into a display television when you have to put away a docking cart piled to the ceiling with crates of videotapes. You don't realize how many movies are *no longer* in circulation until some antiquity of a customer is pounding the counter while you're searching on the computer for a non-talky featuring Buster Baxter Gilhooley.

The more I learn about films, the less I know. I thought I knew quite a bit, but sadly, the majority of the questions are about children's movies or old crusty classics, both of which I know jack about. It never pleases or amuses a customer when I tell them that I'm allergic to black and white. As far as I'm concerned, all the Bogart and Hepburn and Cagney and Welles films should have been buried with them. Customer Service is usually my strong point. I'm damned good at it, if I do say so myself. Ambiguity and stupidity are usually the customer's strong points: "Yeah, it's a movie, I'm pretty sure of that, and it's got Humphrey Bogart in it. He plays this guy who squints and drinks incessantly. OH! And he's really suave around women." I'm glad that you narrowed it down to EVERY MOVIE THE MAN HAS EVER

STARRED IN, YOU IGNORANT CHIMP! 3 out of every ten customers will shuck and jive you into a litany of questions, whether it pertains to your department or not: "Yes, I'm looking for this, and while you're still helping me, do you also have this book, this compact disc, this video game, this air freshener, an ice sculpture in the image of Princess Di, and a twelve pack of sanitary napkins?" Then we get customers on the phone long distance from Canada who could rent a jet, fly down, and look for the damn movie themselves with the money they're spending on hold: "Do ya have the Nine Inch Nails video, Eh?! I think the title starts with a Zed." Zed this!

Cheeky cashiers are universal, so that was no surprise. It's brilliant to see how they hone their sarcasm and condescension to a razor sharp precision that can't be detected by any customer with an IQ under 90 (basically, every customer). Quite to my chagrin, every employee from every department had to get trained on the cash register in case we got really busy. I thought that this policy was demeaning and frightening all at once. There really are a lot of buttons to press, and when you have a line of 20 people frowning and harumphing and whatnot at you, and the person you're ringing out is fishing for a pen to fill out her starter check, the anxiety tends to wash over you like The Blob on espresso. I hadn't felt so incompetent since reading VCR instructions! Thankfully, I always had a wing man/woman at a register next to me to help me hyperventilate into my smock while he/she finished the transaction.

And as with any company that has a sudden surge upward in staff, hormones fire and misfire about as often as commercial breaks on MTV. Romances blossom and crumble in the blink of a four hour shift. At least this year I walked out of the fray unscathed. Last season, I barely escaped two trysts with a feather-light wallet, a trampled heart, and a feeling of pride that had it's tail tucked so far between it's legs that it was lodged in it's ear. It was pleasant this time around just to watch on the sidelines as the innuendoes ricocheted and the flirtations flew to and fro, near and far, whatever. It's almost a syndrome. A gift and a curse, wrapped up in a special gift package.

Groups of people act a lot differently when they're forced to become fast friends for a limited time. I've noticed it in school trips, summer camp, and seasonal jobs. It's all severely carpe diem, live for the moment while you have it. I enjoy the vibe during jobs, though, cause it's a little bit more functional in the friendship aspect. There's a whole one-for-all and all-for-the-good-of-the-company spirit to a seasonal job that fuels me even after a 6 hour shift at my other job. There's a certain excitement to looking out on a mass exodus of ravenous holiday shoppers, and giving my best in serving them, rather then just brushing them by with a perfunctory air. You lose touch with your camp pals, and school trip chums disseminate by the ride home (if that), but I keep in touch every now and again with all of the people at the retail businesses I've worked at in Christmases passed, and there's still a hint of that holiday magic left in the friendship. I don't know, maybe I'm laying it on thick with the sentiment. At the very least, we still have the capacity to make fun of, and mercilessly rip on, the foibles of the customers who pay for our checks in a roundabout fashion. And that's enough.

would the reader please report to the end of this page

for a swift beating,

Tom "I don't need no stinking smocks" Waters

.....And Poetic Justice For Pretty Much Everybody In The Known Universe But Me

My old man always told me that the good Lord didn't make assholes, they had to work at it; and some of them are working overtime. Well this week, they all came crawling (or shall I say slithering) out from under their rocks to pay me a visit. Which is pretty good in retrospect, because I really had no idea what topic I was going to write about, but now I have an action packed thrill ride for my readers. Not only did I get a crash course in law and a correspondence degree in small town journalism. I got a refresher seminar on the human condition. You see, to a cum laude graduate of Advanced A-Hole, when you're sliding around on your belly under a rock, you have no spine (unlike your evolutionary superior, the vertebrae) and the rock starts bearing down on you, you'll hock your own mother on a street corner for less pressure. I'm pretty sure that my own personal Good Karma bus took a header off of a very steep cliff two days ago, so I have nothing to lose. Follow me, but strap on a hard hat first.

Exhibit A: A guy comes into the movie theater over the weekend with a big, cheese-eating grin on his face and a sea hag of a girlfriend on his arm. I was a bit cautious as he shook my hand and told me how he wanted to write down a compliment for a staff member who waited on him during Thanksgiving. This was where my capacity to reason headed south, as vanity is a powerful drug. I told him that Thanksgiving was quite a while back and I couldn't really recall, but he was welcome to write down a compliment. One of the people who worked under me (eager to get kudos, I'm sure) proceeded to give this guy the name of everyone who worked there. He never wrote down any compliments. Thought nothing of it. Assumed that he couldn't pay praise to the staffer who deserved it and gave up. A few days pass. I come in for work on Tuesday and we get a phone call. I give the standard theater phone spiel (disclosing my name), and the person on the other end says, "Is this Tom Waters? Thank you very much, goodbye." Before he hangs up, I laugh hysterically into the phone, as I thought it was either a coward or a prank call. Turns out it was the former. I was a little curious as to who it was after that, but I would've been better off not finding out.

The nine o'clock round of shows rolls around, and oddly, the weekend stranger comes walking up the runway with a paper in hand. Assumption #502: He had written a compliment down and brought it in. I took it gladly and told him I put it in the office, duly noting the return of the eerie, cheese-eating grin. After he left, I looked at the paper and four quarts of blood drained from my head to my toe nails. It was a subpoena. Ordering me to be downtown two days from then. To testify on the behalf of this person I've never heard of. Ain't that a fine how do you do.

Let me just interject for a moment, if I may, how I know next to nothing about the legal system, other than what I can get away with more or less (and we'll get to that shortly). I was called to serve jury duty a few years back and wriggled out of it because I was starting at college. One thing I do know (with my limited lay-person's understanding of statutes) is that when you're served with a subpoena, you are legally bound to show up in that courtroom. Therefore, when I got these documents, I flipped out! I thought *I'd* done something wrong. And I feel vicariously guilty about everything. So I contacted my employer, who made a copy of the document, and contacted his attorneys the next day. He assured me that it was nothing bad with me, and not to worry.

The next day, I called this lawyer. It turns out that some stooge got juiced up before going to see a movie on Thanksgiving, left the film early with his girlfriend, and then proceeded to 'warm up his heater in the parking lot, where he was arrested by state troopers for drunk driving.' If this sounds a little hokey to you, just hold your britches and all will be revealed. This attorney just wanted the manager from that shift to come in and testify to whether or not he saw this person. I'm sorry, but I can't hold back the rant any longer.

WHAT KIND OF MONGOLOID MENTAL MIDGET GOES DRUNK DRIVING ON THANKSGIVING! One of the other things I know with my limited knowledge of law is that, if you so much as put your keys in the ignition when drunk, regardless of whether you're driving or not, you can be arrested for drunk driving. Furthermore, WHAT KIND OF MONGOLOID MENTAL MIDGET harasses and uses subversive tactics on one of the only people who can help testify in the case (namely, me). And you would have to be at the bottom of the barrel, or rather, under the barrel, to a) take this case as a lawyer, and b) think you could possibly win. If I was the judge presiding in this case, I wouldn't let this guy keep his license if he was bribing me while I ate apple pie and received fellatio from his girlfriend! I wouldn't let him ride a scooter after that many black checkmarks on the record. Come on! If you've gotten so many DWI's that you're license is one step away from being revoked, odds are that it's not some quirky coincidence, ok?

So I talk to this hack of a lawyer, who probably got his license off of a box of Wheaties, and he tells me that none of the management staff has been cooperative in conveying the information he needs. First of all, three months is a long time to just drudge up inconsequential (to me, anyway) minutiae such as when I worked. Second of all, if one of the people involved in the case simply had the hubris, or the chutzpah, or the BALLS to come in and ask nicely, they would have gotten the information on the weekend. Thankfully, my employer and his attorneys straightened every thing out and I don't have to appear. This guy is severely lucky (if you overlook the fact that his driver's license is about to meet with an unfortunate accident) that I'm not required to show up, 'cause I'd bad mouth a storm about him over all this grief. I don't even remember the souse, to tell you the truth. We get a lot of sauce pots for the last round of shows. But I'd make stuff up about him after all this. I'd improvise on the stand. "Yes, your honor, I clearly remember him. He spit on me while I sold him his tickets, then proceeded to urinate on the refreshment counter. Halfway through the movie, after scaring a number of small children and a few spinsterly nuns, he left, saying that he would rather mow down some innocent people than watch the rest of the film. And that's all I recall, your honor."

Exhibit B: (As if the previous events weren't more than enough excitement for one week!) The day after I received my subpoena, and the same day that everything was straightened out, I wake up to hear a message on the answering machine. It's my former assistant editor, the bastard, telling me that a certain dentist is suing me for an article I wrote. Do you know how sometimes, every so often, you have a random homicidal impulse that, although you'd never carry it out, you don't brush it away in your mind either? You entertain it for a few minutes? Right then and there, I wanted to just flip out and go on a killing spree, so that I'd have a legitimate reason to go to jail or lose my shirt rather than the worthless turd being discussed. Luckily for everyone in my home town, I'm on medication.

-A Little Background-

Towards the end of the summer, I started submitting to a small community paper. Let's just call them *The Altered Beast*. At first they couldn't keep their nose out of my rectum. I was fantastic, I was a visionary, etc. They didn't pay, but it was exposure (better than the circulation of a college paper, but not much), and a cheap copyright. I overlooked the fact that they ignored all of the self-addressed, stamped envelopes that I enclosed with my submissions, and the fact that they never called to tell me what they were publishing, and figured that I wouldn't rock the boat until my position was secure. I overlooked the fact that my essays were bumped to every other issue in favor of expose's on the town budget to build a new park bench and 3 part series on the healing power of marijuana. All of these things I overlooked. To a point.

One day, after not hearing from these moguls of media for a while, I called to find out which piece they were using for the next issue. They said that they'd get back to me. The aforementioned asst. editor called back to tell me that my submission was terrible, worse than the first few articles I sent them at the start, and that I'd have to do better than that. Well, I didn't think that the piece was any different conceptually or structurally than a piece they'd already published. Personally, this was the most immature, unprofessional critique I'd received in my seven years at the bottom of the literary food chain, and I've worked for college papers, underground papers, everything. Personally, the essay was about local writers, so I'd kind of assume that this forty year old Larry Flynt wannabe took a little offense to it. I'm sure if I was working for a twelve page bimonthly rag that birds won't even shit on that I'd be easily offended, too. I wrote them a letter (after I'd calmed down, of course) and told this asst. editor that if he and his cohorts "couldn't pay me a fraction of the respect I paid them, since they weren't paying me any money", that they could basically stick their hands in their pants and go fish. That if I offended this high and mighty assistant, even though the essay had nothing whatsoever to do with him, then that was just tough nooky. Never heard from them. I burn bridges every time I need to light a cigarette, so it was no skin off of my back. Until this lawsuit.

Apparently, a certain dentist noticed an essay that I wrote about getting my wisdom tooth removed. Normally, I don't use real names (I even said this in the essay), but in this case, since this guy was such a horrible dentist, and since I could prove it, I used his name. The editor in chief told me today that they had no idea that that was a real name. That they were printing a retraction. Way to cover their butt and throw me to the wolves, huh? And I'm thinking, "The ONE time I use someone's name, in a paper that nobody reads no less, and I get nailed for it! Drats!" On another level, I was thinking, "Wow! What publicity!" I talked to a lawyer today and thank god, due to the first amendment, they can't sue me. The responsibility and all of that legal jazz rest solely on the shoulders of the publisher, who should've known better. I was just a poor, defenseless, starving artist, and I had nooooo idea that I could cause any trouble by naming this dentist and the location of his practice (slaughterhouse). So in the future, I'm going to have to be sneakier with the individuals that I slam. It was nice to know that I caused a stretch mark on what little reputation this paper had, though. And that I chapped the ass of that dentist. Good, good, good, good vibrations (now I'll probably get sued for copyright infringement).

I'm reminded of a joke that never gets old: What do you call 1,000 lawyers at the bottom of the ocean? A good start. That just about says it all for this weeks episode. Are we all so legally naive and greedy for cash that we'll sue over the tiniest things, or stupid enough to think that if the town is dragging us to court, that we should drag the rest of the town with us? It used to be that I only despised and distrusted dentists and barbers. And perhaps Canadians. Now I have to throw lawyers into the mix. The last two days have made me want to bury my head in the sand, but they do reinforce the fact that truth is far stranger than fiction. And much more likely to give you gas.

the defense passes out from stress,
Tom "Supreme Court Justice in '99" Waters

Frat Pack

It's amazing how quickly a cult can drain the original characteristics out of a person faster than a dog can suck marrow out of a bone. After joining some warped consortium, free will and individual expression lose precedence over the needs of the group. Before long, the subject's mind is so tainted with the postulations of the group they've been ingested by that they appear brainwashed beyond the point of repair. I'm speaking, of course, about college fraternities and sororities. Over the last six months, I've observed a friend's fraternity involvement (at arm's length, of course), and brother, it ain't pretty. I always thought that they spanked you with those paddles during initiation, but I'm assuming that they break the paddle over your head after seeing the finished product(s). A few years ago, when I asked an old school friend what a sorority experience was like, she said simply and succinctly, "It's buying friendship." There really isn't much that I can say beyond that, but I will anyway.

I've known this guy since childhood. Let's call him, uh, Jim. Jim was always a pretty decent kid, good head on his shoulders, never hurt anybody. Well, Jim graduates from high school, goes off to college, makes a few friends. Over the course of a year, one of these turn-coats offers him up to a fraternity like a roast pig on a silver platter. Now Jim and I are good friends, but we only keep in touch during school breaks and summer vacations, so it's tough to keep tabs on him all the time. Yet by his sophomore year, something had gone horribly awry. Rather than hearing about grades and girls and hockey, he began assaulting me. With horrible, wretched, foul, and vulgar language. Every anecdote and attempt at polite conversation was headed off by, "My fraternity this, my fraternity that, my fraternity, fraternity, fraternity. One of my fraternity brothers and I fraternitied at the fraternity while fraternizing." It was clear that the prefrontal portion of his brain was scooped out and replaced with a Greek encrypted brick.

For the sake of my childhood friend, I had to investigate more closely. That, and he couldn't conceivably do anything in the way of a social activity if the brotherhood wasn't involved in some way. So, like Diane Fosse sitting around some apes with a notebook, I went to the fraternity house at Facetious College, noting the unusual habitat. A wicker basket full of beer caps. Two hollow refrigerators with empty pizza boxes and five month old wine spritzers (in case a girl was ever around). An entire wall strewn with greek paddles, rowboat, ping pong, and otherwise. A black-lit room with so much complicated paraphernalia that the Doozers from Fraggle Rock would have an aneurysm trying to build it. Ten couches in one living room. A stolen construction light on one end of a room, blinking on and off, like the drunken heartbeat of the institution. Obviously, they needed a maid. Or to induct a brother with obsessive compulsive disorder.

Of the few times that I went there, 'pledges' were always being ordered around. For the layperson, 'pledge' is just another term for 'subservient bitch who does whatever we say for an extended period of time until he becomes one of us'. I kind of felt sorry for these people, but I suppose that it was their own stupid fault for going to such great lengths to be in an overblown tree-house club. "Hey pledge, down on all fours since I don't have a coffee table to set my feet on." "Hey pledge, go get me a poached Do-Do egg and some Japanese caviar. You have five minutes." "Hey pledge, get over here and wipe for me, I'm too busy knitting." After what I've seen, I suspect that hazings aren't accidents, they're willful suicides.

Most of the activities that this fraternity funded (I think they were called Delta Kappa Damma Gamma Hi-Fi or something like that, my greek is a bit rusty) were involved with, or revolved around a) drinking, b) property damage, c) anything that would attract mass stampedes of untamed women, and d) drinking, but more so. Cumulatively, they have the liver of a 579-year old man and the lungs of a 70-year old chain-smoking coal miner/driveway sealer. Now I know that every dorm and every college student has played a few rounds of quarters or done a funnel now and again, but these people shotgun whole kegs! They do shots while brushing their teeth in the morning! Whatever became of moderation? Wasn't that a greek paradigm?

I don't know how these people study in this environment, if they study. And if they do study, they're probably sucking down hi balls in the midst of it. Jim was very laid back at his fraternity house. I could never live in those type of quarters because I just can't stand noise and sharing and, well, basically, other people. One thing I don't understand is all of this pretend dignity about the organization. Maybe I'm just not good at swallowing double standards. Pride in something that you're involved in, and contribute to, that I can understand. But dignity? Every time I slip up and make the mistake of calling it a 'frat house' or telling Jim that he spends an unhealthy amount of time with the 'frat boys', he curbs me for a second to remind me that it's not 'frat', it's fraternity. Well lah de dah.

What's so high and mighty about this boy's club? That you have to go to hell and back to get into it? That you have a few friends who are better than the rest of the kids on campus somehow? What does this group really do to contribute to their surroundings, other than stealing streetlights, driving drunken freshmen off of rooftops, and pickling their brains? If that's something to be proud of, then I suppose I should throw a bottle of whiskey into my backpack and bring an assault rifle to freshman orientation week on campus. A cult is a cult is a cult, and the only dignity belongs to people who can think and act and speak for themselves without needing some sort of social security blanket to see them through. Strip away all the rituals and initiations, and fraternities are nothing more than Moonies with beer mugs. Maybe these overblown boy scouts do mold young kids into adults who know how to play ball in the workaday world, but if that's the only alternative, I'd rather bunt.

keep your pamphlets to yourself,
Tom "baboons in the mist" Waters

Seize The Day-Planner

One of the main differences between younger people and older people is the amount of time they spend planning an activity as opposed to the time spent actually engaging in the activity. Don't contradict me, I've seen it! When you're a kid, you or your friend get the impulse to go roll down a hill or eat something on the ground and you go do it. No delayed reaction, immediate gratification. Older couples and friends can take anywhere between five to ten months deciding where to have a cup of coffee. They like to have the freedom and opportunity to flesh out the event, arguing every possible angle and option. Where to have the coffee. Is the coffee good at this place? No, I don't like the placemat design. No, I'd rather drink it at that spot where all the waitresses wear java bean beanies. I'd like to know whether this shift in the formula is a gradual process or happens in tremor-like permutations.

Some of this has to do with responsibilities. If there's nothing tying you down, it's easier to do what you wish when you wish. Youth is a total lack of responsibility. Senility is a total lack of responsibility. Nobody depends on a four year old to bring a two million dollar account home for the company, so if he wants to blow spit bubbles for an hour or two, he's free to do so. An old lady doesn't exactly have to drop kids off at school or put in overtime, so if she wants to blow spit bubbles, she's also free to do so. So why do older people spend a proportionately larger amount of time planning rather than just doing it like younger people? Maybe they have done it, again and again, and things don't have the initial thrill that they used to. Everything's fresh in the eyes of a child, and, as you get a few years behind you, it's nice to stretch out and explore. But during the golden years, you've tried and experienced and discovered what you like, so there's not much deviation. It's comfortable to be set in your ways.

Many times, I choose to do nothing at all, due to the fact that social planning is such a colossal pain in the tuccus. I have the divine curse of making friends with people who have no punctuality, etiquette, or interest in organizing and bringing people together. Actually, that's not fair to my friends. These are just the only people who can put up with me for more than one outing. Seriously, though, it seems like every time a concert comes to town or an excursion is in the works, I end up being the one to allocate funds and remind people and pin down someone to drive. Just because I wear my hair in a bun from time to time doesn't mean I'm a secretary.   I h a v e friends who are constantly late. Figuring this in, I'll tell them to show up somewhere a half an hour earlier than they need to be and they still come tearing in brutally tardy with a makeshift excuse. The oven exploded. Had to thwart a mass murderer en route. Decided to dye their hair before they went out the door. This drives me coo-coo, as I'm the only person from my generation born with punctuality. I figure if you're going to do something, you might as well show up five minutes early or so to get the jump on the situation. I have friends who refuse to go anywhere where you can't use a coupon. I have friends who never get tired of lying around the house and watching edited for television movies and eating naked macaroni. I have friends who are willing to do something, as long as you want to swing from one bar to fifty and dance like an idiot before and after the other thing. This may explain why the majority of my time is spent alone writing, dwelling on evil/impure thoughts, and muttering in general.

Take the Outing That Never Was for instance. There is a certain movie that I've been dying to see since it came out..........TWO MONTHS AGO! I have two or three friends who work at movie theaters who can easily get me in for free, but I don't like to impose. I wouldn't want to hurt their feelings by making them think that the only reason I want to get together with them is to catch a free flick. It may be the main reason, but it's not the only reason, I mean, I'm a caring soul. So, after much bush-beating and eyelash batting and so forth, they tell me that they've a)seen it, repeatedly, but they'd rather not watch it anymore now that I've showed interest b)never seen the movie, it's a piece of trash, and they'd rather see some cheesy b-flick which I personally would rather rape myself with a rusty can of spaghettios than watch or c)they don't know what they wanna do, why don't I tell them what makes them happy (which is a digression I'll indulge very shortly)? So after all these free gigs fall through, I finally bite the bullet, decide to pay, and call a girl I know. Well it's a school night and she has to be home at one, so that would be cutting it close. No, I don't consort with preschoolers, she's a college girl who has a curfew! If not today, how about Saturday. Why not see a film on the absolutely craziest, busiest day of the week for the industry? I love nothing more than being sardined in with the general public. This is how much I want to see this movie.

Saturday rolls around, and I cancel for a majority of reasons, one of them being scheduling exhaustion. This week, I call and she's made plans. Is it wrong for me to expect the people I hang out with to be free on any given Saturday in the event that I call on a whim? I think not. I call a backup girl, we iron out plans, I call another friend whom I haven't been out with in a while, and everybody's so excited that we're all collectively wetting our pants at the prospect of a night on the town together. The backup cancels, too busy with school work on a SATURDAY! Don't ask me where I find these people, they find me. Hopefully, I can remain in the good graces of my other friend long enough that I can see this movie when it's edited for television.

And since there really isn't an appropriate area to insert this rant, I'll just put it here. For as many quirks as the aforementioned have, nothing is more tic-inducingly annoying than The Friend Who Can't Make Up His/Her Mind. They're like an Offspring album, everybody has one, but they'd rather not, they're ashamed of it, and they couldn't pawn it off if they tried. You try to make plans with this sad sack, and the feedback is as follows: "I don't know, what would you like to do? I'm not sure, where would you like to go? I can't really make any important or crucial decisions for myself, let alone both of our fates for the next two hours, and I have no assertive qualities to speak of, so please spare me the anxiety and pressure involved in making a simple choice and I'll follow you around on this adventure like a blind cattle." What the hell is wrong with these people?

It's this tricky middle segment of life where we spend so much time trying to be someone or stay that way once we're there that pursuits of leisure get gummed up in the gears. Careers and family take the foreground while friends and brief entertainments get pushed to the side. It would just be peachy if I had a generic friend from time to time, like the No-Name Brand in supermarkets. He could be a cardboard yellow stand-up, with "Friend" Stenciled across the blank yellow face. He'd be around when I wanted to do something, and overjoyed that I called, and we'd just hop in my car on a cavalcade of wacky adventures. He'd laugh at all of my damn jokes, too. And he wouldn't talk any smack to me either. In his absence, I can only guess to my future, or if I'll die of colon cancer at seventy while arguing over which deli sells the best Danish, and if they have coupons.

party of one,
Tom "The Cotillion King" Waters

Chia-Chick

After years of grueling, thankless, and tiring hard work in the field, it is my finding that love is the only known cure for any form of happiness. It rips out the nagging sense of well being in a healthy subject and replaces it with a gaping bottomless black hole of need, an inadequacy that can only be ebbed temporarily with the presence of the host. Half of the time, what one means to say when they're in love is that they're caught up in some organic lust, but the surplus of seratonin in the brain from an animal act with another person has blotted out any degree of judgment the individual may have had for a while. The rest of the time, 'love' is, obviously, a synonym for 'personal hell I'm going through as an alternative to being alone'. You could shoehorn the greatest philosophers of all time into a rubber room to make sense of, or define, this emotion and they wouldn't be capable of filling a security tag on one of the mattresses that amounted to anything. Love is not reasonable.

The illness seems to retard different areas of the brain depending on the sex. After three months, a woman can't think of going out of the house unless the significant other is involved in body, mind, or spirit. The psychic union is like the jaws of life. And god forbid that the man should get engaged, because no conversation is safe again with the outside clique. Try to start a decent conversation with a marked woman about politics, entertainment, midget tossing, whatever, and, invariably, she will answer, "Well, my fiancee once tossed a midget for our five month and twenty eight nanosecond anniversary." Ask her how's she's doing, expecting an answer that would reflect her state of mind. "My fiancee is excellent, thank you." After inspecting for a remote control antenna or a ventriloquist string, I've concluded that women have the emotional grip of leeches.

Men are no better. It's customary that a couple should spend a couple months deeply involved with each other, a so-called 'new car phase'. But after the whole getting to know you process, the spell goes unbroken. A friend or a brother or a confidant acts and thinks bizarrely, doing things that they wouldn't be caught dead performing b.h., or Before Her. Humming along to an adult contemporary song. Visually checking with the woman before responding to a question that was asked of them. Vowing to give up smoking or lynching or shooting up so as to be a better person for *her*. What especially disgusts me is friends who date creatures that look like they trudged out of the forest or some Scottish moat who volunteer sexual information, as if the emptying of fluids into this unspeakable horror will increase my respect and envy for them. They don't seem to take a hint when you cringe, shudder, or grip the porcelain with white knuckles, either.

Couples travel in herds. They rule commerce with an iron fist. Be it dinners, movies, window shopping, walking, skating, mountain climbing, sky diving, or drive by shootings, they make their presence known. A love interest is all but a status symbol. I can see the commercial now, coming to a web page, radio station, magazine, and prime time channel near you: Tired of not answering to anyone for your actions? Spending money on things that interest you? Going through each day without being sucked into a hyper-melodramatic situation? Wait no longer! LifeMate will put an end to all of these problems, and more! For just the majority of your annual income, you can argue, ostracize your friends, and make an ass out of yourself with a minimum of fuss! She guilt-trips, she flirts, and watch her grow while you have her! But wait, there's more! Act now and we'll throw in a troubled and misunderstood childhood! My button dialing forefinger is twitching already.

Freud closed the book on relationship-related psychoanalysis too soon. What I see most in the love live's of myself and others isn't a matter of mommy or daddy or how many things you like to put in your mouth. It's the one true Loss. The person who you gave yourself to completely and had your soul sliced into so many components that it looks like a construction paper snowflake in the process. The person who understood you more than anyone ever has. The person who got through. And every relationship after that is modeled in kind. Maybe the same build one time. Maybe the same likes and dislikes. They're like faint ripples after a stone hits a pond. And if the other person isn't identical enough, you impose, you try to mold and press and pulverize them into something they're not, and by the time they have changed, you don't like what you see anymore.

Most romances are more of a mutual loneliness than they are an intimate connection. Lost souls scrambling for somebody to keep the sadness at bay. All of this soul mate crap is a myth, something that nobody in their right mind would buy into if it weren't for whirlwind romance novels and pining crooners on the airwaves. I have yet to see a life long and symbiotic relationship, and in this day and age, I'm not likely to see one. The best thing to do is draw up a prenup and sow your oats until you're hooked in by someone else's scythe. Until you can find someone who's conversations aren't dried up in half a year, whose personality hasn't been defined with a chalk outline. What the hell do I know, though. If Neitsche's demise was a prostitute, I'm not likely to arrive at any lasting answers either. About the only advice I can offer is to stay aware of how many times the words 'I love you" really means 'Obey me'. And for god's sakes, if your woman grows a better beard than you, don't tell me how good she is in the sack!

Roses are red, and so are the rashes from crabs,
Tom "Casanova" Waters

Informative, Entertaining, And Incredibly Lethal

Gather round, campers, because what I have right here is the solution to the decay of society. Listen closely, and I'll tell you how to cure all of the loss, unnecessary hardship, as well as any and all unspeakable acts of violence that have been springing up lately faster than Virtual Pets without a contraceptive. If you want to do away with school shootings, parents murdering their children, children murdering their parents, parents murdering their schools, and schools that murder the parents who murder their kids, do just this: avoid all media. Unplug the television, cancel the newspaper, any glitzy magazine subscriptions you may have, and napalm your shower radio. Perhaps you think I'm joking since I've been known to recite dirty limericks while playing a small xylophone and rollerblading through random monasteries. Here's my second, less revelatory insight: I AM JOKING! Only a jackass with a ball of tinfoil in his head on a retarded witch hunt would come to such a conclusion, and yet we, well, at least I, am in the minority.

The media has become the big bad wolf at the end of this century. The bogey man around the water coolers and the man in the black hat that we can all point our finger at. Princess Diana spread across the inside of a tunnel like cheese on a cracker? Damn that media! Couple of kids who hollow out their fellow schoolmates heads with automatic weapons like a weed wacker through a jack-o-lantern? That diabolical media again! A president who accidentally mistook someone's dress for a sperm bank? Former football star carves his ex up like a pan of brownies? Oops! Oh, I'm sorry, perhaps it was only me who followed that train of thought. What's that? That sort of media you don't mind? A celebrity on trial is not part of the problem? Ok then, we'll return to you shortly.

What makes me foam at the mouth and tear clumps of hair out of my ass cheeks is when talking heads, flash in the pan celebrities, and out and out fads put their two cents in concerning this horrid technological beast that sinks it's fangs into the crust of our society. When a TV anchorperson attacks the lens that feeds it, when a syndicated columnist turns on the ink that paid for his house, and when a radio host trades their face in and gropes on to the cerebellum of the mob mentality. This goes beyond the pot calling the kettle and so forth, this is in league with the pot loudly urinating into the kettle in the eye of a black hole hurricane in the middle of the cosmos, telling the kettle how it was a motherless inbred from the Catskills that wouldn't resemble iron after a crate of flintstone vitamins.

Media ashamed of the media. But not the media that they're part of. You just don't understand. It's that other media. The sociopathic media. Media with the hidden messages. That voodoo media with a bad look in it's eyes. You can't really include books in this hypocritical inquisition, or at least real books. I read a statistic from a newspaper article a little while back (funny, after being brain-probed by that publication, my urge to commit mass murder hasn't changed) that less than 1 percent of the population buys more than one book a week. That is really, really sad.   Surely, there's the occasional self-help/inspiration/financial/well-being/angel-experiential/relationship affirmation best seller that pops out of an Oprah type media H-bomb and sells a disgusting amount of copies, but as far as I'm concerned, any book emblazoned with gold leaf on the cover that incorporates the words "Soul", "Soul-Mate", "Co-Dependent", and definitely "Celestine" is not a real book. So literature at large sits this one out. I think it's safe to say that after centuries of blood-shed storytelling and epic war novels that there haven't been any recorded cases of mid-wives shot putting newborn infants after reading Tolstoy or ten year old waifs playing cobblestone tag with a shopkeepers head after reading "Oliver Twist".

But we know what we're referring to when we talk about that nasty, nasty media, don't we? Television, and certainly not PBS. After seeing three hundred billion deaths by the age of two, children all turn into murderous blood thirsty maniacs with no distinction between reality and the overpowering fantasy land of the big black box. I'm so sick of this argument about the deaths on TV. I saw "The Exorcist" when I was in the first grade, "Amityville Horror" in the third grade, and a whole bunch of other gorefests between that time that I'd rather not even tell you about (one of the movies involved a gang of amputee circus midgets with salad shredders super glued to their foreheads). Maybe we should just turn back the clocks, eh? Bring television back to a time of innocence and denial and bittersweet stupidity in a world where death is a completely foreign idea and we can all believe in Santa Claus until we're 40, right? Wrong.

Television shows are the dreams of the collective subconscious someone once said. If it's so rotten, then take a look at the reflection in the glass, buster. If I had it my way, If I were some big wig entertainment mogul, I'd make the all death channel. No cartoons, no dancing frigging dinosaurs, no talk shows, no nature shows, definitely nothing with the Disney seal of approval, no prime time family values crap, just scene after scene after scene of violent gore. Clint Eastwood afterburn on the retina, baby. You say children see 500 million people getting shot before they break in their first tooth? Well I can top it. Just sign up for the "Waters Desentization Network" and after your child kills his first victim, we'll slash your monthly rate in half. That is, of course, if you're not the first victim.

The school killings are too silly to even examine. Children from gun happy family units with no discipline and a fair amount of abuse, I'm sure. Blaming the television is like indicting a china cabinet for an abortion that took place in Tokyo (pretty bad, I know). Making celebrities out of our criminals and revealing our celebrities as the criminals they are might be a little hemorrhage in the fabric of this country's morals, but you can't blame the messenger.

To hammer my point home one last time, if the media is terrible and vile, it is because we made it that way. This is what we wanted. Maybe the Nielsen ratings system is our own private Frankenstein gone berserk. Perhaps it's the advent of cable. MTV. Internet news. I know who mine is. George Clooney, the most narcissistic man in the history of recorded time. A constant smirking no-talent who bit off the thumbs of reporters (I'm sorry, I just can't say the P word, I won't bring myself to adopt a pop culture catch phrase, so get jiggy wit it) when it was the tres' chic thing to do, who cannot deliver any sort of line without incessantly grinning. We'll never get rid of that big bad wolf, though, and you know why? Because he knows how to make us laugh and cry and think when we don't expect anything more than to turn our brains off and relax. Whether it's the morning paper or the prime time sitcom or a radio talk show, that wolf can do a mean soft shoe tap, can't he?

And if, after decades of research, sociologists can find a direct correlation between unjust murders and media desensitization, so what? Maybe I'm insensitive for saying so, but that's population control in the basest sense. Survival of the fittest. If a few stupid people who can't tell the difference between Oscar The Grouch and their homeroom teacher weed each other out, so be it. And I'd bet the farm that Darwin, if he lived in this century, would have a satellite dish. With stereo surround.

excuse me while I kiss my remote,
Tom "1 billion deaths served" Waters

Why It's A Good Idea Not To Taunt The Amish

When I was in Kindergarten it was a tremendously big deal that both of the classes in the grade were going to bury a time capsule for future generations to unearth. I couldn't tell you what we put in it exactly, most likely smurfs, an article about the death of Lennon, and undoubtedly something about those pesky Russians. I couldn't even tell you if it was an actual pill sized capsule, a safe deposit box, or even a cardboard box. What I can pass on is that centuries from now, long after the grammar school I attended has gone the way of the Arsenio Hall show, that our little time capsule isn't going to amount to a Chrysler Building of goose droppings because even if archeologists were looking for a sign from the past or a fingerprint from our semi-advanced culture, they wouldn't be able to find it buried under all of our crap!

The Indiana Jones of 2098 would herniate himself scooping out Pepsi cans, old televisions, empty pens, hypodermics, economy cars, and previously viewed videotapes before he even dusted off the tip of the capsule. In the last two hundred years we've picked up the pace as a throwaway society faster than a contact coal buzz from a runaway locomotive without a driver. Technology, in helping to make day to day life a bit more streamlined, has also turned us into disposable slobs who don't understand half of the stuff we use from day to day. The products we toss, and the reasons for tossing them can be compacted into a few simple categories. We'll begin this empirical abstract right after I drop my box of dead calculators on the curb for the Wednesday trash pickup.

Firstly, there's the *Stuff That Costs Too Much To Fix And Less To Replace*, such as radios, older cars, microwaves, and pretty much everything and anything that's electronic. During my first retail job, which wasn't that long ago, I bought a used boombox from a friend for a hundred and fifty bucks. A simple one-CD, one cassette model. It took me about two months to make all the payments on my meager salary, but I had a sense of pride every time I used the stereo. Now, some six years later, after oafishly banging it against swinging doors and lugging it out into the middle of nowhere in extreme temperatures quite a few times, I can't make mix tapes from CD's because the dubbing is so static that it sounds like hamsters copulating inside of a ball of tinfoil and every time I eject a compact disc (it's a front loading mechanism, for some reason), the front component falls off. It's seen better days, basically. We had some good times, and it breaks my heart to think of just pulling the plug and turning my back on all the weird, freaky music we shared together, but I can turn to any weekend flyer in the newspaper and see that Heimie's House of Electronics has a portable 2,500 CD changer with four cassette players, detachable seven thousand watt speakers and a satellite dish for about half of what I paid for my old faithful. But with watery eyes, I call a repair shop. Where they tell me they'll have to send it to the company. For the low low price of about a hundred and fifty dollars.

Service repair people are lower than the genitals of sewer rats, and I can't stand dealing with them. From car mechanics to blow dryer technicians, there isn't one off the top of my head who goes to school for more than three years (not including mail correspondence courses) and they get paid obscene amounts of money. It's sort of like the sports industry. They can do something we can't do pretty well, and there's a demand for their talents, so we're pretty much at their mercy. It's best to duck walk into the shop backwards while bending over at a forty five degree angle. That way you won't be too shocked when they take your wallet and rape you. After a wonderful experience a few weeks back when I got a new car stereo installed, it was brought to my attention that most repair people get paid sixteen dollars an hour and up. They did such a good job installing the new radio that they left the box, the original receipt, and the warranty sitting on the bench. I can sort of understand why doctors and psychiatrists get paid so much because of the years spent, literally spent, in school, and how much valuable knowledge is in their heads, but paying some guy fifty dollars to wedge his asscrack under my steering wheel and switch a few wires? Perhaps I shouldn't dwell on this. Those bastards! Ok, it's out of my system.

Aside from the toys that are too costly to mend, there's *Stuff That's Better Than The Other Stuff,* such as computers (duh), answering machines, microwaves, and my personal favorite, the dvd player. This isn't to say that the products we have are obsolete, or that the new products are that much of an innovative cartwheel, but they're sleeker, or compact, or just a tiny bit better than what's in our possession. And, with the miracle of advertising, the new stuff looks irresistible. Technology, for the most part, is no longer hitting the glass ceiling, but slamming it's head repeatedly against it like an autistic in a deprivation tank. Breakthroughs aren't really on the same scale as say, horse drawn carriage to Hum-V all terrain tank/jeeps. These days we have refrigerators that are colder on some shelves than others, see-through vacuum cleaners and pastel colored water filtration systems. Computers being a small exception. One tiny, incorrigibly annoying exception.

Computers are still relatively young in terms of evolution. They've become the newest foothold in a long lineage of keeping up with the Jones', from the phonograph to the television to the two car garage. The only difference being that it takes three and a half hours to brag about how much mind-blowing circuitry is under the hood, and about three and a half decades to understand, let alone utilize, all that crap. People are so afraid that their PCs will be obsolete in three years that they buy the most expensive model featuring eighteen thousand things in it's belly that they're pretty sure they need so that when the software and hardware market crank the dial on the evolutionary treadmill they'll still be able to download kiddie porn or run the hemp sandal business out of their homes or whatever the hell else it is that computers are good for. Memory is one thing I'll never grasp with these contraptions. Most of the friends I have can store their entire brain on their hard drives, make a backup copy, and still have room left over to throw in the CIA's hall of records. Megabyte Gluttony. But I digress.

PCs, conveniently, are also part of our next class, *Stuff We're Pretty Sure We Need 'Cause Commercials Tell Us We Need It.* This section changes as often as Joan Rivers on speedball at a Versace estate sale, the trends and fads of today being pagers, cell phones, rollerblades, and the oncoming onslaught of digital televisions. These are products that we didn't realize were crucial to our very existence until ad campaigns, mob mentality, and the personal susceptibility to greed convinced us to acquire them. I'm not saying I'm any better or worse as a consumer or a human being, we are what we are. But I have a personal disgust for cell phones and pagers that nearly eclipses my contempt for Al Roker (that evil, evil man). It's like walking around in a Stepford Wives-type-conspiracy nightmare. I can't go to the end of my driveway without seeing a six year old checking the messages jiggling off of his hip or hearing a senior citizen talking to her gynecologist on speakerphone driving back from a routine cyst check. I'm afraid if I don't buy one or both of these items that I'll be smuggled overnight to an Amish community and banished from civilization to make pies as punishment for my noncompliance.

There's really no use whatsoever for cell phones and pagers, and save your breath, I've heard all the excuses. "What if I get into an accident in the middle of nowhere and I need help?" Yeah, I'm gonna pay sixty dollars a month so that in the unlikely event that I run into a tree in Deliverance County, I can get a total lack of reception because I broke down in a valley and therefore I'm still screwed. When we start leaning on all of these devices in place of our total lack of genetic survival skills, that's a bad sign. Pagers are no more crucial. "I move around a lot and I just have so many damn friends that are foaming at the mouth to get ahold of me at any given moment that I don't want to deny them the distinct pleasure and privilege that is me." Right. I have a close friend who sells both of these infernal gadgets and when his lips curl up and I can sense the pitch coming on, I tell him the same thing time and again. I don't want people to get ahold of me when I'm at home, so why in god's creation would I want to help them find me when I'm not! Between work and home, I use the phone on an average of one half phone call every equinox. As far as pagers go, I have about four close friends, and four or five acquaintances. If they can't get ahold of me, there's a reason for it. Maybe it's just me. Call me a freak for not aspiring to lockjaw from incessant small talk.

All this junk come and gone, mountains of garbage. Literal mountains that they take the stink out of somehow and convert into ski slopes. But how many more ski slopes can we make? Sooner or later we're going to have to sell trailer park communities on top of trash or make really hilly golf courses or something. Don't get me wrong, I'm not some fur-fearing, bead slinging, Greenpeace acolyte, and I couldn't give a damn about the children of tomorrow. If they're wearing pagers they can rut around in the filth we helped create and like it, for all I care. I just wonder sometimes. I took Latin for four years, and other than a handful of Greek Gods and "Alia Iacta Est", I still remember pictures of Pompeii. A beautiful city with delicate works of art, practical architecture, and unfortunate but scenic waterfront property. What's Indiana Jones gonna find from our time? Plastic coin sort banks? Clock radio icemakers? Rowing machines? Hopefully he'll dig long enough to find the time capsules, and, with luck, we won't all look like assholes.

disposable but charming,

Tom "recycle-friendly" Waters

Rooting For The Under- Dog

On the rungs of the holiday heirarchy, Thanksgiving could best be described by it's mashed potatoes. Pretty substantial, moderately warm, and somewhere in the vicinity of the main course. I'd say it's right in the middle of the greeting card barometer, with Christmas being the big badass mother of all occassions, while Labor Day, Veteran's Day, Sweetest Day, Secretary's Day, Take Your Brat To Work Day, and Honor Your Local Brothel Madam all competing for the bottom position. But then, one must weigh the pros and cons to accurately describe this holiday.

I think I'll be zany and begin with the miscellaneous contrasts for a change, if you don't mind too much. We have the average number of people swerving around the roads blasted out of their minds on pills, hooch, fairy dust and so forth. It's safe to say that this is a holiday constant that rises slightly come the following December, but not much. A fairly high number of suicidal, homicidal, psychopathic incidents related to despair, depression, and the other fabulous symptoms of family. While cranberry sauce loses it's shape in a bowl on an anonymous dinner spread, you can bet your booty that a few hundred people across the country are having a main course of shot gun al a mode before their pumpkin pie, using their electric knife to carve up a wronged lover and anyone else in the vicinity, or passing out behind the wheel going two hundred miles an hour head on into a Catholic school.

You can also depend on food, football, napping in cult proportion, and parades, but no gifts. Independance day may have outside light shows and Halloween may have an abundance of sweets, but Thanksgiving has equal parts napping and equal parts eating, which is just jake by me. Whereas one can gain three hundred and fifty pounds from mid-December to early January, here you have one solid meal, a few days of leftovers, and a chemical related coma which also (conveniently) rescues you from having to make small-talk with distant relatives whom you are trapped in the house with. Triptophan, oh, Triptophan, how sweet you are with gravy. For me, napping is not a necessity so much as it is an art form, a science, and a personal passion of mine. And during my napping, the rest of the family is free to talk, watch a football game, some silly parade with cartoon characters I've never heard of and chipper newscasters I could care less about, whatever. Fine by me, my ass is planted on the couch.

And I almost don't mind the football, which probably sounds shocking. For those four or five calendar holidays in the summer, the best that television can offer up is golf, a few eight hundred and sixty hour telethons, and tennis matches which ninety eight and a half percent of the people on this continent don't even know the rules to, let alone have an interest in. The first prize for quality programming on and off cable goes to Christmas, of course, but Thanksgiving tube time is not all that bad. What I love is that on any given day of the year, at any given time, holiday or no, the fifteen stations that Ted Turner owns will be playing "Rain Man", "Road House", "The Money Pit", "Back To The Future", "The Hard Way", and, "K-9" simultaneously without fail. This is pure gravy for the holiday non-football fan. Even the crappy comedies are more amusing when listening to the words a studio gimp came up with to mix over all of the obscenities. For example, "stupidhead", "mothergrabber", and "mud in the ditch". For some reason, Tom Hanks and Michael J. Fox's movies are very syndication friendly, but I digress.

Sadly (for the marketing wizards out there), there aren't too many things you can guilt people into going out and buying to celebrate. No theme garbage bags to stuff with gutter leaves and plop on the lawn, no wicker baskets and plastic grass, nothing. Just the basics. A turkey and maybe stuffing, if you're feeling industrious at the supermarket. You don't have to run around to thirty different places to try and prepare for every little holiday nuance. So that's a plus. Nor does Thanksgiving suffer from self esteem issues in the bunch. It's not some last minute, tacked-on holiday from this century that only psychotic postal workers can enjoy because they get that day off, like President's Day, Secretaries Day, Veteran's Day or Labor Day (the last two which I confuse the dates, times of year, and meaning to know end, because they're worthless holidays!). I think it's safe to note that if you have a Day at the end of your holiday name, then nobody gives a shit about you. Maybe that's just me.

There's a scant or nonexistent amount of religion, which is a plus in my book. Even the goat-beheading pagans who show up sheepishly to chapel on Christmas and Easter can take the day off. No strong religious symbolism, no inner feelings of guilt or challenges of faith when November rolls around. Just a turkey and a cardboard musket by way of iconoclasts. Maybe a little pilgrim stuffed animal with a really bad bowl cut.

My family's Thanksgiving is, well, it's traditional, I suppose. We all eat at the table with utensils rather than the frantic, hurly burly, grab your own t.v. and graze fashion of an average week night, say a mumbled Catholic prayer, and call it a day. Since all of the brother's have been practicing Catholics for less than half of their lives, we sort of take cues from our parent's bowed faces:

"Bless us, oh.....Lord, for these our....gifts, which we are....about to....__ceive; hmm hmm hmm our.....Lord, uh, Amen!"

Keeping with the tradition, my mother asks each brother which of us likes the frozen fruit salad, would like the fruit salad, and puts it on the wrong plates anyways. I don't like anything with fruit, so I always think that this will be the year she doesn't ask, but, there's tradition for you. And on any given holiday, our tribe will go through twenty to thirty pounds of mashed potatoes. My dad spends three quarters of the entire day buzzing and milling about in the kitchen, offering up samples before the meal to the slavering dogs that we are, and finally sits down by the eleven o'clock news. I never understood this. Certainly, it's kind to cater to the rest of the family and then sit, but while my little brother is going for seconds and I'm calling dibs on the couch, he'll still be puttering around near the condiment trays, stirring something here, rotating meat there, and his plate will sit at the end of the table. My only guess is that he's secretly Jewish and waiting incognito to see if Elijah will pop in and drink his half glass of beer and plate of potatoes. That was the only guess I had that made sense, that is. My mother, keeping in line with her side of the family, will chew each piece of food four hundred times before swallowing. It takes her until the next Thanksgiving to finish with the appetizers. Myself, keeping in line with my dad's side of the family, will inhale everything in sight including the cutlery under forty seconds. The key is not to swallow, but rather to hollow out a paper towel roll and insert it in your windpipe for faster consumption.

The history, returning to my mashed potato analogy, is neither here nor there. There's no abundance of factual data. To be honest, the relaxed patriotic arcana thrown together into the mythos is precisely that: thrown together. It's almost like someone gave a six year old a week to tie in our conquests and beginnings on this contentent into a coherent report and we were given a handful of scribbled napkins transcribed from the back of a happy meal. In the grand tradition of winners writing the history books, we've mixed all of America's origins into one solid story and whipped up a few not-so-truths to fill the cracks. To my understanding, Americus Vespucci came over a few centuries ago, took one look at the Indians, and rather than trading spices and pottery and whatnot (as the Europeans had with other nations and peoples), and said "Hey, Tonto! That's my land you're standing on!" Not "hello". Not "Good Day, Mr. Native, I bring you these gifts in a gesture of goodwill." Simply a belligerent conquest in the name of the mother country that turned out to be a welcome mat laid out to escape from the evil monarchy of the mother country. Christopher Columbus, to the best of my knowledge, planted his flag rather ignorantly into a mixed drink somewhere on a sandy island just to the south of the North American continent. This holiday doesn't have any saints, messiahs, war heroes, or overweight comics whom the French strangely adore. Just a few greedy spaniards with metal hats that look like, well, let's not go there.

Rather than bleeding over the homeless or pining for starving children, I'd like to think of the Native American Indian this Thanksgiving, the most screwed race of people on the planet. But how about the Indians? They may have their freedom, but at what cost? Some of our father's father's father's father's (is that the right number?) bilked them out of their land, gave them little pockets of wildlife rest stops to live on (the only alternative being to assimilate), and have systematically been sticking it to them for the last three hundred odd years. As a result of that whole ugly bead affair, with no land to call their own on their home turf, they've all but lost their culture, their pride, and their peoples. What sort of freedom is that? What kind of consolation prize are bingo halls and smoke shops? I'm part Native American, so I'm a little heated on this topic.

Aside from that, I like Thanksgiving. A napping prerequisite is always a plus with me. It's a cozy holiday with decent amounts of all the basic principles. A few days off from work or school, a goodly amount of food, decent t.v., napping, and no church. Pretty substantial, lukewarm, and good

enough for me. But who's to say. Perhaps Give The Crabs To A Friend Day
will really pull out all the stops this year and I'll flip flop.

giving thanks where thanks is due, and in some cases, overdue,
Tom "oops, I found the turkey thermometer" Waters

Deja Misconstrued

It's been argued, or rather, widely accepted, that some institutions are all but dead. Classical composition, psychology, philosophy, Literature (note the capital L and try to pronounce it with a trill in your tongue on the two t's, mind you), and legitimate theater (again, the trill, if you could) are apparently nestled in a some sort of paradigm mortuary just south of Hoboken on rt.77. And to this opinion, I shall reply simply and succinctly by making a statement of my own: Bunk! Total bunk! Absolute bunko! The stodgy belief that all of the good plays have been dried from the quill for more than a century, that all the great thinkers are now great alternatives to mulch, all the painters and poets dust in the wind, and furthermore, that every essential dysfunction of the psyche has been long mapped out by better minds from better eras, is no better than an ostrich with a diploma. One large, pretentious, insecure ostrich, who gathers up his sonnets, his arias, his dogmas, a blue blankey, and proceeds to drill his head into the sand. Under the presumption that he's trying to find the remains of Neitsche or Shakespeare.

I've never believed that ideas dry up, or that they're finite in quantity in regards to the entire history of civilizations. Aristotle argued that there are essentially 24 basic plots for any play or story. I'm sure that's true. But does that necessarily make the first few people to the finish line the winners by a couple hundred years? Should I simply throw up my hands and resign under the pretense that I'm never going to write an original sentence? Run home crying? You get my point. If we're all cribbing from Aristotle's cheat sheet, whether we realize it or not, whether we think it's one of the Kennedy's or not, who cares? I will not concede to the notion that originality is no longer original. It's the battle cry of the born loser.

In league with that school of thought (and I'll try to make this brief, so as to spare you any undue grief from this personal sub-crusade), there are the fabulous and insightful cross section of literati who swear that all roads lead to Shakespeare. I'm actually ripping off an idea he had while on the chamber pot as we speak. Give me a break! You can't tell me that some mud-caked Aborigine out in Australia who's etching a story in the sand has Hamlet in mind. For the love of Pete, if you try enough, and refer to your William conversion charts, you can find Basqueo and Fruitio and the King of Windsordale in everything, but that doesn't necessarily mean that the author of the work had one of his plays in mind, or even that the characters resemble one of the classic, tortured, Oedipal-torn heros from a penny play! It just means that there are a few college professors with Bill on the brain. This is not a Honeymooners/Flinstones type of thing by any means. Certainly, there's more than a passing resemblance between Ralph Kramden and Fred Flintstone, but you can't tell me that, oh, I don't know, Fred Sanford is a direct carbon copy of King Lear. Christ! Drop it, already!

And philosophy, by any other name, is still philosophy. The business of thinking has taken a few twists and turns, but it's still alive and well. This is where we can indulge in a little theory. Popularity. Philosophy is one of those professions that really has no calling left. It's like managed care. It's around, but not in the same sense. It's been cut up into fifty thousand different pieces, and serves the same purpose, but it doesn't pay the bills like it used to. Just hear me out on this one.

In the era of Aristotle and Plato and Socrates, men were bred to be deep thinkers. Raised by their mentors, and sired by rich parents, they had the time and the indulgence and the civilizational means to sit under a tree and dwell on the origin of angst in mankind for a good twenty five years. They'd get up, write four or five three hundred word sentences, and be crowned the new philosopher of Rome. A little ways down the time line, we get our occupational hazards, such as death for your beliefs. Hell, every job has a few risks, but for some reason, this had a negative effect on the profession. I believe it was Galileo, with his devil-worshipping views on the solar system, who was relieved without pay or a steady heartbeat by the council elders. The French and the Germans were traded Philosophy for a century or so, and after Neitsche died from syphilis (that naughty kraut), there was a recession in thought. Things had gone down hill from the Buddhist boom of philosophical orgies running naked in forests, and young men just weren't jumping in on the ground floor anymore.

These days we have motivational speakers with exciting new theories making bucket loads of business conference payola, self-help gurus with revolutionary regimens, and the occasional book from an idle dreamer, which is all there's a call for in our time. For every ten or twenty Anthony Robbins's and Susan Powters and M.Scott Pecks, there's a little bubble of rational thought that floats up from the murk. *The Tao Of Pooh*, by Benjamin Hoff, which, yes, borrows quite a bit from Eastern Thought, is a good example. *Zen and The Art Of Motorcycle Maintenance*, by Robert Pirsig, which, yes, borrows once again from the East, is another one.

What I respect about *Motorcycle Maintenance* is that it was written by a philosophy professor who got fed up, and that takes brass cahonies the size of wrecking balls to do. Every philosophy professor I've known is from the Barber College of Dead Thought, and the biggest contributions they attempt are along the lines of dissection and the minutiae of the greats. Fifty page thesis's discounting one sentence from Heidegger concerning the scatological discussion of discerning bodies of light and the motion of armpit hair in random deities. Anyone that ground into the system willing to thumb their nose back at it deserves a vote of confidence from me. Perhaps books like this borrow a little, but they take a thought further, they refuse to let dead dogs continue to teach, and they think on their feet, which is a point or two in the favor of your dear author's schizophrenic debate.

I never cease to be shocked, appalled and astonished all at once when I hear about the heydays of Freud, the pioneer and grand conductor of psychology as we know it. How he's the veritable End-all and Be-all of every mental process, dysfunction, and coping mechanism thereof. Psychology as a medical practice, not to mention wellspring of creativity, is still quite the toddler next to the other behemoths in this bunch. Anyone who can tell me with a straight face that a hundred and fifty year old profession is tapped out on ideas in a universe that some two thousand years old is either in need of psychological help or not looking at the big picture.

I've said it before, I'll say it now, and I'm bound to say it again, but Freud had a lot of good ideas, and he layed the ground-work for the practice, but there's a lot more to the mind than id, ego, and superego. Here's a man who based everyone's inner machinery on a handful of forlorn, sexually repressed housewives. He hit the nail on a few heads, don't get me wrong. I am going somewhere. Here's a man who proposed to his best friend's little sister, snorted about five barn silos full of pharmaceutical cocaine, and smoked enough of his self-proclaimed phallic cigars that he died of mouth cancer. One or two problems. Meanwhile, Carl Jung, an unrelated predecessor, keeps company with psychics trying to dispel seance myths and charlatans, comes up with a lot of interesting ideas in the field, and is still seen as a kook today. Drugs and sexual dysfunction are fine, I suppose, but we don't like our psychology with two lumps of mysticism, thank you. All those archetypes and icons flushed right down the drain at universities. Poor Carl must be screaming his head off in his pine box, what with Deepak Chopra teaching business mantras to Donald Trump.

But on the upswing, psychology and psychiatry are booming. The Physicians Desk Reference gains five hundred pages every six months due to new pharmaceuticals. Every celebrity, politician, housewife, and cable repairman either has two or three diagnoses, a healthy prescription, or a travel pack of Viagra (I couldn't resist). Psychology is far from dead. It's alive and kicking, and so is it's inner child's inner child's inner.....and, you get the point.

I was listening to a Billy Joel song a few weeks ago and picked up a riff from Beethoven in the piano solo. Just to let you know that this isn't a biased attack on classical compositions, I thought I'd mention that. All the greats are gone forever, aren't they? Bach, Brahms, Mozart, Tchaichovsky, Rachmaninoff, alive only through the miracle of budget bin symphonic reproductions. One could argue that film scores (which are also going the way of the dodo at the writing of this piece, in favor of a string of pop song soundtracks for the merchandising tie-in) are like a modern day classical music, but I certainly won't. John Williams and Danny Elfman have their moments, but there's a profound difference between composing for a story or an idea, and fleshing something from the depths of your heart into music.

Instead, let's take a look at what classical music was in it's respective age. It was popular music with the kids. Revolutionary rock and roll, believe it or not. Amadeus was like the Axl Rose of the Renaissance. The only difference being that nobody threw their panties and corsets at the piano while he was playing. So blasphemy or not, it's safe to say that our popular music, rock and roll, is the classical music of our time. Or that two hundred years from now, it'll be classical. Just imagine; Elvis Presley, the maestro. And he didn't even write his own music. But songs are still being written, and if classical compositions were still in demand, I'm sure they'd be around, but they're not. In Buffalo, where I live, they can hardly keep the Philharmonic afloat because no one goes to see them. Nobody has that problem with Garth Brooks. The mob has spoken, Mozart.

And if the mob's opinion is incorrigible from your side of the page, dear reader, then let's shift gears and discuss the printed page through the ages. Whether we drop the names of Dickens or Shakespeare or Tennessee Williams, they all directly catered to, and were rewarded for, writing what the general populace would enjoy. Shakespeare gave the O theater some blood and guts, Dickens gave his newspaper readers tales of virtue in squalor, and Williams brought the seamy side of sexuality to the early twentieth century. I was always more of a Neil Simon fan myself, but this is besides the point. Ironically, I read about Dickens' methods in a Stephen King novel. He claimed that the endings to a number of his novels were open ended, and that as he submitted chapters to the newspaper, he would gauge the public's response and write accordingly. Many contemporary authors are compared to former giants, but I think that the book world is a tad more forgiving when the death of ideas is concerned. Or sneakier than their words. John Irving has been compared to Dickens for his lengthy novels and his involved menageries of characters. For the last two or three years, every new and twisted male author has been compared to Thomas Pynchon, who was quote-unquote one of the last real novelists from earlier in the century. The death of words is a little bit slower to catch up with the others, you see. We still have some recent heroes to pin all of our disappointments of contrast to, such as Faulkner and Wolfe and Hemingway and Sinclair, virile American men keeping the American dream alive for a few more decades.

The fact that the end-product of creativity in these areas, as well as others, has changed subtly over the course of time is not only an fallible reason to claim that original thought is extinct, but it's also natural. People's tastes change, culture's change, and people in general, well, they change! New ideas spring up with just as much frequency as they did two hundred or seven hundred years ago, but we have a lot more muses to apply them to. I'd almost venture to say that, due to the size of the world's population in contrast to any other era, we have more new thoughts than the tired, wheezy ones that are still ricocheting around pop culture. The very least we can do is try rather than admitting a false defeat. And by doing so, administer a loud, creative, and literary enema to Bill Shakespeare. But that could just be my feeling.

Geronimo!!
Tom "these nicknames have been done already" Waters

Bald Freaks In Pajamas and Other Anomalies

I was thinking last week, which I sometimes do, and it occurred to me that it's been seven solid years since I've made fun of Star Trek and it's fans. Seven years! That's a lot of water under the bridge, friends. A lot of new territory to cover. Perhaps I won't be boldly going where I've never gone before today, but I look at it like this. I am not a writer of sequels, and hopefully, the two people who read my essays (the blind mail man and my mother, respectively), won't see my continuations as such. There are a handful of topics that call me back into the fold from time to time; some subjects that perhaps I didn't really beat into submission quite yet. Universal foibles that are just too enjoyable to make fun of. Hence, Star Trek. Seven years ago, I'm not even sure if I knew what an essay was, let alone how to spell it, and I put down two or three paragraphs on Gene Dingleberry's brain-child, thinking that was sufficient for the subject. How wrong I was. I just hope I don't offend the mail main, as he does make up fifty percent of my reading public. Perhaps I can spill a hot cup of coffee on the braille version.

Not too long ago, the whole craze was manageable. There was a small faction of geeks, one show, two or three movies. Easy to ignore. Now I can't really pin point the exact moment when things blew way out of proportion, but to put it another way so that Star Trek fans can understand it: things blew way out of proportion. There are more movies and sequels about these clowns than I can count on my existing appendages (including my cyst), five hundred current series and off-shoots, seven thousand page encyclopedias on the vulcan culture (with a concordenance), models ships, model Shatner Toupees (scale, no less), more web sites than bones in my body (including the toe growing out of my right ass cheek), and a <u>legion</u> of faithful followers. It's too hard to ignore now because it's everywhere! They're everywhere! They're taking over, I tell ya!

-A Brief Sanitarium Break-

Ok, I'm fine now. Now that we're back to our senses, let me make this comical, yet logical point. Picture if you will, the bulk of the fans (and boy, do I mean bulk). A majority of these people have spent years of their lives and a ridiculous amount of money learning how to speak Vulcan and Borg and all the other languages from the show. Made-up languages. Imaginary dialects. They've studied for the better part of their young adult lives, which they're never gonna get back, mind you, to learn how to speak in something that's no more useful than frigging pig Latin, or baby talk. Now here comes the funny part, so pay attention or you're gonna miss it. If one of these super-fans actually went to school and spent just a smidgen, a tiny fraction, of the time they spent learning Vulcan, on learning a language that exists in reality, a language that sane people use in another country, they could very well be making up to six figures a year translating for some ambassador, teaching auto mechanics to the Japanese, or insider-trading stocks from coast to coast. But instead they pore over space ship blue prints, Klingon newsletters, and take the bubble tape off their newly bought nipple-tasers on lonely nights. A sweeping generalization on my part? Perhaps. Some small kernel of truth somewhere along the way? You're damn skippy.

Speaking of nipples, let's touch, or fondle, the subject of sexual dysfunction in the Trekker, or Trekkie, I don't know what the hell to call them other than saps, so we'll stick with Treck-Offs from here on out. God only knows what the Trek-Off couples do in the bedroom. And they do breed within their own species, so don't doubt that. Can you fathom how damaging it must be for some six year old kid to stumble into his parent's room from a nightmare just to walk into another one? See's daddy with some chrome Marvin Martian Helmet and a taser while mom's spent five hours applying fright makeup onto one side of her head so she can look like an alien mongoloid of some sort? No wonder America has serial killers in spades.

Child welfare must have a field day with that stuff! The latest rift in the craze is Jeri Ryan, who, I'll admit, is painfully good looking. But on the show, she plays an exotic species of something or another, I don't keep track of that crap, and has liver spots on a good portion of her head that would make Jimmy Carter look like the Gerber baby by dermatological comparison. Trek-Offs love that stuff! 'Well, it's a trait of her people's race, so it's very attractive, you know. I read in the fifth novelization of the series that when they mate, these pus-like cheese doodles spring out of the kidney spots and their features take on the likeness of Winston Churchill." I'm so glad that you know that. I thought leather was strange, but this is about five states out of the ball park, my friend.

And oh, what *creative* depictions of aliens! Each one is so incredibly and uniquely different then the other, isn't it? I think we have time for a short anecdote, don't you? I was just going to go right out and steal this idea, but it's too funny to ignore giving credit. A few years back, I was dating a Trek-Off, a real piece of work. When she and I lived together, it didn't matter if there were nuclear missiles headed toward the apartment or a Simpsons marathon on one of the other channels, but she had to watch Star Trek. There was no debating it. It drove me nuts because sometimes that was the only available t.v. in the place, and, since I was smoking enough marijuana at the time to collapse one of Cheech Marin's lungs, I wasn't a big reader. So I was stuck watching a few episodes and I'm never the type to sulk quietly (hard to believe, isn't it?). One day I had a few friends over and we were hanging out on the couch while she watched Star Trek when one of these burn-outs speaks up with and astute, cannibis-spawned observation. Turns his head to her and says, "One thing that's really stupid about this show is how all the aliens have weird shaped heads with human bodies. At least in "Star Wars", they're all alien. How are you supposed to believe this shit?" She.....was.....livid. I burst out laughing just as much from shock that he'd said something coherent let alone funny. And how true! I'll leave that truism at that. It's too beautiful in it's simplicity to mess with.

So anyways, the first show, the original "Star Trek" was harmless. High-camp overacting of a caliber that would shame Al Pacino, a sketchy sci-fi plot, and a little T & A to help boost the ratings. A nation of geeks identified with the isolated, sexually frustrated crew members in the vast loneliness of space, and signed up for the fan club. Five movies in, "Next Generation" begins, and a new army of geeks hops on board. Granted, Patrick Stewart is a stellar actor and a damned good-looking bald man, but the show decided to be serious. They're interacting with cults of aliens and battling fleets of weirdos to the tune of Shakespearean themes. Fantastic. I'm well aware that

Trek-Offs are renowned for their attention to details in individual shows in addition to the general schemata of the plot, so forgive me for not researching this article with Jesuit-like thoroughness. I thought, after seeing a few episodes of "Next Generation", that it was sort of silly, but I could understand why it was appealing to the fans. It had some intrinsic value.

Along comes "Voyager" and "Deep Dish Shameless Spin-Off Nine". Suddenly, cable is flooded with Trek. Every channel on the dial has people running around in red and purple pajamas on missions of peace and exploration. Inescapable crap. It seems to me like they recruited every soap opera actor and ancient sitcom walk-on in the book from the Official Thespian directory and threw them onto these two jewels of modern television. Deep Dish, to my knowledge, isn't even in motion! Why in the *&%$@er &*%$#%ing &%$# would anyone want to watch a space drama where nobody even &(*%$#ing moves, for &*%$#'s sake!? They're like intergalactic gas station attendants!!

And who told Bill Shatner he was capable of writing a book, let alone acting?! That's what I'd really like to know of all things. If I was granted three existential truths from the Sphinx, that would be my first, second and third question. He went off and wrote three or four books, all by himself, with his own shitty sci-fi epic. Something entirely different from Trek. And the Trek-Offs marched out and bought all of them. Star Trek has officially one-upped Oprah. The institution is like an instant Oprah (just add geeks). No matter the medium, no matter the means, it sells. Nobody needs to plug anything shamelessly like the other large institution, because it sells! Trek-Offs are faithful and committed, baby. I read somewhere that these people, the average Trekker, spends upwards of four to five thousand dollars *a year* on related paraphernalia!! Four! To Five! Thousand Dollars! A YEAR! I'd imagine that heroin addicts have more grocery money. That's not a hobby, that's a bona fide illness!

Coincidentally, I was talking to a pretty good friend on the phone today, and warned him of the impending article. He's pretty easy going, so he said "You know what they say, Tom, whatever floats your boat." True, true. This whole thing doesn't keep me up nights, it just bothers me from time to time. If it makes so many people happy, they must be doing something right. I just wish the fans could behave a little bit more and not act so weird and fanatical, because it gives a bad rap to not only the other 95% of science fiction out there, but it lumps the rest of us sci fi fans in with them. Granted, science fiction and it's fans are unfairly stereotyped, but you can't tell me Trek doesn't have just a little something to do with it.

There are those of us who like sci-fi (or as Harlan Ellison curmudgeonly refers to it, speculative fiction) who can properly function in the world and relate to other human beings. Perhaps there are a few Trek-Offs, but I'm not going out on a limb for them. There's *so much* good science fiction and fantasy out there, too! You have to look with a trained eye, but aah, when you find it, it's like a fine goat cheese. I'm a little finicky myself, but I'll always enjoy Ray Bradbury and Harlan Ellison, Robert Heinlein and J.G. Ballard, to name a few. I've heard that Philip K. Dick is good, which I can assume after watching "Blade Runner" a few dozen times and "Total Recall" once or twice. Someone told me a few weeks ago that William Gibson is quite the sci-fi visionary. And I doubt you need a good word from me about Star Wars and it's related empire.

What's unique and wonderful about good science fiction is that it gives us a vision or an analogy of where things are headed, and sometimes, scarily enough, it's right. Most images of the future can be divided into two sections: the sloppy, and the neat. Sometimes it's portrayed as a stinking garbage heap where our overpopulation has crowded us into ski-high cubicle apart, and sometimes it's portrayed as a streamlined utopia where we finally learn from our mistakes and how to get along with each other. Everytime the government does something arbitrary, some egghead pulls

Orwell's "1984" out of his ass, so I'll use something else. Let's get back to that Gibson. He dreamt of the internet about ten years before it even existed! I find that pretty shocking. You don't see that sort of insight in "Bridges Of Madison County" or "The Firm", boy. That's why Newsweek polled a few popular science fiction authors as to where they thought the Internet was heading in the next ten years, as well as computers in general. And dollars to donuts some of their thoughts will be right. <u>That's</u> what's great about science fiction. I just worry that the Trek-Offs will scare people away from the good stuff when they waltz around with loincloths gibbering Ferenghi and nipple-tasing themselves. Whelp, live long and prostrate gland and otherwise, we're all geeks in one form or another. I'm just better at hiding at.

bananas are more entertaining in pajamas,
Tom "viking-strap-on" Waters

No Two Flakes

They say the Eskimos have some 200 odd words to describe snow in all of it's permutations. In Buffalo, where I live, we have 400 different moods in direct correlation with snow. Every psychosis on the Depression color wheel is represented. The weather is just as much a part of who we are as chicken wings, frequently addle-brained football players, and biological makeup. And trust me, if we didn't have snow, I don't think anyone would be hard-pressed trying to find something else to complain about. It's our endearing curse.

What's amusing is how shocked and appalled natives get after the first snowfall every year. A man could live in Buffalo all of his life, for three or four decades, and he'll still be surprised. I can hear the conversations of neighbors in their driveways: "Can you believe this?! Who expected this?! Where in the hell did all of this come from?! This is unbelievable!! It's not like we live near a large body of water or anything!! And I thought the weatherman was drunk when he predicted this five days ago!! Sheesh!" Generally, there's the initial onslaught in the beginning of November, a good sized jolt throughout December to March, and the snow starts to peter out a week or two after Easter. It's been a little wacky the last year or so, but not so out of character that the toothless Methuselah two doors down should have reason to think that he'll be cracking open warm Genny cream ales on the veranda a week after the Christmas tree goes down.

Our weather though, and I'm sure this is true of any town, allows more leeway in small talk with total strangers. We almost buck up under the tiny disasters and exercise a cordial manner that most of us weren't sure we were capable of. Conversations spring up in convenient stores, shopping malls, and over a short breather with a nonchalant elbow resting on a snowblower. Topics consist of Man, It Sucks Out There, Can You Believe The Jackasses They Allow To Drive These Days, It Took Me 72 Hours To Shovel My Driveway This Morning, and I Hear It's Gonna Get Worse Before It Gets Better. Knowing nothing about hockey or football, I'm practically foaming at the mouth at the opportunity to discuss something I actually take part in. And after a half an hour of weighing the pros and cons of Doppler radar with a newfound friend, I'm slightly hurt when they run screaming. Whelp, there's a few nut jobs in every village.

Driving is a special near-rendevouz with death in the colder months. Half of us brush off a fraction of snow off the windshield and expect the wind to blow the rest from the car. This is for when seeing where you're going, what's behind you, or which snowbank you're going to fuse with, is not really important in navigating your car. The other half of the populace drive assorted sports utility vehicles, which I've referred to with great venom in the past. This cross section likes to drive 65 miles over the speed limit to prove that a)they're very cool, b)they have genitals that humble Greek gods by comparison, and c)they are masters of the elements. Now if you mix these two types together, you have a formula for nutty winter hi jinx. I think that one of these winters we should all wear t-shirts with a number and put a sponsors decal on our cars to make this demolition derby official. At the end of the season, the winner would receive a trip to Florida the following Christmas, to prevent winning twice.

The news really does have a field day, too. I wish I was the station director in charge of dropping the rookies into a squall. It's always the reporter wet behind the ears that ends up on the screen, getting thoroughly bitch-slapped in the heart of the snow-belt, doing their best to look journalistic and unfettered by the squall of flakes pounding into their face as they smile into the camera. If I were the station director I would simply send the person out who bought me the fewest number of gifts. A month back or so, during a wicked blizzard, I saw this seasoned rummy of a meteorologist on a cake walk tour of the driveway circuit. He was smiling and interviewing some putz who was wearing speedos, a t-shirt, and a toy hat on top of his poorly trimmed head. Keep in mind that this was a person who probably shouldn't be allowed to wear speedos in the summer, let alone during sub zero temperatures.

A number of times this year I've called the phone number for the local weather update and it's been busy for hours on end. This is how deep the snow runs in Buffalo. What amazes me is that this station has the only update phone number around, and they still have to knock the other two stations. Uncontested in this field of meteorological conquest, and yet they can't help but burn the five other wacky weather guys. The message goes something like this: "Thank you for calling the weather line, and remember, we have the only competent weathermen who have earned more than a GED <u>and</u> tested drug free for two consecutive years in Western New York. When you want a coherent forecast, you know you've made the right choice by dialing us." Ouch.

The collective temperament, throughout the season, goes from slightly amused to mildly annoyed to unbearably peeved to fantastically pissed off to gratefully joyful at the first peek of spring. Studies have shown that a lot of conceptions take place during blizzard climes, and believe me, if I had a nickel for every friend born late '77 with a fall birthday, my keyboard would be tailor made from diamonds. I'm never going to find a climate with perpetual fall, but Buffalo isn't that bad. For all the griping we do, hell, for

all the griping I do, the snow makes for an interesting change of pace. And
it makes us Buffalonians interesting.

el nino be damned

Tom 'don't forget your muffler' Waters

Cough Spot, Cough

With a great affection for all creatures great and small, it's surprising that today was the first time I'd ever been to a veterinarian. After a string of pets, my parents decided, rather broken-heartedly, that we just couldn't handle the loss of another furry loved one, and it was a lucky break that we were given a cat two Christmases ago by my brother (albeit a very odd cat). Therefore, I have to live vicariously through other families' pets. It makes me sick to be so, well, dog-less, when I go over to a friend's and see them taking this sort of 24-hour entertainment for granted. It reminds me of family pool tables. They're all wasted on the wrong people. You go over to their house and the table is coated with about five cubic feet of dust and the inhabitants are using it as a vertical bookshelf/pottery holder/bicycle rack. Severely taken for granted! And this is how most family's treat their pets, except for the family in question. They took a dog that was being mistreated and frozen outside year round by a callous hunting house-hold and gave him a warm home with two playful young boys. So when my friend told me she had to take this adorable little beagle for a few rudimentary shots, my ears perked up with interest.

I cleaned out almost every empty pop container and trace of food in my car and the old boy could still smell gold under the passenger side, bobbing and weaving as he was in the back seat. I suspect it was a stray slice of an onion from a Canadian hot dog I had about three months ago. Once we were steadily en route, though, he started to quiver a little in remembrance. I asked Jen if he'd ever been to the vet before, and she said yes. I asked Jen if he'd been neutered and she said of course. I felt for the dog, I really did. If I went somewhere and they took the batteries out of my unit, I don't believe I'd go back again any time soon. They wouldn't get a favorable comment card, either.

A few short minutes later, we were at the clinic. I've noticed that they all have really outlandish names, too, like Poochie Palace and Amphibians 'R' Us and The Spay Station. I wish human doctors would follow suit. Perhaps I'd fool myself into thinking I was in for fun if I went to Dr.Bob's Wild World Of Routine Colon Cancer Exams. So we waltzed in to a volley of wild-life sounds in varying states of emergency and checked little Stryker in at the reception. It was here that I noticed an honest to god cat lounging on the back of the secretary's computer monitor! He had the whole saucy receptionist attitude down cold, too. He went out of his way to look about a foot to the right of where I was standing as if to say, "We'll be with you when we get around to it, sir. Why don't you just have a seat."

I was about to slap him around a little but I got side-tracked when the vet came in and had little Stryker step on the scale. In the reception office! It was no wonder that he was less than co-operative! What if one of his friends were there making wise-cracks about his weight? Or a cute little Lassie giving him the eye until she heard the magic number? They were really putting this guy through the ringer. After that humiliating procedure, we were ushered into a private room where he was allowed to quiver in mortal fear as he listened to some dog down the hall who sounded like he was ten minutes away from a Vietnamese snack pack. I noticed a cylindrical jar of handi-wipes and told myself to think about the use of something other than the handi-wipes.

In a few minutes, the doctor came in and made baby talk with our beagle to loosen him up a bit. Then she left and a different one whooshed in and, without so much as a Hi-how-are-ya she reached under and grabbed his package! Even in a universe of ass-sniffing this has to be considered rude. And little Stryker just looked around nonchalantly like nothing was happening. My little trooper. After this he was due for two shots. She stabbed the hypodermic into his back side and he still kept his cool front. The next one was the medicinal equivalent of a vodka Chilly Willy, where the nurse sprayed some liquid up into his nose. He subsequently lapped up the run-off and looked at me sitting in the corner like, "You broke my heart, Fredo."

As if this wasn't enough pain, humiliation and otherwise, another nurse came in to help clip his nails. This sounded too painful for me to watch. They said it wasn't a discomforting chore for dogs, but his expression conveyed something other than serenity. It was like a wrestling cage match. The one nurse tagged in and put the dog in a full nelson while the other lifted up his back legs and took what looked like a cigar cutter to his talons. After two legs, the beagle scrambled to the edge of the examining table looking to tag in another partner, but to no avail. One of the nurses lifted him up for the pile driver as the other one chomped away at the front two, and after that, he was down for the count. He received a consolation prize of two doggie biscuits for not being a cry baby, and worked off his excess anxiety by attempting to parasail our narrator with a leash and no chute in the parking lot. For future reference, little dogs have more energy than the Hoover Dam and Richard Simmons combined.

It's tough to be a pet lover stranded in a house with one worthless cat. I can't wait to have a dog of my own for the odd months of every year when all of my friends are on my list. Just think of it! Going out and buying a friend rather than going through the trouble of making one! Someone who doesn't judge me when I wear sweat pants and eat raw pork sausage straight from the roll. Perhaps I've said too much. But some day, when I'm responsible enough to remember to feed myself on a regular basis, it'll be a viable and wonderful opportunity. And we can both ignore our appointment cards.

you catch more fleas with honey,
Tom "mangy" Waters

Rice Cakes In The Round

After dieting for more than two months, there are two things of which I am absolutely certain. One is that your body is your enemy; a heartless, diabolical bastard who will stop at nothing to get in your way. The other is that all women have an honorary phd. in nutrition on par with the food and drug administration. I woke up one sour afternoon in the new year and my stomach already had a breakfast of chicken fingers prepared for us, replete with those fancy linen napkin oragami ensembles you see in the fancy restaurants, and I decided it was time to slim down. This isn't going to be one of those triumphant personal stories of virtue, so relax, because I've only lost ten pounds so far. It's not a hypocritical liposuction of the fast food lifestyle that I'm filing for a trial separation with, either. It's just a menu of the last two months, and the startling discoveries garnished alongside them. Please take note that the "No Tofu" sign is now on.

Ah, the wonderful temperaments of metabolism and genetic predisposition! How was I supposed to know that I could no longer eat five pounds of taco meat before dinner without spoiling my appetite? That I couldn't have a washboard stomach and barbecue elephant ribs at the same time? These things take adjusting to. After growing in my teens to peak height, the four hundred horsepower furnace in my belly switched gears at some point in my early twenties to resurface as the second hand engine to a Shriner's car. I made one promise though, upon near-denouncing my manness by openly dieting. If I was to cut back and eat healthy, a total lack of exercise was the very least I could do to uphold my heterosexual standing. I'll still be a guy as long as I don't wear a headband and buy a step aerobics height chair stand, or whatever the hell those things are. Since I don't turn many new leafs, I thought it best to just rotate it to a ninety degree angle first.

The empire of fast food turned on me with more severity than a civil servant with halitosis. No longer was I to enjoy the hamburgers and the triple battered, gravy sopped chili fried chickens. No more tacos and gelatinous pile ups of beautiful beef! Ok, I better stop with that now. The commercials now bombarded me, soothing and begging me to come back to the non-organic food wonderland of vein-plugging bliss, and I had to turn my head away to hide my tears. Health food is far from fast. You can't get it in a pinch and you can't buy it cheap. Health food takes planning and deliberation. This was discouraging. If, for example, I wanted a cheeseburger, BAM! It would have been digested by now. Throw a rock down a random street and you can get a burger and fries for about two dollars. If I wanted, say, a pita pouch of grilled (not fried!) chicken and fresh lettuce, I would have to hunt down some store that might remotely cater to that need, and if I was lucky, it would be in the neighborhood of eight dollars. Which is really expensive for a nutritious lunch! But it beats the alternative, actually making the meal. And I'd be damned if I was going to eat salads.

So salads it was. Green, crunchy, wet new leafs. After the initial shock and bowel-emptying comedic value that this sort of oxymoronic sight had to friends, they aren't that bad. The trick with dieting is not to take it too far. Upon being invited to dinner a few weeks ago, my accommodating hosts set fat free dressing on the table for my convenience. From my end of the table, eating a salad with fat free dressing is like beheading someone and then giving them a paper cut as an afterthought. There's only so much suffering one should go through within reason! Salads are healthy enough as it is! And fat free dressing tastes like a cross between toe cheese and moth balls. I wasn't going to deny myself the ability to eat without convulsing in disgust every time I took a mouthful. There are many extremes in the world of health and nutrition, and this was just the beginning.

There are those who will consume a coagulated Rubik's cube of bacon fat and then convince themselves that they're eating healthy when they wash it down with a diet soda. I never understood that. We get a lot of people at the theater where I work who will get a bucket of popcorn you can have a family reunion in, turn a fire hose of butter on it, and salt it liberally for fifteen minutes with the flare of a Macarena instructor, who, without a hint of irony, will ask for a small diet pop. There's denial, and then there's people who drink diet pop.

And then there are the fat free, calorie conscious, maniacal deal-a-mealers who swing from fad diet to fad diet like some carbohydrate crazed Tarzan, starving themselves incessantly in the hopes of resembling a heroin addicted supermodel. Maybe it's because I'm from the opposite sex that I don't understand the scam. Every month the women's magazines come out with a miracle regimen that grows in severity as the summer months approach: The Cauliflower and Crouton Diet! Eat Twenty Pounds In a Month And Lose

Five! That would be February. Lose Fifteen Dress Sizes By Deep Frying Shoe Laces! April. Get Into That Dream Bikini With Lemon Water and Legos! You know what I mean. If, by some miracle, one of the ladie's magazines hit the nail on the head, after decades of get-thin-quick plans, then why would they need to keep coming out with new ones? If they found the perfect diet, they'd never have to make another issue! Good Housekeeping could simply reprint the same magazine every month with varying covers featuring Julia Roberts in repose! But instead the supermarket checkouts are showered with bylines that basically say, "I'll hold the yogurt, Charlie Brown, and you kick it."

But there are happy mediums. Tuna fish and chicken and turkey are all good for you, and low fat, in moderation. Once in a while I treat myself to chicken-wing fed veal in a bed of olive oil. Drinking so many damn glasses of water a day is a bit trying at times, but now I have a prostate like hydroelectric damn, so I'm a bit healthier. I could pine about being happy with who you are, but piss on that. I lost ten pounds in so far, which isn't really an overnight success story, but I have more pep and vigor than I'm used to, and the bean bag that forms over my belt when I sit down has diminished slightly. This way, after I've had my first stroke in my mid-50's, and the doctor tells me I need to change my diet and exercise regularly, I'll have enough energy to choke the life out of him. It makes better health sense. no, i'll just have the salad,

Tom 'vinegarette' Waters

The Body of Christ and a Gin and Tonic, Please

-or-

Too Many Jennys

You wouldn't know it from looking at me, but I'm not exactly the wedding type. Some people take in two or three dozen when it's in season, and then there's me. The majority of the time, if blood's not involved, then neither am I. I take after my dad and send a check. It's classy, it's one less meal for the family to pay for, and, of course, one size fits all. Nobody ever sends money back. You can't lose! It beats the hell out of a blender, or bad curtains anyhow. To date, I've been to three weddings. My brother's (where

I stood up, and was therefore required to attend), one of my cousin's (at four years old, I was an adorable ring-bearer), and one of my God-sisters (open bar). Until last week, that is.

I'm very close to my god parents and their family. We go over to their house on New Year's Day every year for a smorgasbord of finger food, meat, and whiskey sours, and my folks play Pinochle with them every couple of months. It was always a running joke in conversation that if my parents were ever to career off a cliff and die in a horrible fashion, they would be my parents. And I've known Jennifer, the bride and subject of this whole silly essay, for the better part of my life. So I felt compelled to attend. Plus I actually had a ravishing date for the shin-dig. Plus there was going to be free beef. And no one wants to miss that.

You see, the O'hares are a very kooky family. Full blooded Irish-men and women, Mr. O'hare worked for the IRS for god knows how many years, and Mrs. has worked at a ritzy restaurant for about the same span. What's bizarre is the domino-effect of the sibling matrimony. It was like a greyhound race or something. The eldest daughter hitched up about five years ago. During that wedding, the only son proposed to his girlfriend at the time and they were walking down the aisle a couple months later. A year or two after that, the second daughter out the gate was shoving cake in someone's face. And now, Jen. After one child slipped the ring on, the rest fell in line.

Since Jen's only a year or two older than me, we used to play when we were kids. And no, not like that. Well, my big brother forced me to kiss her on the swing set in the back yard when I was three, but nothing came of that. Other than that, she's been like a sister to me throughout my life. We saw "The Jungle Book" when I was in the 3rd grade, "Spies Like Us" in the 4th grade, and if memory serves (which it usually doesn't) "Your Friends and Neighbors" a couple of years ago. Jen and I don't see each other that often because we're both workaholics, and she's very socially active (to say the least), but it's not a friendship that depends on constant maintenance and upkeep. What I'm trying to say, rambling on here, is that this is a wedding I sincerely, legitimately *wanted* to go to. All I had to worry about last week was the preparation. I had no idea how much preparation was essential for females who are going to weddings. Ahem.

The wedding was on a Friday, and it couldn't have been a more beautiful autumn afternoon. If I knew then what I found out Friday, I would have started putting my clothes on in August. My Jennifer (my date, not the one saying the vows) and myself embarked from my driveway at about 12:30 to run wedding related errands. Estimated time for the wedding? 4:30. Distance? A forty five second drive. Before I continue, I'll note that I'm a very, very punctual person. Probably the only guy of my entire generation that knows how to show up somewhere on time.

First we went to the fabric store to get new buttons for my suit jacket. Very important. The old buttons were these gaudy, hideous nautical buttons that made me look like a weatherman making poverty level-salary. Granted, this wasn't a royal wedding or anything, but it may as well have been in my eyes, so I wanted to look sharp. After standing in line with fifteen irate women in their forties for a half an hour at a single register, Jen had an appointment to make. More waiting. Forty five minutes, to be precise. I am not a patient person, nor am I good at faking it. I have a tiny allotment the likes of which could be poured into a novelty-sized thimble at the start of each day, and it was gone by two o'clock.

After the appointment, we had to shoot over to her sister's apartment so she could pick out an outfit for the wedding. I had a pleasant half hour conversation with her boyfriend whilst they gushed, cooed, ironed, sewed, and worked whatever sort of magic they had to with the ensemble, because she was a knockout when she came back out the door. Time well spent, but spent regardless. 3:00. Downtown. Then a mad fugue on the thruway to stop back at her place for shoes that weren't there anyway, over to the day care to pick up her boy, zipping back to her house to drop her son off, and back to home base to sew the new buttons on to the suit coat that sparked this insane trek. The time, you ask? 4:25.

We were literally the second-to-last couple into the church. Jen O'hare, looking absolutely stunning in her wedding dress, was on the steps outside, ready to march in, as we (my brother in tow) were jogging through the parking lot frantically towards the front doors. I was so frazzled that I tore down the aisle and collapsed, quivering onto the pew. Since it was a Catholic wedding, I knew I'd have plenty of time to rest and regroup.

Looking around, I spotted roughly 325 assorted video cameras, manual cameras, sketch artists, avant garde Etch-A-Sketch-ists, and one curious fellow using Sidewalk Chalk. There was no way this memory was going to slip through the cracks of time. Jen's best friend and her other sister's were standing up in a fantastic shade of purple, and the groom's side were decked out in very dapper tuxedos. I didn't know any of the guys standing up, but they all had that look of frat boys either just coming from, or on their way to a panty raid. There were about eighty people there, which was fine by me (as if I had a say one way or the other). My parents were a row or two farther down with my brother and sister-in-law, as well as Mrs. Columbo, another close neighbor, so I got to see their heads bob up and down every time we did the step aerobics that is any given Catholic ceremony, i.e.: sit, stand, kneel, rise, bend, and stretch and pray, and so on.

What's funny is how hard it hit me, seeing Jen up there. I don't know if it's because I'm getting mushy and sentimental in my old age, or because I've known her for so long, or because she looked so beatific at the altar, but my throat started closing up and I had to click my teeth for a minute or two to ride out the wave of happiness that hit. At my own brother's wedding, I thought "Great. Okay, he's tying the knot. Cool for him." , and last week I was almost teary. It really was an amazing wedding, so I hope I can get one of the fifteen billion pictures taken when they're developed.

After the service, we went to shake hands with everyone and Jen O'Hare, actually, the recent Mrs. Jennifer Bray, gives me a big, exuberant hug and says "Oh my God Tommy! I was so afraid my parents were gonna make me marry you!" with an exasperated sigh of relief. Because that's the type of person she is. And because she, my Jen, and my mother are the only three people on the planet who are allowed to call me that without being fed to piranhas. Shortly thereafter came the reception.

It's amusing to me how many more people show up for food these days as opposed to the actual ceremony. It was like a clown car of people in tuxedos filled out the reception hall, when about eight rows of pews went untouched at the church. Perhaps if an open bar were set up in churches for any given wedding, the ratio wouldn't be quite so drastic. People might turn out in droves if they could do a shot or whatever every time they kneeled, sat, and stand. It would almost be like a college game!

So for the first hour or so, the bartender was the most popular person in the room. I was jockeying drinks for myself, my girlfriend, my mother, and my brother(s). I half wished I had a trolley or a tray. We loaded up on finger foods and goat cheese and commenced to mingle. The rest of the extended Columbo family was in formation, and at some point, Mrs. Columbo had hopped into a telephone booth between the church and the reception and changed from a smart business suit to a formal evening gown. Greg had praised me for my abstinence from spirits, while Andy, one of the younger twins, was about eight beers in. Yin and Yang, I suppose. The Mr. was taking in the surrounding atmosphere with his usual aplomb: monosyllabic responses and stone-faced acceptance. Mr. Columbo reminds me of the Sphinx in the sense that he plays golf, and he has a good hair do. I have no idea what that just meant. We sauntered over to the father of the bride, and I flippantly remarked that he could sell his tux now that the last of the kids was gone from the house. We traded a bad joke or two and then my Jen and me repaired to our designated table. This whole wedding thing wasn't so bad after all! I've got another one coming up in June, so hopefully I'll be a polished small-talker by then, and still presentable enough to hose off and waltz around in a monkey suit.

I don't think reception seating is ever planned without a tiny bit of mischief. Roosting at table 8 were Jen and I, two Columbo boys, my little brother, my big brother and his wife, and Tara, one of Jen O'hare/Bray's old friends from high school whom I spent a decent amount of time with a few years back. Owing to the fact that neither of us had seen the other for six years, I had gotten a drastic hair cut on my birthday days before, and she looked all respectable, we didn't even recognize each other until about thirty minutes into the meal proceedings. Which was fine.

As it stood, I was getting roasted and filleted by my brother and sister-in-law in front of my girlfriend. It was a slow and painful death involving a)embarrassing anecdotes with the narrator as central character, b)mind-bogglingly anxiety inducing allusions to baby pictures, and c)general quips and knocks to my self-esteem. The entire time I talked to my brother I was thinking about how Jill (his wife of 3? years now) said he felt like a stuffed sausage while wearing an undershirt, and how funny that was. When I got up to grab a smoke before the main course, Tara positive I.D'ed me and we were therefore etiquette-bound to 'catch up' and create pleasantries to share with each other. This is one of the nice things about getting old in non-formal environs; you can decide whether or not to remember someone before you're in the danger zone. We'd both been miserable, depressed psychedelic cowboys when we did hang out years ago, so we had nothing nice to reminisce about and therefore nothing nice to say to each other. After five minutes of torture, we hardly spoke to each other for the rest of the night. I'm pretty sure it was a mutual agreement that was cemented telepathically at some point between the soup and the sorbet. For the rest of our time there, she and her boyfriend/fiancee/whatever the hell he was sat like stone slabs with mandibles. While I was being bombarded with deprecating comments from every other spoke in the damned table.

Now I've been on a diet for the last seven months, so a tender, moist, well-prepared hunk of animal flesh was epiphanic when it arrived in front of me. My fangs and myself howled in delight during the rending of the prime rib. Looking over at the big people table where my mom and dad were seated, I could just imagine my father appraising and rating the meat while eating it, as well as wondering what sort of sauce he was going to throw the leftover meat and bones into at home. The potatoes were, well, I'm Irish, so you can figure that out for yourself. I accidentally missed half of the best man's toast while I was out on the veranda ruminating, and walked in during it, succeeding in making an awkward ass out of myself twice in the last two hours. I'm very good at doing that (making an ass of myself), I only wish that it didn't happen with such alarming regularity. For dessert, they had baked Alaska, which was pretty damn good, and the bride and groom mashed it in each other's faces.

The bride danced with her father to a live band, and I had a tiny little revelation. One of those split seconds that hit you like a sand bag shot by catapult. The lights were dim and we were holding hands and this room full of eighty or ninety odd people were hushed and expectant, riveted to the bride and her fairy tale on the polished mahogany with her daddy. I leaned over to Jen and whispered "This is one of the moments in your young life that they never tell you about, something I'm always going to cherish." Moments like that are few and far between. Then the groom danced with his mother, the whole wedding party danced goofy, and to both of my brothers' delight, the bar reopened. And everyone rejoiced.

We had just enough time to squeeze in a slow dance and say goodbye to the happy couple before we had to pick Eric up from her parents, so we shot out to the floor on my big brother's goading attributed to some freak air bubble of romance, and gazed longingly into each other's eyes and so forth. I cut in on the groom and the other Jen tells me how cute my Jen looks. After agreeing, she says, "So are you gonna marry her?", to which I reply, "Why don't we worry about this wedding, Jennifer." What can I say? It was her day, and she could've have gotten away with saying much worse. Shortly thereafter, she did. Trading back over to my Jen, the bride told her that "We used to bathe together, but we were forced to, and I just thought you should know." Embarrassment and personal discomfort is a rainbow of blushes, and the top of my head hit every color like a Test-Your-Strength meter. A mambo number or some such tempo came on, I got suckered in to looking like the spastic stork I come off as while dancing, and the dream was over, as Lennon would put it. We walked out to the car and the luster and newfound wonder we'd basked in for five scant hours was already leaving us. But it was a nice ride while it lasted.

Most people my age either take marriage very seriously, or they don't put much stock in it at all. I'm part of the former party. Most people my age have grown up in the ashes of a society where nuclear families are an endangered species, a rare and wonderful thing. The problem with the demographic I'm sandwiched in isn't that marriages are that much harder, or that the world is a tougher place to work things out in, but simply that we quit, cave in, or cop out that much faster. My parents have had a wonderful marriage that's been tempestuous, passionate, and difficult at times, but they're that much stronger as a result. This is all par for the course, and I think it makes the good days, the happy times, all the more intense and enchanting in spite of a given fight. They give me hope for Mr. and Mrs. Bray, as well as myself in the turbulent '20s, and who the hell wants to die alone anyways? I want someone to argue with on my deathbed or, barring that, a neat row of Singapore Slings set up next to the holy water for my special day. Is that so impossible to fathom?

I'm king of this house, and my wife is Sgt. Preston,
Tom 'justice of the reese's pieces' Waters

-Dedicated to the O'hare Clan.

It Takes a Global Village To Obliterate What Little Civilized Progress We Had In The First Place

I feel the same way about my new Macintosh as I do about ex-girlfriends (as few as those are): they're esthetically pretty, irritating, and if nobody was looking, I'd toss them out of a fifth floor window. But this isn't going to be an Apple lambasting, this is an internet piece. Well, perhaps a little Apple lambasting. A goodly amount? Agreed. I've been hooking into the net almost every night for over two years now, and I shake my head and wonder why the hell I'm wasting my time every evening that I sign off. I honestly wouldn't lose any sleep if some cyber putz went farther than he hoped and the net came crashing down. The internet is a form of paid slavery disguised as an emerging social medium cloaked in bells, buzzers, and hollow enticements. But before I get carried away with that, let me outline why I want to march around my living room draped in fruit roll-ups with Steve Job's head on a stick.

When I blew fifteen hundred bucks on this circuit-integrated, ergonomic party favor back in March, I was hoping for something fast online, something idiot-friendly, and something with more memory. I promised myself back in 1995 that I wouldn't buy another computer until I got paid and published on a larger scale, and, well, certain compromises had been made. Firstly, I couldn't fit one of numerous internet upgrades onto my archaic hard drive. Secondly, I wanted a computer that I could transfer my lexicon of essays over to with a minimum of fuss. And above all, finding an ink cartridge for an old

Macintosh is paramount to finding a kiddy pool of pork rinds in the middle of a Bris (a cheap joke, admittedly, but they're a necessity in some circumstances).

Apple used to be the underdog with a simple operating system that you could depend on, and when I hooked it up at home, I discovered that I'd bought a PC clone with a big ol' apple on the front. I wouldn't be surprised in the least if there were a screen saver of Bill Gate's misshapen guava head floating around in here somewhere, but I'll be damned if I can find it. If I hadn't spent so much money on this day-glo over-inflated excuse for a word processor, believe me, I would have taken it to the top of one of the Great Pyramids and set it free aloft a skate board a long time ago. Until I get published, though, I suppose this will do. I can make a seven layer cake in the time that it takes to boot this thing up, but it does the job (when it's in the mood), and it goes online fairly fast. As if speed were an option with any computer where the net was concerned.

All the brainy officials and cyber-biographers like to say that this is the awkward growth phase of the world wide web, and that linkage difficulties and downed servers are simply a side effect of the budding adolescence of the technology. I find this hard to believe when such an obscene amount of money is pouring into the enterprise by and large every minute, every hour every day of the year. It's a capitalistic wet dream! A store that never closes, with customers who, for the most part, have a lot of capital and no intention of spending it anywhere else as they never leave their houses unless they need software or toiletries! Toiletries being optional, mind you. No market has ever catered so perfectly to shut-ins and the sociably inept than the internet, and you can see the dollar signs flashing with each advertising banner. There's a commercial with a candy ass kid using a computer that looks comparable in sticker price to a Hum-V taking a picture of an empty pan and sending it via internet back home, and every time I see it, I go into psychotic convulsions. Any silver spoon college boy who has a computer with that much horsepower to it would've pawned it for heroin before he even thought about food. We're an instant PC society, ladies and gentleman. Just add marketing. I'm well aware that I'm included in this mob-mentality, but I'll rationalize a little farther down the road. The money is there, and every get-rich-schtick in the universe is preying on the sucker born every minute. Only now, they take the guys money before he gets his umbilical cord snipped.

I have a small circle of friends both in and outside of this cursed demon box, and a number of them have been coerced, goaded, and hard-sold on scanners in the last year. I see a little advertisement pop up every time I sign on, too, but you don't see me buying one. I'm told repeatedly how invaluable a scanner is, and how, for a hundred dollars, I could send pictures to distant relatives, prepare important business documents, or incorporate it's fantastic wonders into a four hundred dollar photography set up! I may be the king of instant gratification spending, but I won't be brain-washed into buying something I don't want, or that I'm not going to use. My friends know it, and America Online is beginning to get the picture.

The whole scanner scam is a crock, and the only thing people use them for is taking naked pictures of their bloated and grotesque forms and sending them to people who don't want to see them anyways. Like, for instance, moi. The general demographic of hard core net users either look like they've never seen the light of day, or, thank God, that they never have. The fairy tale of an hour-glass dead ringer for Jenny Mcarthy spending her spare time at two in the morning looking for fifteen year old boys who talk like Tupac and act like a keyboard with genitals is, I'm sorry to say, false. The guy to girl ratio online clocks in at about 15 to 1, and of those girls, about one in a hundred and fifty doesn't resemble Roseanne after a C-section and a hobbling case of acne. Which is why I have no intention, nor will I ever, of dating online, or using the net for such means.

I just don't use the net for dating, which cuts me out of around forty percent of it's appeal. I'm not looking for nude video feeds of Dr. Laura Schlesinger, so deduct another twenty percent. What we're left with is actual information, friendly conversation, and bizarre facts. Like any boy, I strive to build the better Batcave. And what's a batcave without a super computer? A database good for cross referencing and investigating is crucial. To erase all doubt for you, dear reader, I have a near-pathological hunger for the peripheral, inconsequential trivia about the world we live in. And the web is a good place to look. At four in the morning. While I'm splitting my attention watching Howard Stern. When I absolutely have to know which exorcism case study took place in Afghanistan. Or how Sheryl Crow got her foot in the music industry as a back-up singer on tour with Michael Jackson. And similar information that most people could care less about.

Not that I don't do some socializing, mind you, but I have rules. The only reason I talk online, as opposed to most net jockeys, is to do just that: <u>talk</u>. Sometimes I wonder if talking (typing) online is a help or a hindrance to my writing, but in the final analysis, it's a help. It keeps me limber, vocabulary wise, and it helps me stay lean and quick. I've had the same close friend for two and a half years online. She lives four states away, we've never met, and we've talked about absolutely everything. A strong net friendship is a great thing, because you can tell someone you don't see every day what's going on over on the flip side, confide secrets, or simply be someone else. They actually seem to evolve faster than real-time friendships, because the turnover is so rapid, and the process is so clear cut. There are a few other people I talk to, but they passed the test. I never meet anyone off-line, because you're just asking for trouble with that one, and if you can't make friends in the tangible universe, how the hell can you make any on the strands of the net? I never go into chat rooms, because it's impossible to have a decent conversation when thirty other people are making the minimum of small talk and the maximum of trash talk. And I just don't do cyber-sex. The concept is ludicrous and desperate in my estimation.

What a statement, though! In the wake of AIDs and the lesser diseases that leave partners with the equivalent of penicillin on their genitalia etc, a lot of people have reverted to the ultimate safe sex: the kind without any contact. How outlandish. You can't get much more sterile than that. Rather than choosing partners wisely, some choose long distance promiscuity. A solution, perhaps, but a severe and frigid one. Which is one of the many long term effects I wonder/worry about. If the machines we hook ourselves up to will turn us into cold and detached machines. I don't remember learning about alluring AOL profiles being encoded into our DNA strands in biology class. Maybe I was sick that day.

A lot of the world's flaws can be tsk-tsked on a number of things, be they newspapers, bad parenting, or the lecherous result of rock music; one detriment that's directly proportional to the boom of the net industry, as far as I'm concerned, is the already-snowballing erosion of proper grammar. In five or six short years of force feeding the positive effects of the world wide web in public schools (translation: payola!), the better part of a generation has been breast fed on computers, chat rooms, and the parent-friendly addiction of logging online with every free second of leisure time. I read in a survey last week that the majority of 6-12 year olds spend 3 hours on line a day! 3.....hours! That's.....a little bit scary, don't you think? I'll admit, I only played outside two or three days a week when I was a kid, but I didn't plug my brain and my freedom of thought into a gray box for the remainder.

So you have this legion of children whose typing skills consist of what they were raised on in Pokemon chat rooms. A cross section of rug rats who think that 'yo homes', 'brb', and 'rofl' are all acceptable terms in the writing process. That grammatical short cuts are a way of life. Teenagers with empty heads and no individual interests, instant-messaging each other just to say "Wassup?" every day, and nothing more. I'd love to see their work resumes when they're in their 30s. Not to mention their conversational skills (or lack thereof). I've seen the future through the mirror of an instant message box, and it's tremendously obnoxious. That's not just the curmudgeon in me saying that, either.

Another one of the internet's negative short term effects is the utter implosion of customer service as a '90s institution (although it's not entirely to blame). A few short years ago, a given consumer had a choice between two or three different locations for a product. Now, thanks to a plethora of web pages, a corresponding site for every physical store, and millions of sites for the intangibles, Fred Q. Customer has gone mad with the gluttony of pampering! Shoppers by and large have turned into spoiled brats, pissing and moaning to whomever is offering a service, because they know that every open field has to work that much harder now to get a buck due to the competition. Once upon a time I rooted for good service, but that's no longer an issue. Good service is out there, it's just not enough anymore for some people. Some people need a good bitch slap, too, but I guess there's no demand for that. Yet.

The net has turned into a rabid monkey's paw of a Frankenstein monster, feeding off of the boredom, the base needs, and the insecurities of a society that stuffs itself with disposable entertainments. Where in the past could someone sell their old gym socks or a Hummel she-male figurine at an auction to the highest bidder? Who would've thought that there would be bidders for everything? That so many people living in your back yard got their kicks from child pornography? When you think about the capabilities of such a doo-dad, it's sad to think about what we've shaped this fledgling giant into. With microcosms of valuable information at the push of a button, in the end, we're left with a cross between global yard sales and overblown dating services for the socially retarded. We're on an industrial runaway train, and our inventions are carrying us away with them. Every gizmo is lauded for the amount of time it saves us. What time? I don't have any spare time! Time saved so that it can be spent jacked into another computer. I like my toys, don't get me wrong. But if the 2000 bug bites, I won't fret. Imagination will never cease to be the most rewarding form of entertainment, and if you need batteries for that, then you have my condolences.

ebay my ass,
Tom "56-K-Y Jelly" Waters

The Tube-Sock Syndicate

I have a solution to the welfare problem, the black hole of social security, and the mess that Medicare has become. It's one simple, straight forward resolution for all three, and it's a wonder that no one else has thought of it before. Maybe it's drastic, but drastic times call for drastic tablespoons. The solution is this: anyone who is over 60 should be jettisoned to a remote, isolated location or, barring that, just segregated and 'involuntarily' 'seceded' to Florida. They've got most of the state as it stands, so it wouldn't be that big of a change. There's plenty of room in the other neighboring southern states for the younger families to move laterally to that receive similar or greater wrestling and Nascar reception. This may sound shocking, but it beats my first proposition, consisting of a new strain of pesticide. Oh boy. I've said too much, and endangered your personal safety. So aside from the fascist viewpoint, which is purely fantasy and a bit extreme for most, I think a tropical or sunny retirement state as an absolute is a perfect compromise for everyone considered. Because old people are a pain in the ass. Well, nine out of ten old people. Let me amend that and say forty nine out of fifty. Actually, after an exhausting census, my final nice senior citizen to miserable old crone ratio would have to be one to four hundred and seventy two. With a one person margin of error. Since I don't have existing grand parents any longer, I can say this in good conscience.

The elderly are a wicked, crotchety, incessantly whining leech on the change purse of the system, and I for one am jealous and tired of it. In a day and age where longevity is upheld and revered mere decades after a financial loophole was created to give the retired and useless a meaty allowance with no strings attached, something has to give. Namely, the retirement program. I keep hearing in the news that I'm not going to have any social security if and when I make it to 55. I say we head those shenanigans off at the pass and just Priority Mail every available old person to the Sunshine State. Every time I wait in a grocery line (strike that, a line of any kind), or get stuck behind some tank of a Lincoln Town Car that looks like it's being driven by a two foot blue bee hive, I'm reminded of two things. One is that my taxes are sluicing out of this person's pocketbook or money clip at the speed of sound. The other is that senior citizens are irrationally rude to everyone but themselves.

Back in their day! When they were younger, in their time, in simpler times.......ad infinitum. You've heard all of the stories and I'm sure you have a few of your own. When dinosaurs roamed the earth and for some strange reason the world was paradoxically slanted so that every walkabout was somehow uphill, be it to school, work, or church. Back in a given sarcophagus's day, people could drop out of school after the fifth grade and get a steady job with benefits, security and a pension for the rest of their lives. I'm almost vicariously nostalgic because in their time, you could look forward to letting the state carry and support your wrinkled and liver-spotted ass for the last twenty plus years of your life. Granted, some elderly actually did put money and hard labor into the system of retirement. But how many women from the forties and fifties never worked a day in their life? How many senior citizens go the doctor three hundred times a week just so they can talk to another human being and use up my benefits at the same time? I don't understand how old people have the right to complain about the obscene rate of inflation (which may seem obscene if you've watched the cost of living shoot up over the course of ninety years) when it's not even their money that they're spending!! The federal government has a big community chest that the country dumps their taxes into, and all of the rudimentary doctor visits and placebo medications are draining it faster than a headlining stripper with a body shot of Jim Beam. Whoops! Forget I said that. Is it any wonder that I feel like I've been jail-raped by a gang of Aryan bikers? Not only do I get to watch the elderly spend my money, but I get to hear them complain about it! My generation, and every one after that, is getting it from both inputs, without lubrication. I've been violated.

Why are they so incorrigible? Maybe it's because their time in the lime light is over. They no longer count as a demographic, and no one pays attention to them for the most part, so they feel like they have to kick and scream to get attention. If I had a nickel (or what a nickel was worth when these people were my age, as they're so fond of pointing out) for every time I've had to sit idly in public and listen to some parchment corpse whine and lament at length to some helpless service person who stopped listening after about two minutes, I wouldn't have to worry about squirreling cash away for a retirement account. Nobody cares what some anonymous ancient wretch has to complain about, because they always complain! It's not so much boy who cried wolf as the old lady who bitched about the inflated cost of tooth paste. If I had half of a penny for every time I wanted to bludgeon one of these people over the head with the nearest blunt and/or rusty instrument, I'd never have to work for the rest of my life. Before I forget, let me mention that this essay is being written for the old person newsletter at my local community center.

There's a sort of a reverse-vulture effect with old people. After a certain age, relatives and total strangers, uncomfortable with illnesses and the reminder of their own mortality, steer clear of septagenarions, octogenarians, and the rest of the Al Roker jet-set like rats off of a sinking Frenchman. After being isolated socially, they go out into the world and cause a ruccus to synthesize what passes for a connection with a world they no longer have any control over. The isolation drives them mad! Well, that, and a pharmaceutical regimen that would put Hunter S. Thompson into cardiac arrest. A regimen that everyone my age pays for.

After being separated, old people enter into a Howard Hughes-type symbiosis with their radios and televisions, hard wired to the news and the weather stations in some futile attempt to keep track of what's going on around them. Other than current events, they don't watch or listen to anything that's been recorded for the last thirty years because they have no connection to the culture being represented. Young people (better known as any one under 300 yrs old) are seen as threatening because of their different value systems, style of dress, and slang, and consequently scowled at. It's pretty fun and cheap to aggravate old people, due to the fact that it's really easy. Whenever some cane-weilding ghost gives me the 100 yard stare, I just smile back and it sends them scrambling for a pill. If it seems like I'm making grand, sweeping generalizations, it's because I've lived in a neighborhood infested with old people for most of my life, and because most of them are true. So there.

The elderly have a strong bond with adolescents, since they're both on the outskirts of the workaday world. Old people see non-threatening innocence, and the chance to mold an impressionable child into something that resembles a decent human being, whereas children see someone who's loose with money and takes a proportionate amount of naps. It's sort of nice to see two sections of outsiders who find comfort in each other. Neither group is responsible for much insofar as participating with what's lies beyond their doorsteps, and they have a penchant for sweets and long-winded, self-invested monologues that most people aren't remotely interested in. The writer will now take a breather to surgically shove both feet in his mouth. Oomphgurgbleg...........

I'll go to bat for those one or two nice old people hobbling around on the face of the earth, or the wizened Nobel laureates, physicists and composers. But as for the rest of them, what good are they? They have no jobs, they're unconscionably rude, and they're spending my money! They can't function behind the wheel, they can't do anything at a faster pace than say, a snail with a morphine drip, and for as bad as I come off, they hate me just as much as I hate them. I hope their pacemakers go haywire at the turn of the century and we get a couple who drop like so many seagulls over Love Canal. We have to save Ben-Gay as a natural resource for the born-again toothless of tomorrow.

What would be so bad about Florida? The bitter and crippled love hot weather, as they have bad circulation and the humidity is good for their leathery complexions, so it isn't as if they'd suffer. When you think about it, the state is designed like a big retirement home. Bingo, shuffleboard, wading pools, and a gold mine of antique crap. Everybody dresses like they're color-blind, Cuban, or time travelers from the Hoover administration, so assimilation isn't an issue. And as far as I'm concerned, they can <u>have</u> Disney World, part and parcel, I don't give a suspender-wearing, circle-eared rat's ass! The rest of America could chalk it up as spoils of war and build an additional evil amusement empire somewhere else. So it isn't like old people would suffer if they got farmed out to Florida at 60. Washington could treat it like a commune, or a non-profit organization; separate, but part of the nation nonetheless. Senior citizens could have the fat of the land, and what drug cartel or immigrant boat would have the courage to face down a platoon of lobster-burned, topless hairy men in checkered shorts and ankle high socks? It's an ideal solution! I'd never go south (geographically, anyway), but if I play my cards right, perhaps I'll get banished or have to flee to another country by the time I'm in my sixties. This is known as 'pulling a Polanski'. Or was that what they said about George Michael? I can never remember.

The main reason I abhor the ancient isn't about the money, though, or that I'm going to have to work my tail off to grow old gracefully (if that's an option); I'm angry with them because they're allowed to act the way I wish I could act most of the time. An old person can get away with screaming at a total stranger in the face for twenty minutes without any fear of reprisal. If I had varicose veins and a walker, or one of those funky shopping wheelchair hybrids, I could coast around town, go up to a person, spit in their face for no apparent reason, and not get the mortal crap kicked out of me. Life just isn't fair. I came into this world an asshole, and sadly, I have to wait for the better part of my expectancy before I can act like one. In the mean time, I'll just have to tolerate the tired, the weak, and the aged, and they'll have to do the same with me. Mexican standoffs aren't so bad. When they're not in the seven items or less lane, that is.

Art Linkletter for Florida Governor,
Tom "where the hell are my glasses? Oh, on my head" Waters

I Think;
Therefore I Suffer

Be it a central trait of Scorpios, middle children, manic depressives, or strikingly handsome men in their twenties (tongue resting toward cheek there), I am constantly redefining and over-analyzing myself. Who is this person? What is he made up of? What makes him who he is? A third person perspective isn't crucial, mind you, but it adds more melodrama to internal dialogues and arguments. The contrasts between identity and ego could fill a landfill the size of South America, but it's safe to say that ego is a minimal yard-stick in the introspective cosmos, and that identity is the boundary around which all else is contained.

Whether the business of letters is a profession or a slight entertainment for me remains to be seen. Yet I am constantly at odds with words, their meanings, and their perfection (or imperfections) in a given sentence. I grapple with them. Lose sleep from their tortures. And Sigmund's definition of ego just doesn't convey the infinite concept of self that's been gestating in my head for the last year. This is not to say that I'm a better psychological thinker by any means, because that's just asking for trouble, but that the temporal restrictions of the term ego are far too confining in contrast to the scope of a limitless and permanent identity. My war-torn thesaurus claims that it's synonymous with individuality. I guess paperback reference books don't have a pat answer for everything. Personality, childhood trauma, self-esteem, status, caste, and rank are all bouncing around inside, ever-changing to mold the parameters of who the 'i' was, is, or will be. For the practical intentions of this work, the word ego will be used in an almost mirror sense with the term Identity, but only with the working knowledge that it is utilized with a greater implication than the textbook standard. Identity is less of a fad than a pillar of stone that wears away imperceptibly with the passage of time. But what _is_ it? While restrictions are still fresh in your mind, forgive my naivete in the realm of existentialism. I am a novice; instantly and easily outclassed by greater minds a few hundred years my senior. This is more an indulgent train of thought than the attempt of a boy playing old men's games.

The best way to define the timeless essence of yourself is, I presume, the same way you would define all other ethereal ponderable; by examining them when they aren't looking. By peering and squinting and dropping down on your haunches to get your mind around the sharp edges and tiny flotsam rather than letting yourself be overwhelmed with the sheer looming enormity of such a thing. Eliminating the variables helps. It's a lot harder than you would think to validate what identity most undeniably isn't. Almost just as hard. But a good starting point, at any rate.

No one is really what they own, although some would like to be. A car. a house, a computer and a bank statement don't make you, well, *you*. They may be byproducts of an identity, but certainly nothing more. Possessions are no more permanent than a phone call or a sneeze. They have little or no influence on who you are. If an Italian villa is the proof of how unique and incomparable you are as a person, what's to say that someone else with a villa next door isn't you? Cognitive indian-wrestling, surely, but to a logical end. Materialism is more of a sway or a hindrance upon discovering your identity than any real and valuable component. When people get caught up, tied down or, hmm, possessed with the clutter and glitter around them, they get side-tracked from any sort of affinity or cultivation of identity. A common mistake, but no less reprehensible for it's recurrence. Status symbols, like a full head of hair or a first edition novel or the latest compact car, fade away. They have no permanence and, therefore, no bearing on identity.

Social standing may be close to the mark, but not close enough. Who we represent in the rest of the world is not really who we are. People wear a lot of hats for a lot of reasons, and even if you stack them on top of each other at the end of the day, there's a lot that's unaccounted for. If there's a Doctor, Mrs., or Honorable at the beginning of your letterhead, does that define the whole of you as an entity? Is there nothing more? For instance, a physician can be a father, a brother, a member on a softball team, and the head of the P.T.A in his town, but all of this isn't necessarily and singularly him. Titles may dictate the most important roles and obligations we play in the world, but the sum total of the parts, at best, form only the boundaries of self.

Hobbies and interests are unique to each person, but they merely add to the overall ingredients of one's makeup. A passion or special interest gives insight insofar as their tastes, depth and gratification are concerned. Someone who has an obsession with vintage baseball cards is less likely to have a dark and maudlin soul than, say, someone who locates the death masks of indigenous tribesmen. Past times are mere clues in the collective alloy of persona.

Talents and accomplishments are better defined as byproducts of the individual. The results of identity. They may demonstrate much about who someone is, yet even crowning achievements don't illustrate the big picture. Edgar Allen Poe, for all his mastery of the macabre, was tortured by love as well as by fear. The story goes that he proposed to three different women on the same day. But trying to extract that sort of human nature from one of his vignettes is near impossible. Propensities illuminate the best in ourselves, rather than, well, the rest of ourselves.

And what of the individual's convictions, opinions, and morals? These are the foundations of identity. Ever-solidifying, one's attitudes and feelings are more intimate, more inimitable than any other trait of consciousness. Just as each person's daily existence is unique in and of itself, so are his or her's feelings and reactions to the society around them. No response, no conviction is alike. Two different people will look and divulge two different things from the same situation. They'll walk away from a given situation slightly and irrevocably changed in two distinctly different ways. So the core of Identity, I suppose, has much to do with personable paradigms.

Biology and upbringing have just as much of a claim in the floating ego as mores and grown postulations. Conversely, you could say, without hesitation, that they create belief systems. Nature is not at war with nurture in this instance, though, but rather interwoven. Harmonious. It's widely held that the first six year's of anyone's life are the most formative, and that whomever you become, however you turn out for the sizable remainder, is largely and irreversibly a result of this pupal stage of childhood. I wouldn't necessarily go that far. Many integrated habits and emotional patterns are instilled in infancy, but it's cynical and small to presume that they can't be broken, or that they'll be carried out ever after. The other biological side of the coin has to do with physiological nuts and bolts, the raw stuff of existence. These are certainly influential in formulating the 'i', but they aren't iron-clad indications of origin. The ego has a mind of it's own, literally, and grows to suit itself rather than following a set pattern like so many metaphysical connected dots.

Circling back to convictions, environment is a tremendous stimulus on one's sense of self. Persons raised in one portion of the world have a distinct cultural, temporal, and religious (if any) attitude compared to other climates. For example, Icelandic culture designates a holiday every year with the purpose of encouraging adultery. This may seem wildly outlandish to you, but you haven't lived with that belief system as a norm in your community. Environmental influences can be as inconsequential as traffic laws or, in the case of politics and family, as arbitrary as a patriarchy/matriarchy standard. These outside matters do hold some sway in terms of self.

To further complicate matters, what of the detached reality of the ego? The Russian-doll-like nature of this madness makes me wonder how, even if I could plainly define who I am right at this instant in a shining moment, would it match the bare analysis? Do we see ourselves as we really are? The majority of the time, we don't. Maybe it's better that way. We trod through a flurry of distractions, be they emotions, external cursors, or physical ailments, and they all get in the way of rigorous introspection. Most matters can be defined by objective or subjective method, whereas identity is split right down the middle. An informed bystander can't divine who you are any more than you can, which renders such a study both pointless and lifelong at once. It is impossible to completely separate yourself from yourself, and if you allow opinionated triggers to inform your dissection, then the riddle itself is being utilized! Clever.

The sad and fantastical truth of the matter is, we will never be able to cut the 'i' open because it is always in flux. With change as the only constant, every other component of identity is a spontaneous metamorphosis unto itself. To realize that is to appreciate imperfection. To appreciate our imperfections takes us one step closer to utilizing what we are, as well as what we're capable of, skulking about this cold body in motion. Spending a life's work in constant self-revision is the only choice a decent writer has. As with anything, I'll do the best that I can with the resources I have, or die trying.

shying away from hemlock,
Tom Waters

Perpetual Money

Money \'mun-e*n, pl* 1. : something (as metal currency) accepted as a medium of exchange 2. :wealth reckoned in monetary terms 3. :the art of being insatiable without trying.

Believe it or not, up until a month ago, I had never trolled the collective chum nets of the evening singles scene. Not once had I sat on a barstool during last call as the sun peeked up from the horizon and prospective special friends, peg-legged and otherwise, suddenly looked more interesting to each other while some wretched Bob Seger song played on a beer-stained jukebox. For two years, I was alone by choice most of the time, and was certain I knew desperation. A month ago, I received a formal instruction in despair by every lay person (now that pun wasn't my *fault*, damnit!) in the field. This probably doesn't sound that alarming, unless you take into account that I'm a stout lad of 24. This is my journey from daylight into darkness back into daylight and, oh screw it, here's what happened.

My prior dating philosophy consisted of waiting for nubile young coquettes raining from the sky to fall into my peripheral field of vision and, by nature of proximity, in desperate and sweet, sweet love with your's truly. For your own sake, this method isn't the most effective. Least effective is a better description. Dead right worthless is perfect. Now certain boys and certain men have the innate gift of picking up anyone, anytime, anywhere, be it a supermodel at a yard sale or the much sought after girl-next-door in the grains and nuts section of your local convenience store. It goes without saying that I am not this certain type of boy and/or man. It goes without saying that most men aren't, and most men wish that this sort of person would perish viciously in a freak soda machine explosion. Some people play it wholesome, and try their damnedest (bless their hearts!) to find love and it's common denominators in haunts without alcohol, such as a library, a church service, or the occasional cross stitching club for straight men in their early twenties. First of all, I hate libraries, and most of the women who frequent bookstores are, at the risk of sounding uppity, a bit on the, eh, Homely side. Secondly, being that I pay worship to the pagan deity of retail every Sunday as opposed to God-fearing folk, I don't have the opportunity to get in on any pious action that may go on thereabouts. And lastly, my stubby, hairy guy fingers just aren't conducive to any macrame related activities. Conventional means of dating just weren't going to work, so it was clearly time for last ditch efforts.

This is the point where I was dragged, kicking, screaming (and generally biting anyone that got within a mile radius), out of my happy pocket of seclusion and into the dismal and poor lighting of the lounge lizard stratosphere. I am neither an extroverted nor zany person in the presence of strangers, so the club life was always an option and a lifestyle that was looked down upon. How foolish it is to despise something one knows nothing about when you can research and divulge each revolting tentacle for it's singular foulness (in addition to the overlying revulsion). Like this Greek dude who descended into the Underworld to bring his true love back from the dead, I wandered down into the very gutters of the velvet rope and escaped with something far more valuable: validated parking.

Being that I have led, for the most part, a sheltered and suburban life, city and inner city conduct was never my field of expertise. This isn't a very good thing, either, as most pan-handlers and run of the mill raving lunatics tend to prey on, and gravitate towards, people without this field of expertise. I'm not sure if it's because I have a face that's misleadingly kind-looking, gullible, or naive, but the homeless home right in on me. Within five feet of leaving my car, some poor, ruddy vagrant will pop out of nowhere and begin with a cockamamie tale of woe so far-fetched that I can't help but reward his flair for creativity with the 38 and a half cents that the story was contrived for: "Yo, man, my grandma got crushed in the steam press at the laundromat and I ain't got no case quarter to take a rickshaw to go see her at the hospital in Baltimore. You got a case quarter? You gotta cigarette? Wanna buy twenty kilos of heroin?" No thank you. I suppose this sort of obstacle comes with the territory.

Awful techno music is another necessary evil of clubbing that has to be tolerated as there is no alternative. On one evening, I heard the original version, house-trance remix, and 12" extended vinyl of a song that I think was called "Smack My Bitch Up" at every club we frequented. That's part of the charm of going out and dating, though; you go somewhere where you don't want to be so you can pretend that you're having fun and not looking to meet anyone in a place that's too loud, disgusting, and crowded to talk to someone even if you did make an acquaintance! A daisy chain of inevitable logic!

And then there were the Gothic, or 'Goth' people. They make up the ruling majority of the actual dancing type clubs. Goth people are a strain of trend with some bouillabaisse of an ethic and system of beliefs that would make the Mormon code look cohesive. They dress in black to convey their spiritual numbness and/or angst at their parents. Ditto for nose, nipple, eyebrow, and prostate piercing. Some of them either pretend, or legitimately believe that they're vampires. I wasn't aware that vampires were typically five foot men with skin problems and lipstick, or three hundred pound girls with pewter crosses and hairy arms, but...fair enough. The musical collective prefers rancid techno with men screaming through speaker distortion about serial killing and other such nastiness that makes them, by virtue of listening, feel nasty. I don't plan on turning into a Goth person any time soon. It sounds too exhausting. Plus even I can't pretend to be that angry all the time.

Every club, lounge, and dive had it's own charm, or prepackaged lack thereof. In club-speak, *ambience* is a term that's synonymous with 'shit-hole that a lot of interesting people for some unexplained reason keep going to'. At one of the darker clubs, the toilet was little more than an open hole in the ground sheathed in darkness, where one stood in a voluntarily unidentified puddle (I wasn't about to investigate) and tried to aim for the desired target. The place had great ambience though, because a lot of lesbians danced and groped each other there, which, admittedly, does not bode successful odds for the single male, but is entertaining regardless. Plus it made up for the outlandish cover charge.

Every woman at every bar had a special tantalizing feature that stuck to the roof of my mind like so much mnemonic peanut butter, whether it was an interesting back pack with copulating children's show mascots, a nose ring bigger than any you'd ever see this side of a toreador, or in some cases just an ass that left my eyes out of their sockets and my tongue along the rail of the bar. It's a fascinating atmosphere, with it's own ethics and a corresponding band of acolytes who go faithfully into the night, without fail, until they find that fake someone who hits home with the little fake person inside of them.

Certain days had themes attached to them in the club utopia. At one bar, on Tuesday nights, only Englebert Humperdink cover bands graced the small plywood handicapped ramp that doubled as a stage. Some bars designated Sunday as Sexually Conflicted Day, where closet gays, asexuals, and the occasional Eunic were allowed to get out, get down, and get dirty with each other, no one, or their catheter, respectively. And I'm certain it's widely known that Thursday is the day when people the world over place sponge candy in their underclothes and somersault the length of the bar onto a pool table full of Vienna sausages, but I was never privy to these things before. Just like I was never privy to dancing.

(Audible and extended sigh of disgust) I will never dance, even for the sake of finding action. No Bump and Grind, Slam Dance, Macarena, or other pasta-related dervish. There are some men who dance, and enjoy dancing, and these men are known as gay. I myself am not gay. If I were gay, maybe I'd enjoy dancing, but gayness simply isn't in my genetic encoding. It's sort of tragic how women love to dance, are always looking for guys who want to dance with them, and have no alternative other than: gay men. Sometimes drunken men dance, or desperate men, and you can still see how uncomfortable they are with their sense of coordination, self consciousness, and overall burgeoning embarrassment regarding the fact that they're dancing badly. If I could make it to the bathroom without tripping over a level surface, or get on and off of a barstool without catching my jacket on a nail on a post that's three feet behind me and ripping the lining out onto the floor much to the amusement of my friends and any other strangers who aren't blind to wild, stunted spectacles, perhaps I would venture it, but I can't, so I don't. I did the twist once at the age of 13, when I didn't know any better, and the original videocassette, as well as any copies, were destroyed tragically in a freak gyro copter crash some years ago. One of the other things I learned was not to trust a straight man who dances well, as he is a professional, and therefore he is trouble.

There are lifer's on every notch of the gender rainbow in clubs, and you can spot them by these easy guidelines. If you meet someone who's hair is glazed, greased, or so perfect that they look like they should be endorsing a product while they're talking to you, that's a pretty good sign. If a woman is playing tiddly winks with a handful of diaphragms and an empty margarita glass, this is also a good sign. Persons who don't have a general air of shame and self-disappointment are almost always cold-blooded, no-nonsense, hit-and-run swingers. This isn't necessarily a bad thing, but it depends on your designated prey. Do you want a disease or a drink? A one night stand, four month relationship, or an interlude in the alleyway next to Bob the Hobo? It's an unforgiving meat market, and there are many different cuts of beef hanging from hooks in sub zero temperatures wearing nylons and pumps. You just have to know how to grade your beef. Fortunately, I lean towards the Upton Sinclair school of evaluation, as opposed to the Tijuana State Board of Excellence in Iguana Remainders.

That's not fair, though. One thing that I learned among many is that in life, there are diamonds in the dust, and the club scene is no different. The other things? Perhaps a roster is in order. Thomas' Rules Of Lounge Order, as it were. Relegated by the order in which they were discovered. Take note, and if it sounds silly, or outlandish, remember the source, and bear in mind that much pain and hardship was incurred for the sake of this invaluable scoopage I am imparting to you for the low introductory price of, well, free.

Rule#1: ***Bring A Decoy-*** This works on multiple levels. Not only do you not feel pitiful and shunned by the opposite sex, but you're gaining valuable information from the enemy lines while in their midst like so many Diane Fosseys giving rectal temperatures in the chimpanzee house of a city zoo. This is a crucial, crucial rule. Aside from learning how to speak with the fairer sex without stuttering, mumbling, blushing, and spilling food and assorted drink on yourself in a blind rash of anxiety, you appear wanted in front of actual targets. Women at heart are lovely and sweet and all of these things, but women, when dealing with other women in the realm of dating, are vicious vindictive psychotics who would put John Wayne Gacy to shame. If they see that you're with someone who's having fun with you, their natural instinct is to go and ruin whatever jubilation said girl is having simply for the sake of messing up another girl's good thing. The decoy actually gets something out of it too, as men are testosterone fueled atom bombs who will stop at nothing, including hitting on someone else's 'girlfriend' to strike it rich. But this is, of course, an irrelevant and unimportant side effect that makes you look more sensitive than you, in reality, actually are. This rule is a keeper.

Rule#2: *Nothing Ever Happens On A Monday-* This was obtained the hard way, and anyone with a brain in their head would have figured it out without unnecessary shadenfraude. Since bar folk and their ilk are perpetually in motion, it's patently obvious that after a wild Friday, a bombastic Saturday, and an Interesting Hat Sunday, Monday would be a good day for all around recovery and subsequent rehydration. One also has to factor in the possibility of the general after-parties that those in the know go to after their dive of choice shuts down at the legally enforced dawn hour(s).

Rule#3: *Recognize A Good Thing When You Have It-* When you're clearly on the road to pleasant chemistry (not including a drink with a quirky umbrella that changes colors every five minutes), follow it up and ride it out. Please see the attached.

Rule#3a: *Don't Blow A Good Thing-* With the exception of men whose first names are John and last names Travolta, you are not the universal swinger. Trading up is frowned upon in the bar malaise, and should never be performed in the same night, at the same club. It's conceptually impossible to make someone feel as if they're the only person in the room and make lascivious gestures and eye winks to someone across the room at the same time. Trust me. This is just plain rude, and I for one am disgusted at anyone who would do such a thing. Other than me, anyhow. Actually, I'm still riding a stationary shame cycle from my incident. Just don't do it.

Rule#4: *The Harder You Try To Score, The More Bleak Your Odds Become-* In a space age futuristic world full of more aphrodisiacs than people who have a use for them, it is my firm belief that confidence is, and always will be, the greatest hook with women. Desperately grappling for intimacy after the witching hour with anyone who happens to stumble or get sick next to you is not an example of confidence, but rather a dead end exercise in futility. This operates under the same universal principles as Rule 3 and it's footnote: If things are going well, put some effort into the catch. If nothing's happening by 4 a.m., odds are nothing's gonna happen. Best to cut your losses, fold, and drive home with some dignity rather than a second cousin to Ilsaa the Bearded. Unless, of course, you're into that sort of thing.

Rule#5: *Travel In Packs, Preferably Well-Wishers and Hangers-On-* It's murder out there, and one needs as many tricks as are humanly possible to gain the hometown advantage. In place, or addition to a reliable decoy an entourage adds to your personal star status and proves that you're admired and adored by many. What we're trying to avoid here is going somewhere completely by yourself and going out on a limb for someone only to get shot down horrifically by not only the intended princess but her two slightly heavy and overly giggly friends as well. Women <u>always</u> travel in packs, and so should you. One more time: Women <u>always</u> travel in packs. You see them marching like a battalion in malls, on the streets, and even to the bathroom in groups of 20, so bring some reinforcements. If you're lucky, your friends will recognize when you're interested in someone and help to build you up as the wonderful mystery that you most certainly aren't.

Rule #6 *Perfect A Look-* As in comedy, and also with dating, one must have a schtick. You can't open with something that's outlandishly out on a limb and expect consistent results, so it's best to flagellate with a routine that works. This sounds cliche', but it doesn't have to be, and when in Rome, be the fake toga wearing bastard that you can't stand. Or in this case, the Plebeian who says he 'enjoys Dave Matthews for his political impact on the 21st century, as well as his ingenious world beat innovation'. The horror of it all. I feel dirty just writing that. Before I lose track, make sure to have a look. Lounge chicks usually go for a certain type, so it's best not to confuse. There are many options and looks to choose from, up to and including 4! You can be the leather clad bad boy who's an embarrassment to the girl's parents, whom she's trying to punish for spoiling her all of her life. Or perhaps you're more the sensitive charlie brown-pullover wearing new age man with a buzz cut and penny loafers of indeterminate color? This works on gold diggers. But then of course you can be the strikingly individualistic beret/beanie/handlebar mustache sporting, tortured misunderstood artist for whom life is painful and creation is bliss (translation: college chicks). If these sound like too much of a stretch, you can just be an asshole with a sizable wad of cash, which is not too shockingly the house special of the day any day at any bar in any town.

Rule #7: *People Who Slur Are Not Even Close To As Charming As They Perceive Themselves To Be-* Circling back to the confidence game of all confidence games, if you want someone to feel uniquely desired after, the last thing to do is funnel a few liters of absinthe and deliver your soliloquy from the heap of cigarette butts and ground cheese doodles at the floor of the bar. Women like to feel needed, not lusted after by virtue of their biological bits and pieces. It's best in dating to stay on top of your game, which basically means that you shouldn't phonetically skip every other vowel in a given sentence while forming a basin of drool out of one side of your mouth. People who are drunk to the point of unconsciousness are more liable to get a ride home in a white van with big blue lights and a stomach pump rather than in the lamborghini of some blonde viking. Utter inebriation is an agenda in bars, but shouldn't be mixed with dating, ever. Aside from a complete lack of charm, drunken people have a tendency to pretend that their conscience has taken a vacation when in fact and in most cases, it's simply their sense of balance and/or bowel control.

Rule #8: ***If You Don't Have an Ugly Friend With You, Then You're The Ugly Friend-*** Fetching females collect them like so many beat-up plastic barretts under a vanity chest, and will look at you and your surrounding friends in the same manner. If the majority of your friends look suave and dapper, it's best to hang out with them on off nights and make an acquaintance with someone who has a growth on their neck, supplemental nostril, or similar disformity that will draw more attention to your own beauty. Granted, inner beauty may be important, but who are we kidding? If women were drawn to boys with flippers, we'd be sanding off our forearms right now.

Rule #9: ***The Sensitive Male Schtick Stopped Working About Five Years Ago-*** Now that everyone has the hang of it, the knack to understanding 'where she's coming from' and how you 'know how tough it must be to find your individuality in a male dominated world' in addition to the way you 'have psychological water retention that makes you feel psychically bloated in a succinctly feminine manner', nobody cares. As a man, pretending to be responsive to other's needs is about as current as wearing platform shoes and a tie wider than Marlon Brando. It's a fake out to our natural instinct, namely conquering and plundering. You know it, they know it, and there's no use trying to dress up your approach by limpening your wrist and discussing the crying jags you had while watching a Sandra Bullock movie. Masculinity is in, thank God, because we're not very good at anything else.

Rule #10: ***Lie About Your Job, Even If You Have A Good Job (And You Probably Don't)-*** That's right, I'm an analyst for one of the city's largest subsidiary brokerages. I handle off-shore accounts when I'm not cramming for my LSAT's. You may not believe this, but I'm an advisor for one of the lesser Popes, it's not really a big thing. You get the picture. Just as decoys reinforce the fact that you can behave yourself in the presence of the opposite sex, a fake job can be save you from a raving psychopath, as well as reel in the abundantly plastic persons you may be in the mood for. Leprechauns are easier to spot than anything vaguely truthful in the small talk that sifts through the air in a crowded club, so why should you be any different? After all, perhaps you actually did have some government stealth jet experience in a former life and you're simply getting in touch with that.

Rule #11: *If At All Possible, Don't Go Out To Clubs For More Than Three Months At A Stretch*- If you can drudge up the ability in yourself as a person to be outgoing, attentive, and confident in the presence of interesting women, drop out! If the attitude is there, females will pick up on it. They're much better at these things than we could ever be, and if you put out the subtle mystique of confidence, you can meet someone at a jug band cotillion. It's a cruel, relentless festival of carnality out there, and it's fun and it's fantastic, but it's not for everyone. I knew that I wasn't one of the beautiful club people going into it, I just wanted to see what I'd been missing, or hadn't been missing, all these years. Bars are a lot like the Largest Standing Cast Iron Replica of Andy Rooney in Salt Lick, Wisconsin: It was a nice place to visit, but not to stay. That, and no one can feasibly look at a scale model of eyebrows that abnormal for an extended period without having therapy-inclusive nightmares.

Pardon me, but who's that you're reading, gorgeous?
Tom "Valentino to the Impaired" Waters
-Magnanimous thanks to the Flying Bolis brothers, Melissa, and Lindsay, for patiently and diligently helping to create the monster at the end of this essay.

Introspective Cage Match

With a quarter of a century fast at my heels, I cannot help feeling content with who I am, where I've been, and what I've accomplished with my life up until now. No great feats, really, no grand voyages, but it's been......enough. It's enough to have lived long enough to be grateful for what you have, and, in the same turn, patient with what you don't, as well as stoic about everything that's been lost. The first blush of adulthood is setting in, and it's calming. My early twenties found me shrugging off a lot of the blind anger with the world, discovering the pain of loved one's (and their passing), celebrating the marriages of others willing to take that step so soon, and weathering more than a few stormy romances of my own. Two thoughts occur to me now that I'm too old to be considering a young man and not quite old enough to merit the respect of one who's features are molded with the years: The less you care about what others think, the happier you'll be, and that there is nothing mundane about an ordinary life.

The first piece of advice came from the parent of a friend. Easy to digest, but much harder to follow. I know a lot of people who strive to make others happy and end up shortchanging their own desires and dreams in the process. In the same token, I've spent a lot of years cursing myself for a lack of progress in the things most of us get on with after school, and including school. I've yet to get a degree from any university, whereas peers and otherwise have gone on to masters diplomas and bachelor diplomas, and this no longer bothers me. Many of my friends have had lasting relationships that led to marriage, and I seem to be a bit difficult to outlast a month with the same person by my side for some reason. I don't mind. Letting comparisons and status symbols (figurative and literal), nag at the back of your mind is a fruitless exercise that only magnifies the slights and barbs we build up in our hearts. Progress is subjective, and at any rate, I've got a lifetime to achieve my dreams and desires. And if I don't?

Another parent told me once about on of his friends. A landscaper or a groundskeeper for a country club, in his forties. A janitor, for all intents and purposes. He was married, and didn't really make a lot of money. I'm sure tending the grounds to a golf course wasn't his life dream, but he was content with what he had. Read voraciously in his free time. I think about that guy sometimes.

What happens to our dreams if they aren't nurtured or rewarded? Do they die on the vine, taking our hopes and thoughts of serenity with them? Do they take another form or outlet when they aren't given the full attention of a career or a family? Or are they reduced to mere hobbies, with all the passion and pluck of an old maid's tea party? Ever since I found what I loved, and even before that, when others saw a talent in me that I hadn't even realized fully), I have wanted to be a writer. Paid or unpaid, adored, revered, or admonished, it's taken precedence over everything else in my life. And after a decade of erratic print, notable and unnotable, impending lawsuits, spotted accolades and enemies earned, I have yet to break into a passing resemblance of a big break or a prestigious publication. But I keep at it. The encouragement has faded away to a twinkle, and I stay the course regardless. Why? Because it still gives me the greatest joy in life. A hundred pages of new work sit patiently on top of my bookshelf, and the pacing of my cycles has ebbed off into a slow and deliberate pace, but it's enough for me right now. History soothes me with the knowledge that most writers don't come out with a bang, that it's a long and arduous road, and that 30 is considered a young age to make any sort of literary debut. It's a bit of a late start, but I suppose one needs to live a little before imparting any sort of wisdom or sharpened creativity. And laughter, for the time being, will keep going. Laughter is the siren song of my work; it manages to lure me back to the typewriter time and again. The words will always be the best sort of therapy I could ever indulge in. The creativity is often all I ask for, and all I'll ever need. Perhaps dreams never die, but simply sleep or gestate or disseminate, spiraling off into a thousand smaller outlets. Hobbies and children; Sunday activities or evening escapes.

An ordinary life used to be the bane of my existence. I dreaded the thought of a nine to five life with a textbook family and years lost paying off a house only to spend your remaining years, the leftovers, withering away and watching the world contort into something you no longer have any affinity with. There's more to a cliche life than the cliche, though. The thought of having children is no longer light years from my mind, and recently I've found myself thinking of baby names before stopping and musing at the absurdity of the human cycle. It's funny to have changed so much. To grow. Birthdays become small evolutions, and my values bleed into each other with every passing year. An ordinary life just might be rewarding in it's own right.

Our hearts hardening and swell in turns and the blood that ran so hot years ago has cooled, and the simplicity of happiness in a compromised world dawns upon me. So much time left to experience things I haven't, with lifetimes behind me. And in between, the unmitigated thrill of never knowing what's next.

contemplatively yours,
Tom "work in progress" Waters

Mild, Medium, Or Doomed

At the risk of sounding psychotic or schizophrenic (and give me a few paragraphs to back this up here), I have it on good authority that the boom, franchising, and bust of chicken wings as an institution (much like the industrialization, slow rust, and the spread of a retail virus in this town) are directly proportionate to the second or third or fourth downfall of Buffalo as the thriving Metropolis that it dreams of being. Twenty years ago, no one had ever imagined that the delectable sting of hot sauce, or the bland neutralizing power of blue cheese would have such a striking kismet with chicken, the universal of all meats. In the same span of time (and no, I didn't say twin span, for chrissakes), once upon a time, we could all fall ass backwards out of high school into factory jobs with cake pensions and social security to feather our retirement nests. Or, if so inclined, we could go on to higher education, and after pissing away obscene amounts of money on collegiate core courses, find a guarantee in our major of choice. Coincidence? Let me persuade you otherwise! Before we continue, note that I am frying up a few dozen wings in my futuristic home cooker as we speak. For company. Actually, a few friends. I'm sorry, I lied. I'm a gluttonous, fat bastard, and I'm cooking up two dozen wings for myself. Shame, thy name is Tom.

Buffalo Wings, in addition to the brief and embarrassing stint that Mark Twain had here finishing up Huck Finn, the Bills, and the narcissistic mediocrity of Vincent Gallo, are among the few native creations (or mutations, in Vince's case) that we're privy to calling our own. In a national sense, mind you. I was never a big historian, but I know that chicken exploded like Oppenheimer with Montezuma's revenge at some point about ten to fifteen years ago. And since then, our humble town has gone the way of the lemming. Economy has flagged, the Cheektowaga Police Department has gotten nastier than they already were, and sub rate retail positions have eclipsed stolid factory placement for those of us without benefit of box top diplomas and so forth. The choked cholesterol of a thousand jumbo drumsticks clogging the gears of a bustling town. Crime in Italy!

This is just another example of a local creation that's been whored away to the rest of the states where we stand idly by in mute terror as it's been homogenized and ruined in the process. I won't name names, but a certain pizza chain (which was actually funded with Sabres dollars as a startup company many moons ago), has Buffalo Wings that are bastardized and so many times removed from the aesthetic and basic beauty of the concept (rhymes with pantyhose, and it's a game in league with checkers), that I would rather deep fry week old, room temperature ham-hocks than digest such a travesty of a miscarriage of justice! Watching file footage of the last Stanley Cup that we completely whiffed on, one sees a backup goalie spasming in disgust as he tries to masticate his first morsel of, in the rest of the free world's opinion, one of our wings!

And what of the goddamned peace bridge? If it weren't for our cholesterol soaked, wing-weighted fat asses, maybe, just maybe there wouldn't be as much wear and tear on the border between our fair city and Canada! The entire debate, the horse and pony show of mudslinging and rabble rousing could have been averted for another ten years if person's (like myself) hadn't spent so much time choking down bucket after saturated bucket of deiciously seasoned white meat! The bridge bodes warnings in the tons. We'd be better off warding away the wing-hogs such as myself.

So much valuable time and creative energy we waste looking for the perfect hot sauce, the perfect size, shape, cooking and texture for our favorite repast. After twenty five years, I've grown fond of Pizza Supreme's fingers. And Tony's Pizza in Cheektowaga has tremendous subs. Mazias in the Clarence hollow has sublime wings that stand head and shoulders above every other wing I've tested in my quest for the perfection! Agh! Would Samuel Clemens (if he'd lived in this day and age), be able to finish the last fifteen chapters of Huck if he were so preoccupied on the malaise, the veritable monsoons of hot sauces and twenty cent wing dings? Would we have to suffer through two possible, grueling, and hideous years of Hillary in a Senate chair if she weren't aiming to fatten her philanderous husband to the point of being unattractive with our phenomenal snack treats? Such an Eastern Koan, this one. If Buffalo Wings were never invented, would we be happier? And, on a much more personal note, would I name my first ulcer after something other than Durkee Red Hot? I'm beginning to hemorrhage, so it's best that I leave you with that.

gastrointestinally yours,

Tom "give me Wishbone blue cheese or give me death" Waters

Mrs. Bush Goes To Washington

If Scott Bakula were allowed free reign in our universe, outside of a failed television series, what would happen if he had performed an impromptu sex operation on the infant George W. Bush? A poor pilot episode or a bizarre turn of events? You be the judge! Picture a world full of liberals and Nader acolytes. Picture a universe full to the brim with pro-lifers and socialists. You have just entered...........the Alt/Zone.

First of all, if George Dubyah were female, she wouldn't be Republican and she never would have made it far enough in the ranks to the presidency, nepotism and otherwise. And nepotism does not work! I know this first-hand, especially after working at a locally owned family chain. Politics is nepotism cubed most of the time, and it's baffling to think that we've backslid so far in our voter apathy turnouts that we would reach a day and age where someone's scam-artist son could run for the same slot his dad did not two terms after he stepped down. I'm sorry, she. Georgina, in this little sketch cosmos, wouldn't have committed grand, grand larceny with a savings and loan scandal that daddy's little girl funded. For further reference to spoiled presidential offspring, please see Chelsea. She's certainly not that difficult on the eyes. Or perhaps Reagan's daughter, who not only whored herself for any broke, inappropriate tough guy who came along, but wrote an autobiography stuffed to the brim with smut to boot. Perhaps she would have run up the national deficit on a shopping spree that would make Imelda Marcos look like a twelve year old mall rat with a two dollar allowance, but nothing close to the foolishness that we've all swept under the carpet.

Since she'd be one of a small circle of females at the top of the heap (Janet Reno doesn't count, mind you), would she go with Lieberman? Being a minority herself, perhaps out of irony she'd choose some alpha male for a running mate. Or, if she ran on the donkey ticket, Georgina could opt for a full minority sweep comprised of three or four smaller demographics. A slight, four foot Hispanic man with a lazy eye! Bush/Lopez. She could run with a child for a gimmick. Strike that, reverse it! A ten year old boy with a club foot. The sympathy vote! I see a catch phrase, t-shirt, and bumper sticker already. Bush/Smith in 2001, go to the ballot boxes, limp or run! The ad wizards would have a field day of spin on that one! Or an African American man who was street smart but not too much so that he didn't scare off ultra conservatives. This conjures up (to me at least) how most cinema aficionados collectively wet themselves over Bulworth when it came out. We all thought it was a joke at the time, and then Beatty tried to run himself. I guess he didn't get the joke.

And coke snorting! What woman has time to do lines up her nose when it takes an hour and a half of facial prepping just to leave the house? And if she ran for president (the author is reminded of an annoying Olive Oyl song from the sixties), she wouldn't have to lie. She could simply sport some gams in a few liberally slanted papers (are there any other kind?) and she'd be golden. She could talk about doing morphine drips out of the spines of infants as long as the papers got a good photo op. Our representatives have been reduced to after-images of themselves; sound bytes and ghost traces of personalities that might represent someone in the feasible world. Forget Nader this round, I'm voting for Max Headroom.

How lazy and shiftless we've all become! How lazy and shiftless that swamp of a cesspool of a political epicenter Washington has become! It might make things interesting if we had a female Republican Bush running! Hillary just isn't cutting it. Plus, I'm sure the debates (that no one really watches unless they're gung ho political aficionados who plug their cortexes into pbs) would pick up half of a half of a ratings share if we could witness a cat fight with a budding bitch president and a budding bitch senator. Psuedo lesbian conflict draws voter sympathy! Wouldn't you rather hear about the plight of the homeless if two of our prime candidates were squirming with each other in a vat of macaroni and cheese? It may be surprising after that litany to discover that I'm not a huge feminist, nor chauvinist, but I think it would be interesting to give women a chance. This is coming from a conservative, too, by the way. Stuffy suits and monotones are getting a bit old. How about some flare and panache, for a change? But finding a Republican Female is like finding Marilyn Manson at a Kingdom Bound Conference. Not gonna happen. The on-again off-again game of naked twister that big politics has become (on auto-pilot, no less) is growing tired. Democrat, Republican Republican. And so on. And the third party guy stands in the corner like the third man, or a wall flower at a really bumping party. He's there, but who's really paying attention to him? Nobody cares. He's a nice guy, but he gets no play from the girls near the keg and he's got no moves when the real music kicks in towards the end of the night.

Am I the only person who sees this chain of events? Senile, Bedtime-For-Bonzo star with Dry-As-Cork Vice President. Vice Prez takes the cake by default and pulls off a little bravado before end of term. His marathon at the maypole ends and, two skirt-chasing terms later, we have the same polluted gene pool clogging the pipes of the system! I don't normally use this many exclamation points, people! I am so sick of politics. Why can't it be cake, cookies, or potato chips instead of the devil or the deep blue sea for one election year out of one hundred? It appears as if platforms and personal views no longer take precedence over a decent hairdo and a good photo op. So George/Georgina will probably win, since Gore (with his last ditch attempt at drudging up a personality) comes off like a substitute student teacher, unsure of himself and trying desperately to trick his classroom into thinking that he's confident, and in charge. I'd be the first kid in the back to shout "Heads up!" while he was writing on the chalkboard, as I sent a small marble paperweight at the back of his chisel-shaped head.

Whether we vote green, bleeding red, or........what the hell? Is there even a color associated with Republicans? Or is it just black, mirroring their souls? Anyway, whoever we vote for, we're screwed. It's simply a crap shoot, and when the lottery pays off, we have one of three choices. Would you like an obscene tax hike or four years of stasis? Some health care at ridiculously inflated prices, or no health care? A cute little war so that we can pin all of our internal struggles on an enemy outside of the nation, or a few well-dealt-with riots or floods to win the country's sympathies, and our hearts (awhhhh!). Maybe a few more well-planned and extensively filmed school shootings, with numerous references to Harry Potter and Eminem. If it sounds like I'm cynical, then you won the hearing test. Too many paradoxes in voting. Or not enough. Heck, I'm a paradox myself. I'm a conservative for the most part, but I do have compassion (it's somewhere in my glove compartment, I assure you). I'm pro-choice and pro-capital punishment, and I'm sure that just won me a couple hundred new best friends. Whatever. Kill 'em when they're young, fry 'em when they're old, and let one of the gods sort 'em out. I don't believe in letting emotions rule legislative decisions, but then again, I've never voted. I believe I'd like to vote for Lazio, if I can proceed with the necessary paperwork it takes to vote this year. I'd like to think that a woman would be allowed to make it far enough to the presidential elections, though. Jesse Jackson must be getting exhausted trying to grab the minority ticket. Forget Nader, vote Jackson! This poor guy's been trying for what, twenty or twenty five years?! I feel sorry for him! Whitey's had his turn. White males have had more than their term. Rich white males who were born into money, preened into power, and have no conception of a normal life, and we expect them to make decisions about a lot of normal lives. Hopefully we'll see a woman in the catbird seat on 1600 in our lifetimes. And hopefully she won't look like either George. Oof.

Puff Daddy/Nicole Kidman in 2004,
Tom "grass-roots" Waters

-This piece is dedicated to Michael Calleri, who continually refuses to give in to the belief that I try not to write about politics, as doing so pisses too many people off. Thank you for the exercise.-

The Atomic Lightness of Being

I made it for ten full years before I fell off the wagon. I didn't even think about it.....too much. And then one day, a buddy from work comes in and starts talking about it. The fun, the adventure, the escape of it all. You'd think he was a representative or something. He could see the old glimmer in my eyes, and once he got the scent, he wouldn't let up. I told him I wasn't into that sort of thing anymore. He could tell I was lying. Told him I'd moved on to other hobbies, that I was better off without it. All it took was two incredible graphic novels to rook me back into the world of comic books hook, line, and sinker. And then I gave up. No more fighting it! I was old enough to get away with reading my vintage issues of <u>Mad Balls</u> in public. I was too distinguished and too big in stature for anyone to make fun of me for carrying a tiny Bat Signal pen light. And even if I wasn't, the stigma was gone. I am, and always will be, a comic book junkie.

Right out of the gate, this new kid at work lets me borrow his beat-up trade paperback copy of *Kingdom Come,* by Mark Waid and Alex Ross. I didn't have a prayer of resisting after that book. It blew me away. Had I been away for that long? Had I turned my back on comics for so long that the rules had changed that much? I had, and they most certainly did. <u>Kingdom Come</u> is a masterpiece of modern art, and boy, do I mean art. It's an astonishing yarn about the loss of faith in the old heroes. About how heroes lose their faith in the people they protect. And the succeeding, animalistic, ultra-violent generations of super-humans that take up the mantel. Superman, beaten and secluded by choice, is drawn back into the fold to restore traditional justice to a world of crime fighters who instigate more chaos than control. The old school is rallied up, and an alliance is formed. The new mavericks don't go easily. All hell breaks loose. Asses are handed to their owners, sonic bitch slaps are administered, and we find that Bruce Wayne is just as much of a cynical badass as he's ever been. And that wonder woman, stretch marks and all, is still a goddess. This book was easily the best story I've read (of any kind) for the last two years.

So the rules had changed in the DC and Marvel Universes. The punches that were pulled by the big companies in 1990 were now let loose, bare knuckles and all. In the '80s, common death, mortality, and murder were introduced in titles like *The Punisher, Batman:The Dark Night Returns, Daredevil,* and the masterpiece we all know as *The Watchman,* which was so far ahead of it's time that I was surprised by the first printing date when I read it in the fall of 2000. We'll circle on back to *Watchmen,* though. By the '90s, I was out of the racket, for all intents and purposes, but I kept track for a few years when I worked at a bookstore. All of a sudden, our heroes were being mutilated to boost sales. Some muscle bound monster broke Batman's back. The iron man was paralyzed for a little while. The second Robin got pretty much vaporized by The Joker. And Superman was dead. For as long as it was profitable. Reality was seeping through the cracks in the mythos, and we all begged for more. Hence, *Kingdom Come.* Watching everyday people get gunned down was all well and good, but just not enough. And seeing our childhood legends hospitalized with super-bed pans and so forth was getting closer to the mark. At the close of a century, a millennium, we wanted more. So we get near-extinction. Total apocalypse. Either everybody dies, or the fittest survive to limp away and fight another day. Pretty fitting for a world that was horrified about Y2K, but too cool to admit it. And it made for an amazing graphic novel.

Taking a zip cord back down the time line, the next book that pulled me back in was Alan Moore's *Watchmen.* Now it's one thing to expand on an original. To billow out a story, or a world that's been around for sixty years. But it's an act of prodigy to create an entirely new roll call of super heroes altogether. At 25, I wish I were Rorschach, the David Mamet-dialogued, ass kicking, gray area sociopath who forgets to shower because he's too busy breaking fingers and getting answers. Or Ozymandias, a former league member who markets his fame for the convoluted and coldly intelligent plan for world peace. Much brighter men have written at length about this ground breaking story, so I'll leave it at that.

And what is the deal with Batman's ears? They oscillated obscenely throughout the '90s. In some issues, they're the length of string cheese; in others, they're little nubs the size of pretzel bites. God I'm hungry! Is it a sociopolitical thing? Economic? Perhaps when the Dow Jones soars, the ears follow suit, and when the market plummets, Bruce Wayne busts out of the cave with stubs over his cowl. The Joker's psychosis seems to mirror the insanity of the moment as well. A stand up comedian with the capacity to commit mass murder, he often quips current affairs between the violent deaths he imposes.

In the realm of amusing violent deaths, there's *Reid Fleming, World's Toughest Milkman.* Easily one of the funniest books of any kind that I've ever read. Reid drinks a lot of whiskey. Owl Rye, to be precise. He beats the hell out of the people on his route. The ones who give him lip, anyways. And in every single issue, he manages to wreck his milk truck beyond the point of repair. Let me count the ways: automotive death by head-on collision with a moving locomotive, a falling Skylab satellite, a falling meteor, and a run-in with an in-ground swimming pool. Ried's one endearing trait is his near-religious need to watch his favorite soap opera, "The Horrors of Ivan," every single day, no matter who's house the tv set happens to be in. Ivan is a talking skeleton in a business suit. He doesn't really seem to do much but rather lets the world interact around him. *Reid Fleming* employs a style of dark comedy that isn't used nearly enough. Sadly, it's nigh-impossible to track down any of the original comics, but I scored a few trade paperback reprints.

Luckily, anything that Neil Gaiman and Dave McKean work on together (Sandman) is reprinted infinitely, so that those of us who were out of the game can catch up on the best of what was missed. Before, during, and after reading *The Tragical Comedy Of Mr.Punch,* I knew I'd never look at the lovable marionette the same way again. A twisted tale about the most vicious puppet passion play in history, it tells two tales exceptionally well. The narrator discusses childhood issues of death, deformity, loss, and lies told out of turn by parents and relatives while he interlaces the complete story of Punch and Judy. It's an ode to sadness, youth, and the pain one goes through in order to become an adult. That the artwork was breath-taking certainly added to the book. This is my favorite one-off by the team.

Every hobby has a boom and bust, or at least mine do. And then, after the bust (preferably She-Hulk's), I streamline my stock. CDs get traded in to buy better CDs, books get donated to the school library, video games are swapped for nicer video games, and comics are hocked for graphic novels. I always figured in the back of my head that I'd move onto ridiculously priced photography and art books, but this is a much more entertaining detour. So, come fall, after the one-two punch of those two books, I headed straight for the first comic store I could find. I was planning on trading in my old comic books for cash, buying a few graphic novels, and then leaving. Since I can't stand a certain comic store downtown, fortune smiled as I meandered into Don's Atomic Comics. I met Don, the proprietor, and he proceeded to chew my ass about the condition of my private stock. I was yelled at for a few minutes, and then he said 'Trade only!" But after talking to him for a couple minutes while I made my selection, he instantly came off as the nicest comic dealer I'd ever met. Because most of them are snakes. Especially the Canadians.

Within a week, I'd dropped in the neighborhood of three hundred dollars. What's great about being an older collector is that you can do things like that. Plus you have the refined taste to track down the really good stuff, rather than just plucking every single title off of a pharmacy spin rack when you were twelve. He kept recommending titles, artists, and writers, and I picked those up right along with my steady diet of Batman and Sandman titles. To say the least, buying comics at Don's is a unique experience. Since I'm a regular, I depend on, and look forward to, taking crap from every employee in the establishment. Within two minutes of coming through the front door, a verbal fight ensues between either Don and myself, Don and Sherman, or Sherman and me. Don and Sherman are the two guys who work there most of the time, and Ian is the floater who's actually the cool head of the operation. What amazes me is how Don and Sherman will scream at each other in the face for an entire eight hour shift! They're worse than an old married Jewish couple. Don will say something like "John Byrne really sucked after the seventies." And then Sherman will jump back with "If you ever had any taste in comic books to begin with, or got your head out of your ass long enough to look, your chimpanzee brain would recognize some of the great mini-series he worked on in the '90s, you douche bag!" The flyers invite you to 'come to the fall-out shelter'. The flyers weren't kidding. It makes for a great show while I'm perusing my titles, though.

Men are creatures of habit. We like to go to the same store because of the comfort factor. By the time we reach our mid to late '20s, we've most likely selected a barber, a tailor, and a florist for life. I have my comic book store now. They know who I am when I call or come in. And they bust my balls incessantly about buying less comics than I special order. And I take it all with humor and good cheer. Or, barring that, I scream back just as good as I got it. The reason comics are so compatible with guys is because a)we don't have much of an attention span, b)all the female characters have monstrously large breasts, and c)we don't like to read too many stories without pictures. Don pointed out to me that comics are part of a very, very long line of expression and non-verbal communication, going back to cave drawings. It's too bad that they're in sort of a dark age, not fifty years after the golden age of the '50s. I have a feeling I'll be reading and rereading comics well into my '60s. If anybody makes fun of me for it by then, I'll just pick my shotgun up off the porch (next to my beat-up easy chair, and just to the right of all the neighbor's stray baseballs and footballs) and put some buckshot up their ass.

madballs in my jockey shorts,
Tom "world's toughest essayist" Waters

Lovelorn Confessional

I remember a luggage commercial from about fifteen years ago with a gorilla and a set of stairs. The gorilla rides down the steps with the luggage, bounces it off of the walls, and generally does his best to beat the suitcase to smithereens. The advertisement was selling the durability of the product. Now, whenever I think about that ad, it reminds me of emotional baggage. We've all got war-torn stickers, nicks, cuts, scratches and mildewed compartments. Everyone has baggage, and it's never in mint condition. For the last year I've been on a romantic roller coaster at breakneck speeds, hell bent on finding monogamy again, but lost on the trip. I have no idea where I'll end up, and I probably shouldn't have taken a seat towards the front. I've been lost in a fantasy land of impulses, infidelity, and forgotten dreams. Sadly, there's no emergency brake, and believe me, I've tried. Somewhere along the way, I tried to stop, and ended up going deeper into the recesses of amorous pursuit. Hopefully, I'm half way through my journey by now. How did it start? When, where, and why? Sometimes, it's tough for me to even remember. Other times, it's the only thing I turn over in my mind.

About two months before my 24th birthday, my childhood sweetheart came calling. She was my first date. We'd known each other since grammar school, and had kept in touch through thick and thin down through the years. Two or three years would pass, and one of us would turn up. For some reason, since that first date, we never tangled with each other. Either she was seeing someone, high school got in the way, or I was off on another quixotic crusade, and too busy for emotional pursuits. It always seemed like the only times she was interested in me were when I was doing very well in my life, when I was with someone else, or both. Well, fortune finally smirked.

She'd had a child at the age of 19. Adorable little boy. And when she came to visit that last time, she'd had a wild summer. Reckless abandonment, a throwback to a second youth she'd always thought stolen from her, and another pregnancy, which she decided (or was told) not to keep. None of this made me think or feel any less for her. We'd started spending more time together and, after two years of solitude, I gave in. It was all fireworks and passion from the jump. Destiny and fairy tale endings woven together. But Jennifer was split down the middle. I enjoy duality, I really do. It's sort of a religion for me. But I choose to be paradoxical; half of the time, she wasn't even aware of the way she acted. Half of Jen wanted to pick up where we'd left off before her darling son came into her life. And the other half was fine with our little triumvirate; breakfasts in bed, cartoons on fridays, and little talks from a male figure who wasn't in and out like a swift wind. So, in an effort to control the life she thought she wanted, she cut me loose. This was to be the first break up of many, and the last time I would be faithful to someone for no reason.

Enter a redhead. One very opinionated, mouthy, pompous one with intelligence and talent. In my mind, I thought that she was gorgeous, and that in hooking her up with my best friend, I was keeping her out of my field of vision and helping them out at the same time. How vain of me. My friend soon grew tired of Melissa, and they'd never had any sort of, how shall we say, intimate involvement together. She proved to be clingy, and slightly psychotic, and ulterior in the sense that she only spent time with you if there was something she could prize from you. No matter, though. Fresh from being dumped, I was infatuated. It didn't help that Mike told me he was going to get rid of her. Or that she reminded me of the one girl in my life who lasted the longest. That wasn't a very healthy relationship, either. So in a mad dash of spontaneity, I raced out to get her phone number, called in the middle of the night, and got her machine. Left a message that I had to talk to her as soon as possible. Wracked with lovesickness, I penned a five page letter telling her how I felt, how I wanted to be with her, and how I didn't quite think that things were going to work out with her and Mike. I wasn't about to sell him up the river just yet. The next day, on a drive, she read it, and shot me down in flames. It's a trend, this. Following my heart only to find it wrong. And, eventually, they come around long after I've stopped giving a shit. Bitter? Not really. Missy said she wanted to see how things would work out with Mike. Very mature and all that. A week later, he'd dumped her, and I was getting bedroom eyes.

Some people can't bear to be alone. I rather prefer it. After being off to myself for so long, it's soothing. No ups, no downs, no ground zero fights or melancholic battles in public places. I don't think it's all my fault that I've gone the last year from one to the next. And half of the time, I wasn't even looking! But that's how it works, doesn't it? Other people, like the aforementioned Melissa, can't bear the thought of being alone. To them, it's a sentence. And yet, if you can't be happy by yourself, how can you expect to have a healthy relationship with another person? I never got that, but then again, the monkey bar swingers seem to deal with these things a lot better. After a lifetime of entanglements, it still hurts when I leave someone, or vice versa.

So after those two, I'd made a last ditch attempt on another friend. I'd known her for a year and a half, and there was certainly some chemistry. Pissed to the gills in a bar one night, feeling sorry for myself, I tried to swoop down and kiss her in the parking lot. The swoop down method was a guaranteed winner before that. Didn't work. I ended up feeling lower than I did before that, which I didn't think possible, and spent the rest of the night on autopilot, looking past her when she tried to reason with me, and mutely watching the tv in the corner while she flittered about, kissing random friends and pretending to have a blast. After a week or so of this, Jen and I got back together. I was miserable without her, and I tried to meet her on her own terms. Promised that I wouldn't call every single day just to chat, and then get aggravated when she wouldn't return my calls. I'll admit that I'm difficult to be with, too. Sometimes, I want to spend every waking second with someone. Other times, I need a lot of time to be with the guys, or work on my career, or just have a night to myself for a change. These phases last for a couple months, too. We're were going to try spending time together in small doses, since she was so terribly busy with being a single mother, and working a salaried job, as well as church choir, friends, and family visits. This lasted a few weeks. Then the fights escalated, with both of us screaming at each other over the phone, nasty things were said, and we broke up again. I've lost track of who broke up with whom how many times, but I think we're about even on that one.

I had a crush on this adorable cashier I used to work with at a seasonal job. She reminded me of Bjork in some way that you can't quite put your finger on. A tiny brunette with a little button nose with dark, sparkly eyes who gushed innocence and allowed herself to giggle. After everything that had transpired in the previous months, I figured I had nothing to lose. I asked her out to a friend's house for a party. We had a wonderful time together, and I was getting strong signals from her. And I was a gentleman, or tried to be. By this time, it was December. Eventually, we went on a date. Dinner and a private movie screening. We cuddled a little bit, talked about the movie afterwards, and both of us were horrified, because we knew that an end-of-the-night kiss was imminent. It was wonderful, and she was sweet and innocent. Erin had Wizard of Oz paraphernalia in her room, and loved the muppets at the age of 21. Plus she had a lecherous side. It seemed like a nice mix at the time.

Whelp, four weeks before Christmas, I'd spent an entire paycheck on a locket for Jen. For some reason, I didn't think it would be right to return it, not to mention the fact that I wanted to make her feel guilty, and the goddamned thing was engraved, so why not? So before the holiday itself, I gave it to her. And she either saw a few dollar signs or realized the error of her ways, because we got together for dinner. A friendly dinner, I told myself going into it. After a nice meal, she repented and told me rotten she'd been to me, and how she missed me with big, full blue eyes. I couldn't resist. We ended up kissing in the parking lot, and going back to her apartment. Driving over there, I was trying to decide what to do, as I do have a conscience squirreled away somewhere in the back of my head. So I went over and confessed. After all, I had the upper hand in a relationship for the first time in my life! I told her that I'd met someone, and that she was a wonderful person, and that I had no intention of leaving her just because she'd changed her mind yet again. Whelp, we ended up doing something anyways.

This is where things begin to get complicated. I tried to play outside of the rules. I was with Erin as a boyfriend, and spending time with Jen otherwise. Jen was fine with this, and Erin didn't know about it. In my mind, it made sense that if Erin and I had fun together, and if I could be there for her in every sense of the definition of a lover, then no one's feelings would get hurt. I may sound like some sort of big time player this far in, but I'm not. I always end up getting hurt. Which I prefer, or maybe even deserve most of the time. This whole circus came to a head on New Year's Eve. By this point, Jen was torn (again) between wanting to be with me and playing second fiddle to a younger girl. And Erin was starting to wonder why I was so busy all the time. At the beginning of the night, I went to Erin's house. We watched some tv, had dinner, and goofed around a little. By eleven, I told her I wanted to ring in the millennium with my family, and tried to be as vague as possible. I hauled ass to Jen's house to play charades with her and her family. How fitting that was, in retrospect. We had a very long talk on the porch, and reconciled a lot of things. By the midnight bell, we were in each other's arms. And then off to Mike's to start partying by one o'clock.

In lieu of making it up to her, Erin and I went down to my cottage the next day and tramped around in the snow a bit.

Tensions rose. By late January, Jen was no longer amused with our arrangement. And the ante just got upped. Mike introduced me to Beth, one of his high school chums. I couldn't stand her at first because she was such an unconscionable flirt, but I was interested. She was absolutely gorgeous. I prefer redheads, but for some reason, most of the time, I wind up with brunettes. In my opinion, anything beats a natural blond because, well, they're blonds, and they think they can get away with murder because of it. Beth had dark, dark black hair and these sublime brown eyes. We'd railroaded her into coming out with us the first night I met her, and I worked it. Relentlessly. We had one of those hyperconversations, where it felt like we'd covered ten years worth of small talk and tiny truisms in the span of six hours. It was like she was the only person in the room to me. I was smitten.

She had a boyfriend, I knew that much, but she never brought him up. Riding back to Mike's in her car, I told her about my sordid history. After she left for the night, I told my best friend that I <u>had</u> to see her again. After prizing her phone number out of him, I called her from work in a few day's time. We talked about everything again. She said she had to leave in a few weeks to Washington for a conference. Did I mention that she was in medical school? Slipped my mind. So Mike had another party at his apartment, as he was liable to do at the time. And she showed up. I was ready this time. I'd studied her personality enough that I knew which angle to come from. We ended up attacking each other halfway through the evening, then hugging indefinitely in the parking lot before she left. I thought I was in love.

In a week or so, I talked her into going out to dinner with me. We had one of those wildly spontaneous dates, jumping from one place to the next, and buying roses for her from a street person just because I could. Bear in mind that I was still with Erin. Things heated up a bit later, and there was a very wild and unconventional interlude in my car. In a small parking lot. I was impressed. We spent three hours talking afterwards, and before long it was three in the morning, and she had to get back, as her flight for Washington left the next day. We decided to break up with our respective others (all of them, in my case) and start building on a relationship when she got back the following Tuesday. And then we went to a diner and held hands while we talked about how crazy the whole situation was. She couldn't bear to leave me. Nor could I leave her. But we had to, and the next day I talked to her before she left. She was spending three days in another state with a boyfriend that I trusted her to break up with. And I had complete faith in her.

After I got off the phone with Beth, Erin came strolling in to visit me at work looking chipper and cute, as always. She did the sweetest thing with me once upon a time. When we were together, she'd tickle me if she wanted to start something with me. I have a suitcase full of these memories about every girl I've ever been with. And here I was breaking up with her. She sat down and it killed me, but I told her that I needed to be by myself for awhile. Disgustingly, Erin was the only girl who didn't know about the others involved. I had a hickey on one side of my neck while I was having this talk with her. It was on the side she was sitting on. Either she didn't notice, or she knew all along that I was a heel, but liked me anyways. We spent that night watching a movie at my house, because we did have plans and she was doing a very good job of being cool about things. Through tickling and utter disgust in myself and my behavior, I behaved.

Then came Jen. I told her that I was seeing someone who meant a lot to me, and that I was going to be monogamous for a very, very long time. She went ballistic, threatening me with tales of Aids and unwanted children and so on. After what felt like a scolding from a parent, rather than an interim love interest, we left things at that. I never really expected to come out of this whole situation (with either girl) without a few bruises, though, so it was par for the course.

The rest of the weekend was agony waiting for Beth to come home. I felt like I'd found an equal for the first time in my life, and now she was taken from me. To make matters more guilt-inducing, Erin came in with a handwritten letter for me, explaining that she understood how I felt, and that it was ok that I needed time to sort things out. Including her, I've broken up with two girls in my life. I'm not very good at it, and it makes me feel rotten. This made me feel worse. I realize now that I never gave things a fair chance with the two of us, and that I'd been too busy goofing about with others to really appreciate what we had for the time that we did. We had absolutely nothing in common, but she was sweet, and kind, and a terrific cuddler. On the eve of Beth's return, I was counting the hours and praying for sleep.

And the day arrived. An hour after her plane was supposed to be back, I started to second guess myself. Was she all right? Did she change her mind? Had I made a grave error? The plan was to spend an entire day sequestered off in a hotel room with each other. I'd told all of my friends how deeply I felt for her, and how if she had to move out of state in the fall to pursue her career, I'd seriously think about going with her. Well, I called her house. And she was home. And she had changed her mind. She'd made a mistake. She broke up with the other guy, but she'd acted erratically the week before, and was ashamed of her behavior. She was sorry, but she just couldn't see me for quite awhile. Could we be friends, though? Borrowing a line from a Jack Nicholson movie, I shot back with "God I hope not." If someone hurts me deeply, I don't care about the pain. All I care about is hurting them back even harder.

I was crushed. It felt as if, no matter how I tried or who I tried it with, I could never find someone who'd accept me for who I was on a regular basis. Was I too tempestuous? Too unpredictable? Did I smother them? Or not give them enough affection? It was a tough spot, that one. Beaten and resigned, I lied to Jen a week later and told her I was ready to come back, and that I'd dumped Beth, not the other way around. She took me back. Things were beautiful for a week and we were fighting again. The father of her child had a sudden interest in spending time with his son, when it had never mattered before. I was livid over this, and worried that she might be romanced away by this clown. Somewhere along the line, back during the whole Beth mess, she let it slip (at the perfect time, as well) that she'd seen someone on the side as well. Jen had a way of doing that, pushing my buttons and playing coquettish when she knew it would throw me into a blind rage. Had a soap opera set formed around me when I wasn't looking or what?

Whelp, I spent a week or so alone. Well, not completely alone. In the company of friends. One of them happened to be female, but don't worry about her just yet. I called Jen up to apologize and she'd gone prioritizing again. Wanted to get her life, as well as her son's, on the right track with this father. This father who couldn't have cared less for the first five years of his life. Who wouldn't even admit to being the father until now. And it was going to take awhile. It was early February by now. I was so tired of this solliptical bullshit that I accepted her situation. It was always about control with her. It is with most people in relationships. I'd rather just be in love, and leave the fine details up to someone else.

What's funny is how many people thrive on control, no matter what form it is. Some don't mind being beaten up by their lover, as long as they get their way in the end. Others go outside of the relationship to find a little fraction of control with someone else, whether they tell them or not. And some let their partners languish in substance abuse, because it gives them the upper hand, as well as an easy target in a fight. So many dysfunctional pressure points we have. I'm sure there's a 4'000 step Jacob's ladder that I haven't even heard about, let alone experienced.

So for the majority of February, I'd thrown in the towel. I was a beaten man, and I'd had enough. I hung out with the guys constantly. I stayed away from women, stayed away from home, and stayed as far away from having to deal with the previous five months as was humanly possible. I was on the lam from the entire relationship nightmare. It was all rented movies, three hour cold pizza, and crashing out on Mike's couch for a little while, there. But I had an enemy in the midst. An understanding shoulder who'd been there all along who went by the handle of Lindsay. Lindsay was 19 at the time. She was mind-blowingly good looking, agreed with pretty much anything anybody said, and laughed at all of my jokes. What a fine mess my heart was turning into.

Yet another night, she was helping to nurse me back to health emotionally. Just having her around was comforting. I'd had a stray eye on her for going on a year, but never thought I'd had a chance. Now my heart told me I did. Women: 20, Tom's Gut Instinct: 0. What made things worse was that she was so mature about letting me down. More so, in fact, than any girl who's dumped me. She said she'd be cool about things after that night, and surprisingly, she was. That was far from the last of it, though. We'll get back to Lindsay.

March rolled around. I had a new job, and my self esteem was slowly building back up. The new job didn't take, and I had to go crawling back to my old job. I'd felt worse emotionally, than I had for a very long time. I was severely depressed about life, love, work, and the other essentials of happiness that one should be working on by one's mid-twenties. It felt as though nothing, absolutely nothing was on the track I wanted it to be on. I was sleeping thirteen hours a day and loathing myself when I was awake. And my best friend at the time was moving out of town. I had no one to care for, and shortly, no friend to confide in. Plus my job sucked. Mike was having a going away blowout soiree at his house, and he'd invited all of his friends to see him off. When I got to the party that night in July, I'd found that he invited Beth.

I was severely upset, but holding it well. By way of coping, I sat as far away from her as possible, and ignored her. I couldn't believe that he invited this bitch who stole my heart and then pulverized it at the blink of an eye! Whenever she tried to talk to me, I either stuck with one-word responses, or jaded insults. I told her I liked her new granny glasses. That she still looked good with the weight she put on. And that hospital scrubs suited her frame. Within an hour, we were making out against the door of Mike's apartment. In one hug, I'd forgiven everything. She was sorry, and it felt like home to be with me again. We embraced for what seemed like forever, and made promises to call each other. I was floating on a pink cloud going back into the apartment.

Here we have April. Beth and I were having hour long conversations on the phone again. I was still depressed, but wanted to be with her again. She was hesitant, but listening. One night, I finally wore her down and she agreed to come over and 'study'. During notes, I was allowed to give her a back massage. The hour was late, and she decided to sack out there. You figure the rest out. She'd gotten a half hour of sleep, and had to intern at a hospital the next day. We were both ecstatic and dopey eyed. One small problem. Somewhere along the line, Beth had gone insane, and I didn't pick up on it until the day after.

She was neurotic about anyone knowing that we were involved. I would have to promise, repeatedly, that it stayed between us. She had developed an annoying habit of chewing with her mouth open when she was talking to me because she knew it annoyed me. She would do Jabba the Hut impressions. I was told to supply the set-ups to punch lines in bed before sleep. She'd have conversations with my cat. And five million other things that didn't really get to me until June or so.

I was happy to be back with her, I really was, but once I had her back, she was completely mine. Calling me at work, calling me at home, showing up unannounced at one in the morning because she was 'in the neighborhood'. Showing up at work unannounced because she was 'shopping for something'.

Staying at work for entire shifts. Not leaving my house when it was obvious that I wanted to be alone. Beth was, hell, is a gorgeous young woman. And she had other.....talents. If she were anyone else, I wouldn't have tolerated her as long, and if that comes off as callous, then I'm sorry. But eventually, everything about her became annoying, and I couldn't even stand the few things about her that men never get sick of! And then Lindsay kicked into second gear.

I don't know if it was the night, or her mood (actually, I have no idea what variable it was), but she was feeling amorous. We'd remained friends throughout everything, and she'd become the friend that I could tell everything to, just like she was before the mess I'd gotten myself into. I still had feelings for her, but I kept them stuffed away deep down inside, never to see the light of day. We hung out all the time, we talked on the phone constantly, and late at night, we'd trade insults online. So one day, she wanted to go out to the bars. We went to my place first. We're very fair handed that way. Right out of the gate I knew something was different with her. She started flirting with me. She was rubbing her foot against my leg when we talked. We went to her choice of bar next, and she wanted to make a deal after I mentioned shaving my goatee on a whim, perhaps. If I let her shave it off, I could kiss her. Feeling self-confident, I told her that she could do so only if I could kiss her before as well as after. It was a deal.

We went back to my house, and I felt like a kid before her. I'd had Lindsay on such a pedestal that she was out of our atmospheric system by then. I was breathless and nervous, whereas, with anyone else, I had no problem. It probably had something to do with the honesty issue. I was the same way with Jen. She knew too much about me, Lindsay. I told her everything about everyone the entire time, and she still wanted to be with me, if only for that night. It scared me. And when we kissed, it was...incredible. I swooned. I felt like I'd left the material plane for a brief time. And when I came back, she was shaving my goatee off. She'd done a terrible job of it, too. It was so embarrassing that I had to shave the rest the next day. But well worth it. And I was completely in love with her. Again. There was something so innocent and intangible and beautiful about her that I'd never seen in anyone else before.

She'd stressed the importance of the evening being a one shot deal, but everything was different for me. I could never look at her the same way again without thinking about how her kiss felt. Every time I hung out with her, my heart tugged a little bit further. But I'd given up on my heart after so many disappointments. I did my best to behave and act as if nothing had changed, when, in all actuality, everything had changed. After two or so weeks of that,

I broke down the walls online and told her. I love you, have since I met you, and it's brought me nothing but pain and hardship, but I can't bear to spend a day without you, basically. That sort of thing. She was touched. But didn't feel the same way, either.

I tried keeping the two animals separate. Sharing my feelings with her when we weren't together (be it on the phone or online), and keeping things completely platonic when we did hang out. I'd written five poems in a row for her which was a first for any girl. Eventually, I couldn't keep the two separate any longer. I cared too much, and felt helpless. There was a string of emotional outpourings, and more than a few tear-soaked nights spent in parked cars. She loved me, but as a friend. If it was going to work it, it would have. She just wasn't attracted to me. I didn't get it. It didn't make sense. So I bided my time.

August rolled around, and Beth kept coming around. She'd been spending time with me throughout the spring and summer. I've got to hand it to her, she was around when no other woman could stand me, and when I didn't have the confidence to look for someone outside of my dating circle. I would hate myself for being so openly nasty to her, and be the most despicable person I could think of in her presence. Neither seemed to make a difference. A ray of hope appeared in the form of acceptance to a big time medical school internship. She was leaving! Hopefully for good! I told her how much I'd miss her, and clicked my heels after she left! Perfect. She was out of my life. Christina waltzed back onto the scene, entering stage right.

I doubt you remember which girl Christina was, do you? She was the girl who refused my attentions after Jen had broken up with me the first time back in November. Confusing, isn't it all? After that incident, she'd forgotten my phone number. I was hurt at first, then aggravated, and eventually, I became so occupied with other pursuits that I forgot/didn't care. But sometime in August, I called her house at three in the morning (as guys are apt to do) and her father answered. I'd forgotten all about it a week later when she came strolling in to work to apologize for being such a shit all this time, and that she was a horrible friend. Beth was gone, things with Lindsay were sketchy at best, and I started going out to clubs with Christina and her friends again. We were having fun, and it seemed like we'd gotten closer somehow, although I couldn't put my finger on it.

All of a sudden, September. We'd spent the night club hopping, and we'd found a dive to close the evening off. Christina started asking very direct questions. I answered them unflinchingly. Now Christina has a very sensual quality about her. To me, at least. She just seems like a girl who's cool, knows how to have a good time, and she has a very chalky, sultry voice. We ended up making out against a brick wall next to the bar entrance. I was impressed. She she always thought that, when we hooked up, she figured it would be forever. Pretty heavy small talk for a first encounter, but I rolled with it.

Whether you know it or not, sometime in September my first book consumed my life. It cost me my sleep, my sanity, and eventually (and rather thankfully, mind you) my job. Once the hype and the b.s. started gathering momentum, people started looking at me differently. Women started looking at me differently. I was spending more time socializing. I was no longer depressed. I was going out every single night of the week. One extraordinary night, and I forget how this transpired, a whole rogue's gallery of friends had come out with me. One of them was Mike's ex-girlfriend. The one who really did a number on him.

Now everybody has one person who messed them up for life, but good. One person who, better or worse, you base every relationship thereafter (for quite some time) on that person, in one form or another. Maybe you date a girl with the same hair color, or the same build. Just maybe you see somebody with the same attitude, or the same background. Any number of variables. This was Mike's girl. Mike was in deep shit with me at the time, and I always thought that Sara was attractive. I've got a thing for redheads. I hadn't seen her for a number of months, and hadn't spent time with her socially for at least a year and a half. In that time, she'd grown up to be a stunning, sexy, amazing young lady. For the last year of her relationship with him, Mike was a right bastard with her. I'd been on the sidelines the entire time. Not to mention the fact that they'd had nothing to do with each other for at least a year and a half. You can tell that I'm trying to rationalize what happened, so it's best that I don't stall any longer.

We hit it off famously. I didn't care who else was there, I was riveted to this amazing person sitting next to me. Maybe I fall in love too easily, I don't know. Innuendoes flew back and forth, and, before I knew it, we were glued to each other in the back of a friend's car. I'm not one for lurid public displays, but it was animalistic, and I couldn't have cared less. The night ended quickly, and the two of us sped off from the bar in search of other things. Somehow we ended up at my house. I didn't get a whole lot of sleep that night. I was physically ravaged by the time I got to work. For different reasons, Sara and I never got that close again. Mike never talked to me after he found out about the tip of the iceberg. And you know what? It was well worth it.

Around late September, things had become confusing again. Christina had flaked out on me another time. Had something to do with the fact that she was playing hard to get, and I trumped her at her own game by playing the field while she was playing hard to get. And Lindsay was driving me bonkers. Whenever we went out, she would get hit on. And flirt back. With me sitting right next to her. And she knew how insane it would make me. Now I'm not the jealous type, but for some reason, she made me want to hospitalize complete strangers just for offering drinks.

One night it escalated. We went downtown, and she said she was going to the little girl's room. After twenty minutes, I got worried, as she's such a teetotaler. Upon going to investigate, I saw her chatting it up with two college geeks. I walked up to her, told her I was leaving, and stormed out. There was a big scene in the street. She bullied me into staying with her long enough to go to another night club, and as soon as we got there, I shook her from my tail. Beelined it straight to the farthest recesses of the dance floor, and sat in a chair, pissed off beyond any form of verbal communication. The friend we'd met up with took off, afraid of the look on my face after trying to talk to me. Eventually, Lindsay found me, apologized without really saying sorry (women are so <u>good</u> at that!), and went to get some bottled water so she could level out. Ten minutes elapse. Fifteen minutes elapse. I wonder where she is, agitated already, and I find her talking to two more brain dead morons from her school. This time I wasn't as pleasant. I leaned into the closest kid and tell her I'm calling a cab. After she kicked and screamed (as the club was emptying out for the night), I went back to her car with her. Another brutal session, tears pouring down both our eyes (and this from a man who cries on an average of once every seven years). And that was that.

We're still friends. Matter of fact, after that, the pinnacle of my chase, I'd given up. Closed that little section of my infatuated brain off for repairs. What's funny is that I've learned a lot from my tanglings with Lindsay. That not every guy can handle having a friend-girl. And that having a friend of the opposite sex is possible. She's become my best friend after Mike, which is a first. The two are completely unrelated, too. She's very attracted, but that doesn't matter. And we share everything with each other. And we swap dating stories and laugh over them. Who would've guessed in a million years?

In the two months following this legacy, or rather, crash course in heartbreak, I've had a string of dates. Some have been great, some have been disasters, and some have been all right. It could be my age; maybe I've reached a point where the relationships and flings that I have are alarmingly quick. If it's the type of women that I'm interested in, I either haven't caught on to it yet, or the traits are so infinitesimal that they can't be measured by modern science. I do fall easily, though, I know that much. And I bruise too quickly. The ages have gone somewhere between 19-37, surprisingly enough, and I'm 25 now. A decent spread. It's no matter, though. It may take a thousand dates for me to toughen up, but it beats the alternative. And I still love women. I love everything about them. I refuse to be one of those guys who's forever embittered after making his big power play. I love their smell, their kiss, their taste, their mannerisms, their bodies. There isn't much about women that doesn't catch my eye or my heart. And if my heart's been broken terribly every month for the rest of my life, I won't regret it. Because one telling smile, or one naughty giggle, will suck me right back into the fray. Every single time.

addicted to pain,
Tom "don't do as I've done" Waters

The Steering Wheel Of Fortune

Automotively, this was the worst summer I have ever had. That anybody in my family has had, for that matter. Where to begin? As for the rest of my family, their misfortunes sound cartoonish and surreal; certainly nothing that could happen to an average motorist! My little brother rear-ended an eighty year old woman and her nurse's aid on the way to work. What are the odds of that one? My mom (the god-fearing member of the family) was holding her weekly prayer meeting at the house when one of the blue-haired ladies who holds court for these shin-digs backed her minivan into my mom's car, which in turn went sailing in the garage and slammed into my dad's '77 powder blue Chevelle. He would sooner see his first born child's arm sheared off before allowing any harm to befall that car. And then there's me. Between June and August, we all got really familiar with mechanics, insurance companies, and on occasion, the long arm of the law. Welcome to my nightmare.

In the first blush of summer, I went to my friend Dave's bachelor party. They'd taken out a private suite at the baseball park for drinks and debauchery. When I got there at three, the party was already well under way. Card games, old men smoking cigars and laughing about the stock market, and frat boys slapping each other on the back, funnelling beers into each other's mouths. We consumed about three kegs of beers, two trays of roast beef, five pizzas (with the works), pizza fingers, chicken wings, nachos, chips, dip, and enough cigars and cigarettes to re-pave the parking lot to the stadium. I can't stand baseball games because they're boring, but nobody was watching the game anyways. By eight o'clock, after the game was over and last call was announced, we made a mass exodus to the brewery down the street where a row of pool tables and an infinite tab were waiting. The sight of us all was preposterous. Thirty to forty burly grown men stumbling down the street together with novelty-sized baseball bats howling, singing, and swearing like sailors.

At the bar, I'd swindled my old boss out of forty dollars in a few fast games of eight ball. The groom was holding the bar up as best as he could while everybody in the establishment was doing shots with him. A few hours elapsed. By about ten, I was exhausted from the day's events, and decided to take a quite rest on one of the benches. It seemed like a good idea at the time. While I was napping, the best man took a picture of me snoozing, half on and half off of the bench, gut hanging out of my shirt, and hair sticking every which way but down. By about midnight, I woke up, refreshed, and decided to go home before causing any more harm to my internal organs.

It was a long drive home. I'm not very good with directions downtown, there was a food festival going on, and when I get lost, I usually drive obstinately until I find a street that I recognize. Did I mention that I'd been driving on a donut for three weeks prior to this bachelor party? No? Well I had been. This isn't really a good idea, in case you didn't know. Thanks to the wonderful road work that's going on indefinitely throughout my fair city, the donut blew. Then it wrapped around the back of my car axle. I rode half of the way home on the rim of the axle, spitting sparks and bumping up and down in the car like I was on the tea cups at Disney World. A logical man would have called a tow truck. I am not a logical man. I just wanted to get home. It had been a long day, and I figured I was more than half way there anyways.

When I was ten minutes from home, I got stopped by a police car. He was a nice guy, and he asked me to go across the street to call a tow truck. I followed his advice. After watching him drive away, I set out for home again. Barely two minutes away from my house I got stopped AGAIN! Clearly, my luck had run out. I got a ticket for going 55 in a 35 with a flat tire. The cop was so nice to me that he let me gather my things and chauffeured me home. Cost of bachelor party ticket? $50. Cost of total repairs to the car? $350. The expense of a really good anecdote? Priceless. I lucked out with the town court, and ended up with a traffic school appointment, but that's down the road.

In late July, I went to a birthday party at a friends. I've had to tell this story about forty times, so I'll give you the nutshell version. It was a great time; we had steamed clams near a bonfire and all of my old comrades were in attendance. Upon leaving the party, I decided to go downtown. For reasons I'd rather not disclose. But on the way back, I noticed a flat tire. Rather than go back onto the thruway, I took a side road to investigate the matter. Having just watched someone change my tire a week or two before that, I figured I was ready for the hands-on experience. And after ten minutes of prying, swearing, and exerting myself (in the rain, mind you), I couldn't get the goddamned jack off of that stupid holy trinity of tire changing that they put in my Dodge. It's some sort of tire jack/tire/crowbar combo that's about as relenting as a Chinese finger trap. At two in the morning, I gave up and walked to a phone to call a tow truck. In one of the worst neighborhoods in downtown Buffalo. I hadn't been there before, and I certainly won't be going back anytime soon.

After calling a truck, I walked the block or so back to the car. Or where it was when I left it. The Dodge wasn't there. The Dodge wasn't there! I wigged out, then tried to make sense of it. Perhaps by some spatial fluke, it was transported to the Dark Ages ala *Army Of Darkness*. No, that wasn't it, the car was stolen. Somebody had taken my car. And yes, the keys were in the car. I'm an idiot, no disputing that, and I have no common sense to speak of. I looked around the block. There were a whole bunch of unsavory characters out and about past the witching hour, and they all looked capable of folding my vehicle into their back pocket and walking past me on the sidewalk without so much as a sideways glance. Upset and befuddled, I walked around for a while, chain smoking cigarettes and wondering how far this thief could've gotten on a flat tire. Far enough would be the appropriate punch line.

I was the only well-bathed white male with all of my original teeth walking around this section of town at four in the morning. Everyone else was either on crack, strolling around with a 40 in a paper bag, or drumming up other business propositions that I didn't even want to know about. I had no idea what the hell I was going to do. I remembered calling my dad in the fifth grade after my bike had been stolen from the mall in the bushes next to Woolworths. After telling him that it wasn't locked, he said "Good!" and that was basically the end of the conversation.

At one point, near dawn, I considered taking all of my money out of a cash machine and leaving town. That wouldn't solve anything though, other than having to deal with my parents. I did a lot of thinking that afternoon by the waterfront, and smoked more cigarettes. My car had been stolen. Something had to be done. I was going to have to go home eventually. I called the police to report the theft, and they stopped for about three minutes on the way to another matter, laughed at me when I couldn't tell them what my dad's birth date was (he was the legal owner of the car), and then drove off after giving me the station address where I could file a report. Super. I called my dad finally, and he came to pick me up. Driving over to the station was an exercise in silence and defeat. I hadn't slept in over twenty four hours. And somehow, it was my fault.

After a week, the police called to report that the car was recovered. When we got to the impound the following Monday, I was sucker-punched at the sight of my baby. The mini-disc had been taken, it was caked with mud, and the entire front column had been savagely ripped out. All the paperwork that was in the glove compartment was dumped on the floor. And there were gnats flying around inside the car. It smelled like an animal had lived and breathed and attacked the inside of it. Ironically, the only thing of value that hadn't been taken was a book that I had in the back seat. I guess phonics hadn't reached this section of the 'hood. I was pissed off, disgusted, and violated. The cops told us that the car was 'drivable', and we couldn't even turn the engine over. It was towed to an auto shop where, after three weeks of Allstate Insurance investigators passing the buck, it was deemed completely totaled. And then the fun really began.

At the end of August, I took my vacation down at our summer home. My family was kind enough to buy me a new car. It was used, but in very good shape, and it a smooth ride. '93 Buick, I believe. A real boat of a car, and whisper quiet on the roads. I was happy with it. Throughout the summer I was clinically depressed for the first time in my life. I have manic depression, this is nothing that I hide. But I'm generally on the manic end of the diagnosis. After going back to a job that I couldn't stand, going through a lot of emotional difficulties with various females, I was in a tail spin. I'd been partying like a rock star, not really caring where I ended up the next day, or if I made it to the next day at all. None of these events that took place helped to buoy my spirits, either. I'm not blaming my behavior on anything other than myself, just giving you some decent background here. Setting you up for the fall, as it were.

Perhaps I was waiting for the fall. For the other shoe to drop, and hard, at that. About two weeks after getting my new car, I hung out with the boys after work. We spent the beginning of the night next door at a tavern, and then we went to a pub. I sang Irish folk songs with two old men who had acoustic guitars and a similar love for the sad ballads of Bob Dylan. We took pictures, and traded jokes. It was a nice night. Then I went by myself to my favorite strip club. Where I had far too much to drink. After leaving the club at two or three in the morning, a fence got in my way. Funny how those fences just sneak up on you, isn't it? In my state, I didn't think much of it. The thing rolled over the hood of the car and I just kept driving. It didn't seem to phase me or the car, so why worry about it?

After stopping at an all night greasy spoon, I noticed that the front headlight was hanging off of car by a wire. Hmph, that's peculiar. On the way home, I got stopped. My luck had clearly run out. This was the end of the line. In a town where the police weren't really known for their wonderful demeanor. I took the test on the side of the road, and failed. They cuffed me and led me to the back of their car. I went without complaint. There was no getting out of this one. I spent the night at the station in lock-up listening to these bastards giving me a hard time. They treated me like a criminal, and I guess, for that night, I was. I got finger-printed; they took a mug shot, and I every time I tried to sleep on the cold, hard bench of the cell they had me in they'd holler over for something. I was ashamed of myself, and this was what the cold granite of rock bottom felt like. I'd screwed up, but good.

By morning, I called in a favor and a friend picked me up. I picked the car up from the towing company the next day, and tried to figure out what I was going to do. I called a lawyer. Enter Keith Perla, Attorney at Law! He was a smoothy, and apparently, I was just under my limit for the breathalizer. When we met outside the courthouse, I was surprised by his rather small frame. He was a slight, balding man with fierce blue eyes and a smart gray suit who was three sentences ahead of whatever I said. The whole ordeal cost me my entire nest egg (about $1500), but he got me off with no points, no fines, and a trip to a DWI Impact panel a month later. I promised to buy him dinner sometime, and we still keep in touch. Before the panel, I had to go to traffic school, though. For the bachelor party fiasco. Almost forgot about that one, didn't you?

I went to driving school as a kid, but this was a whole other ball of worms. Try and imagine detention for the adult demographic. Detention that lasts for four straight hours. I got off to a good start by entering the one way entrance the wrong way. There were two classes going on in the same building, and all of the really good looking women were in the other classroom. The A-M classroom. Dumb alphabetical luck! I was herded in with junk men, suburban princesses, foreign cab drivers, college boys with white baseball hats, some Wise Guy, and a man who strangely resembled Kris Kristofferson. A real Rogue's Gallery. The school was conveniently located 20 feet away from the thruway. Throughout the course, we got to hear the scolding whisper of twilight traffic reminding us that we f*&%$ed up.

The instructor had a perfect hair helmet, the kind that football coaches and problem drinking weathermen keep for their entire lives. He was rambunctious, and spoke like some fired-up 3am motivational speaker on tv. We all filed in and paid the fee for the class in front, and someone paid with a roll of quarters! With only three girls in the room, I wondered if the old ax is indeed true about 18-24 year old males: We've got lead feet, and we know where to find trouble. I just couldn't believe that I'd gone seven years (after getting my license at 17) with no tickets, fines, or convictions of any kind. Either we all have a finite amount of luck that runs out, or our cruel deeds go punished if we keep at them diligently enough. The punishment for a speeding ticket is terrible films. Not the cool ones with blood and carnage either. I would have stayed on for another hour if they had those ones.

Movies with sub-rate production values and b-list actors from the '60s. Legions of leisure suits, mutton chops, porn star mustaches, Super Tramp feathered hair-don'ts and disco ball afros. And they were interlaced with these attention deficit friendly mini seminars sporting the corniest anagrams I've ever encountered. A.lways S.top for S.ignals and H.ail the O.fficer or L.ane worker at E.xits. And so forth. There was a certain brain-washing quality to the short films, what with repetition and all. Along with a revival of the Crash Test Dummies, those two guys from the 1980's public safety commercials. After two hours of these films, I was ready to drive my car up the flight of steps and into the TV/VCR. Then we moved on to the 15 minute feature length presentation, "Road Rage: When Tammy Needlebaum Attacks!" followed by the short edutainment clip, "Respect the Car! Tame The Foot!" I don't even believe in road rage, personally. It's just another retarded politically correct term for something that's been around since cars were invented. It's not a diagnosis, and it's not an epidemic.

Regardless, the film had a very Jedi-like theme throughout: "Don't let anger cloud the issue, Luke. Count to ten and <u>then</u> reload your weapon Crack the guy in front of you over the head with a Louisville slugger or not; there is no try." The examples the instructor gave were outlandishly funny. Scalpings, Tommy Gun shoot outs, babies being shot-putted at other cars in motion, etc. After the film, we had to tear through some work sheets. One of them was an anatomical diagram with the effects of x amount of drinks on the human body. The one arrow actually said "Mouth-Alcohol is Drunk". Epiphanic, is what that is. Then we were subjected to a 'pop quiz' with 'difficult' multiple choice questions: Is it best to a)flip someone off when they do something stupid in traffic, b)mutter obscenities with pitch-perfect enunciation, c)shake your head in disgust, d)perform a small ventriloquist act in which you sodomize a dummy that resembles his wife with a large turkey baster filled with napalm, or e)all of the above? About a month and a half after the driver safety course, I had to attend the Drunk Driver Impact Panel.

The panel was painfully effective. After an hour of listening to stories that you'll hopefully never have to hear, I walked out feeling worse than all of my parental scoldings and principal office summits put together. I was moved that the judge for the courthouse stayed on at the end of the day to listen, and that he took a personal interest in drunk driving. That meant something to me. A lot of people say that all judges are evil, or that all cops are a-holes, but that simply isn't true. There's good and bad wherever you go. Sometimes the bad outweighs the good, but sometimes a few dozen years of seeing the same damage puts a little cynicism in your stride, too. Finally, I understood the other side of the court room.

Throughout all of these mishaps, I'd been working on getting a claim for my stolen car. Allstate Insurance should change their names to Asshole Resurgence. At the time of writing this, it's been four months and we still haven't received a check for the value of the stolen car. From August to October, I gave a phone interview, twenty page notarized statements, personal statements, and an interview under oath. Why would anyone try and total their car, or get their car stolen, when you'll never regain the original cost, let alone the sentimental value? How does that make sense? Scores of people drive around without insurance. Many more get into accidents and don't report them, or settle it without bringing the agents into it to avoid the hassle. We did everything by the book, to a t, and we're still suffering for it. Justice isn't blind, She's just an accountant for an insurance company. After paying for just such an eventuality over the years, we can't get reimbursed. Why should I be made to feel guilty for having my car stolen? I may have to get my hot shot lawyer involved, and then it's going to get ugly. And not for me, either. He's very good, talks very fast, and he <u>always</u> wins. We'll see what happens.

A friend of mine (a full-fledged Buddhist), had a theory about bad luck. He said that the Eastern belief concerning luck is that the bad variety lasts for a year. Not that it travels in threes (that would be comforting), or that your luck runs out and never gets replenished; just one solid year of getting your karmic ass handed to you. Either I'm paying for things that I've done in a past life (if you buy that sort of thing), the stupidity I indulged in over the summer, or making a down payment on a year or two of good luck. That would be nice. By Confucius' watch, I've got about six months of this left. And I'll be damned if I'll tempt the fates anymore. Best just to drive sober with my fingers crossed, and count the months. It feels like I've suffered enough, but, being raised Catholic, I always expect suffering. Some of my misfortunes were just plain bad luck, some could be chalked up to stupidity, and the rest of it was downright tragic. Luck is too ambiguous; I'd like to think that you make your own consequences, and that you have to deal with them no matter what. A new calendar year is right around the corner. I'll keep a horse-shoe in my glove compartment just in case.

right of way more often than not,
Tom "cruise control freak" Waters

Lord of the Broads

Try as I might, I can't fight it anymore. I've reached an age where I have to frequent (and know what the hell I'm doing, mind you) the supermarkets. At 17, I made a vow that, when I grew up, I'd live the solitary life of a bachelor and get the lion's share of my groceries from overpriced convenience stores or fast food chains. With a handful of years left until 30 smacks me upside the head, the food marts are winning the battle. My will has been broken. My dignity forfeited. Hand me a cart, and I will push it. I can actually tell you where to find cake frosting in a set aisle, for instance, or where one can locate an asbestos colander. I give up. All the Tops and Wegman's of the world have presently made me their bitch.

Among other things, what unsettles me about food shopping is the mob mentality. As a single person, I'm in a niche of a pocket of a minority. Most of us shop on the off hours, shuffling around like zombies and mumbling to ourselves at two in the morning. We don't have a file folder stuffed with coupons. We don't even have our hair combed most of the time. I can identify with the shoppers during the witching hour. They're either alcoholics, workaholics, or the terminally, socially inept. We grab four or five random items: a bag of hot dog buns, some cheez whiz, a copy of GQ, and perhaps a candy bar or a horoscope chart in the impulse lane. There's no set agenda or method to our shopping madness. Rhyme and reason go out the window after midnight. We let it all hang down. We shop in our pajamas, at any rate.

Daytime shoppers, drive-time shoppers, would put Genghis Khan to shame with their attack plans. The housewives have the floor, and they do not relent. I'm outnumbered, out-hair-sprayed, and just plain out in the open. I'm a target. Bee hives buzz past me at forty miles an hour. Menopausal brick houses shovel carts loaded with four hundred pounds full of rice cakes, Slim

Fast diet drinks, and bags of cat food. It's a waking nightmare. Women wearing colors brighter than day-glo hunting clothes holler at the staff for large slabs and slices of beef and cold cut counters. And, at the risk of sounding cliche, they hold up the checkout lanes.

I'm cursed when it comes to supermarket cash registers. My friend Richie pointed that out to me. Whenever he had one quick thing to pick up on the way home to the wife, he'd stop somewhere. With me. And, like clockwork, he'd find the item, phone his success into the better half, and we'd end up in line for two hours in the seven items or less lane. If it wasn't a starter check, it was some three thousand year old man with a six pack of Schlitz and two jacket pockets full of pennies. Or a Welfare check and some congenital moron who had a driver's license that was drawn with a crayon. Sometimes it was as simple as an employee running out of register receipt, their supervisor too occupied flirting with the acne-scarred sixteen year old newbie on the front lines. And other times it was a logistical horror. Scenarios and schematics that would put Rube Goldberg to shame. The law of averages do not apply whenever I whoosh through the automatic doors of a food market. The lane that looks the fastest is always the slowest. The price puncher who appears friendly from twenty paces will bite your head off when you inquire about the locale of surgical gloves. And so forth.

My dad was the main shopper in the house. I used to go on runs with him as a kid and ride in the cart on weekends. Now that I'm older, I realize that weekends are the worst time to go food shopping. My mother would leave a grocery list that appeared to be written in some chicken scratch/16th Century Hindu Sanskrit and we'd go wheeling through the aisles, my father whistling all the time. I caught myself whistling in the aisles today! Perhaps it scares away those shoppers who tend to block an entire lane with their cart, their fat ass, and their attention deficit screaming children, who knows? It does keep you in a chipper mood, though.

Dad shopped seven days a week. He'd go to thirty stores in a three hundred mile radius if he could find a better deal: "SureFine Baby Carrots for thirty cents a case at the Food Lion in Utah! You can't beat that! I got a two liter of Pepsi for three cents and a song at the Wegman's in Alaska! Where do you find values like that?!!" Apparently a few states away. The thrill of groceries, I suppose, is in saving cash. Cutting coupons. The finders fee of combing flyer deals on the toilet and then embarking on the adventure of a given weekend.

Speaking of toilets, that's where my credit has gone lately. So, to salvage my approval rate and pay off debts as quickly as possible, I've come out of retirement in the field of aluminum futures. Mainly, returning cans. This is the main reason I go to grocery stores. These new machines came out a few years ago that make Playstation2 seem like a butterfly yo-yo with no string. They're so much fun that guys line up and compete for endurance and speed side by side. I love these daffy can machines! You have the option of either the aluminum can set-up, or your plastic variety. I prefer both at the same time. A row of degenerates (myself included, obviously) fire/feed whole barn silos full of beer cans and soda bottles into the hungry maws of these large metal beasts, breaking a sweat and enjoying the sheer thrill of going into overtime. Perhaps I enjoy it too much, but it gets me into these cursed citadels of suburbia.

I guess the supermarkets aren't too awful. When I'm middle-aged, I'll hit on the cute register girls too. Hell, I hit on them now! If you know which times to go (essentially between 3-5am), nobody bothers you. You don't have to deal with double price comparison coupons, blue haired sweat-pant wearing crotches with fire in their eyes, or thoroughly whipped, bespectacled husbands watching the hours of their adult lives shuffle away in a 5'oclock traffic lane, two carts of disposable diapers, cranberry juice, and sanitary napkins in tow. Find your market and work with it, right? My new goal in life (as far as nutrition) is to get in and out of the grocer's as quickly and efficiently as possible, without getting popped over the head for squeezing the fruit too longingly. And, failing that, to avoid being swarmed upon, chopped up, and partitioned off in butcher's paper to the housewives.

ten cents an essay, this weekend only!
Tom "pimento loaf" Waters

A Fistful Of Loonies

Aside from the strip clubs, I wouldn't be upset in the slightest if Canada, by some freak tectonic shift, fractured and sunk like a stone into the ocean. They're a colony of liberal wackos with no tangible culture and too many tree huggers. But god bless the lackadaisical stripping laws. Only Nevada, with their predisposition for legal prostitution, can top the topless, bottomless, lap dancing beauty of The Mediocre White North. As a Buffalonion, going to the nudie bars is more than just ogling naked flesh; it is a male rite of passage. It's an introduction to the provocative wiles of women, and all the mysteries that lay ahead in a man's life. Plus there's the ogling of naked flesh. We call it the Canadian Ballet. This is the code word for those with untrusting wives or smothering girlfriends who wouldn't understand the wholesome fun that can be had by a platoon of men fortified by strong drink and scantily clad, barely legal Nova Scotian women. I'm still recovering from my sojourn yesterday, but perhaps it would be best to start at the beginning. My first time.

A good conservative estimate regarding my number of trips to the land of sin would be three dozen, but I'll never forget my introduction. I was a freshman in college at the time who befriended a Senior who, how shall we say, went as often as he could, whenever he could, by any means necessary. So naturally, after the a very small degree of coaxing, I hit a bank machine and rode up with him. It's only a forty minute drive to the opposite side of Niagara Falls and the outskirts of hedonistic bliss, so my new acquaintance Scotty was predisposed to driving up between college classes during the day. We went on a weeknight (with me babbling all the way up with all of the fervor and excitement that only the soon to be initiated display), and I was shocked, embarrassed, and excited as soon as we entered the first club of the night. I mean there we were, sitting down and drinking not four feet away (in any direction, for that matter) from shame-free, instant and lascivious nudity! Gorgeous, gorgeous women with tremendous bodies were disrobing at a rate of one nineteen year old per song! I didn't know what to do with myself! I blushed for the majority of that night, torn between looking away out of embarrassment over my own uncomfortableness, and joining the herd of wolf-like drunken men in cat-calling, howling, and finding interesting ways to insert money into other human beings. I was clearly hooked, and deduced that I'd have to go again, and again, and again, to overcome my embarrassment, for one, and to wrap my brain around the scene. To try and understand it completely. I mean, it's obvious that sex sells. That much is a given. It's also blindingly apparent that men will travel as far as another solar system to see nudity, no big surprise there. But why men compulsively frequent these clubs without any healthy sort of romantic involvement (or degree of intimacy with other women in general), is another thing. Plus I was curious about what sort of girls would work at a place like a strip club, and for what reasons. This was all strictly for the sake of observable social science, and my own personal enjoyment was sacrificed in favor of the greater good. And if you bought that last line, I've got some fantastic bridge property in Brooklyn you'd be interested in.

For the last five years, I've been up and back with less frequency and for reasons individual to the trip, as well as my main study. Some times, it was just nice to get away from everything and bask in the carnal glow of nastiness that runway lights, spinning tassels, and assorted body oils (edible, glistening, and otherwise) represented to me. I have a very dark, chaotic, side to myself, and pleasure-domes appeal to that side. Once (out of charity), I took a boy who, in my estimation, would have married the first girl who found it in her heart to bed down with him. I thought it would open his eyes a bit to the rainbow of possibilities out there. The bastard ended up getting a lap dance from Miss Manitoba, the headliner, and was asking on the ride back if we could return the next day, so, mission accomplished. Now I'm at a stage where, twisted as it sounds, I go to get some perspective on things. When I want to escape from civilization and general stress, I drive to my summer home for a day. When I've had it up to my eyeballs with the horse and pony show that dating and courting can often be, I go to Canada. It's not a substitute for a healthy love life by any means, but it's a thoroughly enjoyable pit stop, and a dazzling quick fix.

Why do most men go, though? There's a large margin of difference between fantasy and reality, I know that much. Some guys aren't fortunate enough to enjoy the company of beautiful girls. From looking at a crowd on a typical month, this is pretty accurate. If your loved one looks like Orson Welles in a sun dress, you'd be more susceptible to getting hooked. At a good club, on a good night, you can find a handful of archetypical chicks who mirror your innermost superficial desires. And then you have to factor fetishes, personal tastes, and consequent individual perversions into the mix. From school girl uniforms to full body latex to corsets and garter belts, every turn on is represented. Not everyone is comfortable with their interests. Ironically, if they pay someone who they'll never meet again, they have no problem. Some like whips and chains, some like leather and lace, and then there's me with my predilection for women who can cook Egg's Benedict in a full Civil War costume while singing selections from Mary Poppins. People have secret kicks is what I'm saying, and some have no aversion to their longings while others hide them in a dark place. Or at the end of a dark runway.

For my money, it's explosions, costumes, and musical numbers are better than any contrived Andrew Lloyd Webber revue. It is an amusement of a sort, on the fringe of a dark, sexual eclipse of all things male and wanton. I've seen girls do things with the brass poles at angles that defy the conventional laws of physics. Once, a woman slid down from the ceiling, upside down, leaned back at a right angle, and winked at me! This is a valuable talent that should be rewarded! The dancers go the extra mile in terms of innovation, originality, and ingenuity. Bear rugs, assorted fruits, puppets, snakes, female partners; there's something new every time I go up.

There's a definite rush to the scene. It usually hits five minutes after arrival, once you sit down.

I become overwhelmed. Drunk on sensory input; bass from the music permeates your rib cage along with the funhouse black-lighted fluorescent panorama of colors and excessive, *excessive* lust, gorgeous women walking around, dancing in front of you, dancing behind you, to the side of you, and good-natured hollering combined with the general sense that a good time is being had by all, that this is wrong, but we're all doing it anyway. There's just something about a stripper's ass, too. It's a phenomenon in league with the aurora borealis. They aren't exactly firm and they aren't really fat so much as they're.....perfect.

So it's the taboo that's the catch. Husbands sneaking away from their wives for a dangerous thrill. Boyfriends hiding what they're specifically forbade. And other assorted degenerates slinking off in an era of political correctness and throwback gender equality to a place where they can treat women however they want. For a price.

The price this trip was steep. I was taking a friend up as part of a twisted Christmas gift, so the tab for both of us rested solely on our poor narrator's head. But just as you don't go to Disneyworld just to use the water fountain, there's no point in going into the temples of sex simply for a look. My friend Jon and I left at about 9:30 when we stumbled upon our first catch: neither of us had any goddamn *idea* how to get to The Sundowner. We both knew where Canada was if prompted to point to it on a map. We both knew to take the Thruway. It's sort of silly, because I've been up there numerous, numerous times, but I've never driven, and I never once paid attention to what roads were taken, or any other helpful visible indicators that would have aided the situation this time around. I was always expectant of the nudity, or bathing in the afterglow of the nudity, and didn't think that departure routes were that critical. Until this trip. In the time it took Jon and I to get there, a normal person with a functional sense of direction could have humped it down to New Mexico on a pack mule. Even with the law of averages, we consistently missed every proper exit, turn-off, and glaring green sign along the road.

The main strip on the flip side of Niagara Falls is difficult to ignore, too. Since a ritzy casino was constructed, tourists and compulsives of all kinds gravitate towards this area for all their base urges and compulsions. Clifton Hill looks like a mini Las Vegas, draped in fifty foot neon lights, franchise restaurants, and scores of picture-taking Okies ambling through clogged Canadian streets. As you keep driving, though, the marketing mood drools over into nice hotels, which bleed off into holes in the wall for a few bucks a night, and finally, an infinite row of strip clubs. Pure Platinum, Maxines, Mints, The Concorde, and I even saw one called Barely Legal that must have just opened up. With a name like that, I don't imagine they'll stay open that long. Pedophilia appears to be the last Western taboo that hasn't been accepted, homogenized, and whored about in advertising. Once that's gone, I have no idea what's left.

Jon had never been to The Sundowner before, and there's only so much cajoling I'll do to convince anyone before I abandon them in search of a more worthy candidate, but he was game, and therefore rewarded with the best line up of ladies north of the border. I told him before we left to imagine five beautiful female archetypes heretofore untouchable to his wants and needs. Then I told him that they were at The Sundowner at this very second, getting ready to go on stage. He was a little skeptical, which was fine.

After our three hours past the border and up the strip, it was only a matter of making it inside. On the weekends, there are bouncers taking door charges, but it's pretty loose on a weekday, so we just strolled into the fray. Upon getting drinks and taking a seat towards the back, he turned to me and, drool coming from the right side of his were-wolfesque leer said "You were soooooooo right, Tom!" And then two strippers in white fluorescent skivvies sat on the couches behind us for a quiet moment. There's always something new.

The setup at the club is very accommodating, depending on how close you want to be to the action, and what level of interactivity you plan on involving yourself in. There's a main runway, with round tables growing off of it for separate table dances where lesser dancers give free dances occasionally. A few feet away from that (to either side) are regular tables with silver chairs. Sort of a dead area where the floor strippers make their mark and the waitresses grift the real problem drinkers for everything they're worth. This is also the area that frat boy caravans and corporate expense account packs carouse at, as their numbers and proclivities for getting touchy- feely are less likely to get them bounced at that distance. Branching off from this is a smaller, circular stage with a band of followers glued to a b-list girl who makes small talk while she dances with the voyeurs and/or customers.

To the other side of the main stage is a second level, with plush couches and ornate coffee tables. This is where we chose to sit while we took in the initial vibe of the evening. Obnoxiously, there was a group of rednecks in front of us who brought their pock-marked girlfriends along for the thrill while they whooped it up. There was a surreal moment where I wondered if they thought their behavior was comparably acceptable to a rock concert. Well even at rock concerts it's really retarded to stand up from your seat and hoot like a dog at what's going on onstage. A good stripper is an artist at work, and unless a dollar bill is involved, these people should stay the hell out of my way! They moved closer to the stage after a few minutes, though, and in doing so narrowly avoiding getting my drink winged at their heads.

Thursday must be a big night for ugly people to drag their girlfriends along, though, because the merry band of jackasses that briefly sat in front of us weren't the only ones. I never got that, bringing a spouse. Are they trying to show them how good looking they're not? Or what good looking really looks like? It just seems uncouth on all accounts. If the girls are *interested* in girls, then what are they doing with a boyfriend? It just seems like the wrong setup in an inappropriate setting. Or perhaps it makes me more aware of my own intimacy issues. Best not to dwell on that.

So we hovered at our couch while watching a few dancers on the main stage. Jon was propositioned for an average of twelve lap dances per every five minutes, owing either to his fashionable neck-tie or his patented air of standoffishness. I was just glad that I wasn't marked as a soft touch for a change, and left free from the range of savages to peruse the main drag. One little girl routine, one Italian fox, one lesbian set. One stripper typically goes through three songs. One song mostly clothed, which leads to topless. The second song is where everything comes off. And by the third song, anything goes depending on what the rail perverts are willing to cough up, if anything. I'm a bit too much of a bleeding heart for this scene, as I begin to wonder how unwanted these poor girls feel according to how much money they don't get. Granted, they probably get an hourly amount from the club, plus lapdances, plus whatever the pittance is that ends up on the stage, but some nights you only see two or three dollars hit the floor during the length of the set. And these beautiful creatures knock themselves out for a gratuity!

The really extroverted, or the very drunk often belly up onto the stage with a folded dollar bill in their mouth to be taken in a number of crude, degrading (to the man), and blush inducing manners. Once I saw a man on his bachelor party get completely emasculated in front of his buddies. The headliner (some adult star with breasts the size of two lesser planets in the solar system) lashed this man's arms to the pole with his own tie, ripped the buttons off of his shirt, and wrote 'asshole' on his hairy stomach with fire-engine red lipstick. I sort of shied away from stage tips after seeing that.

After a few beverages and the standard period of adjustment, we wandered downstairs to the third stage, which, we found, was pretty dead. In the past, the basement was the spot where the really freaky stuff went on, but I suppose there wasn't enough clientele to fill three stages worth of stripping bliss. As soon as we got downstairs it was obvious that nothing was going on.

One hornball was slithering onstage with a dollar in his teeth for what looked like a third world peasant girl who could only passably seem attractive in low lighting. The vibe had changed in the basement, and somehow the balance of rube-like charm passed over to me, as I was talked into buying a shot for a waitress wandering around soliciting beakers of fluorescent goop. This is just an out and out scam. Some girls who, for some reason or another, are not dazzling or extroverted enough to be strippers (but too manipulative to just empty ashtrays and shill drinks), walk around the club and ring up shots of varying sexual degrees. There are body shots, where you can drink the shot from between someone's cleavage, and other kinds involving muscle control, chocolate syrup, or a pyramid of triplets with afghans and lassos. But there I was, spending six dollars to buy an employee of the club a watered-down test tube. Lost to the mob mentality. Jon and I couldn't get up the stairs fast <u>enough</u> after that.

The only quadrants we hadn't covered by midnight were the secondary stage, the lapdancing salons, and the pool tables. Since playing pool in the presence of blatant nudity is ludicrous, we sat down a few feet away from the b-list dancer and commenced to making a selection for a 'private dance'. The lap dance is the be-all and end-all of the gamut, and it's advisable to save it for the end of the night, as the rest of the club is anti-climactic afterwards. Jon, drunk not on Canadian beer but his own sense of business-like power, found that the dancer he was initially interested in had finished her shift at least an hour before he decided to hunt. Tough luck. Indecisive, he frantically scanned the girls weaving across the floor of the club for a decent candidate. I was beginning to wonder if I looked too good in my skin tight jeans, because only one dancer had approached me all night (looking intimidated and defeated on the upswing), when a woman with dazzling eyes sat down next to the two of us and started working the sale. And it really was her eyes that I noticed first. Seriously!

The illusion that the dancers exact in the requisition of a lap dance is making the situation seem like a genuine date. This works on a lot of lonely guys. They make small talk with you, ask about your life, and pretend that it matters when you respond. Then you're asked nonchalantly if you'd like to 'dance'. It's cute how money is mentioned as an afterthought. At the risk of being misunderstood as sarcastic, stripping is a difficult job. They have to be therapists, healers, untouchable (most of the time) objects of drooling male worship, and the understanding girlfriend when they're confronted with total wrecks. We come into the clubs with agendas, ambiguous issues, and wallets bursting with cash (and an 'exit only' stamp on the side). All they have to do to get that cash is listen. Aside from the gyrating, the costumes, and the nakedness, that is.

I decided, in a vain display of self control, to tell the dancer who was working me to come back in twenty minutes. What surprised me was that she did! If you watch the entrance to the private lounges, some girls swing in and out of there like busboys at an expensive restaurant, whereas others bob and weave the room for the majority of the night hoping to get in there once or twice. This is where the real money is made. Twenty dollars a dance, doesn't matter if it's American or Canadian currency. And seeing as a dance lasts the length of a song, it's very possible to either a)lose track of time in the wake of this seduction, or b)get rooked out of more money than you have or expected to spend. I was at a dive once when some Oriental girl suckered me out of forty bucks. I'm a little too compassionate in these places, felt sorry for her, and followed her into the back room. Before I knew what was what, she turned to me and said "That's two!" I had to borrow money from my friend just to make it out of the club. I just shook my head on the ride home and told him I got bilked by Yoko.

This time around, I actually found someone I was interested in. In my experience, there are two schools of thought in choosing a lapdancer. You can either choose someone who really does it for you, and risk their total disgust and a rotten lapdance, or you can pick someone who's semi-interesting (as well as semi-interested in you), and get the works. Since this girl came back, I figured I was in for some fun. I was right. We went to a little cubby hole in the back and talked a little bit more, while she waited for a song to start. I read in an article somewhere that paying up front was a wise choice, as the dancer wouldn't have to worry about it and therefore put more energy into the dance. It made good sense. I took my jacket off and set it aside on the little half couch we occupied, and she began. The boundaries for the dance are a little gray, to say the least. Sometimes they can touch you but you can't touch them. Other times you aren't supposed to move at all. It depends on the stripper and the rules that the club imposes. In some cases they can get fired for inadvertently getting too involved with a customer. It's bad for the business. This time, I was allowed to do whatever I wanted. It was very nice. I've had about two dozen dances from two dozen different girls in my life, and I'd file this one away in my top three.

It's a bit quirky that I would rate a woman, or a dance, but therein lies my enjoyment of the scene. I'd equate it to meta-fiction. In the business of letters, there are some who are aware of the rules, and the traditional manner of writing, but choose to step outside of them anyway. When I go to a nudie bar, I know that women aren't objects, and that there's much more to them than what you see for five minutes, but it's nice to be entertained. Sure, these are somebody's mothers and sisters and cousins, but no one put a gun to their head to get on the stage! It's a very lucrative career, and if anyone is getting short changed, it's the men.

Oddly enough, in October, I got to see beyond the silken veil of the clubs. Matter of fact, it was ripped away forever. Here's where the story takes an even stranger turn. After the release of my book (and a certain degree of b.s.ing), the entertainment director from Madamoisselles (a Ms. Lucie Savage, great name) agreed to give me FULL ACCESS in exchange for a certain degree of notoriety. All I was angling for at the time was a free t-shirt, and I was given the veritable keys to the kingdom! I didn't know where to start! I was introduced to the house DJ, a Mr. Tim Hastings (better known as Timmy!), who patiently walked me through some rules. I wasn't allowed to go backstage on fridays or saturdays, because it was simply too busy. I could take pictures, but only with express permission. He was going to talk to that week's headlining stripper and see if she'd grant me an interview. This was my kind of journalism! Forget covering Mrs.Smith's recovered cat, I was granted a glimpse of paradise, front to back.

This was where the other end of the stage came into play. I'd been to Madam's quite a few times before my privileged tour of duty, so I knew the basic layout. It opened about a year and a half ago, and they've obviously made back their money ten fold. Since I live in a very 'moral' town, some of the dancers were wary of me, thinking that I might be some undercover cop trying to bust them on a silly technicality, like the liquor laws or some sort of unsavory business in back (which, to my knowledge, I never saw). The bouncers took me in with beefy, open arms. This was the cool section of the club. All the guys showed me self defense moves, and we joked about how I could get kicked out in the most dramatic fashion possible (one scenario involved going through a window). Sadly, I'm a pretty peaceable fellow, so the subject hasn't come up.

The dancers are split up between the staff (or 'house' dancers) and the head-liners (or features). The staff girls were very nice, and all of them lent me their ear when they weren't busy making money hand over fist. The majority of them were, as I suspected, single moms, students working their way through school, and girls with jobless scum bags for boyfriends. I was surprised at how down to earth they were when I talked to them. They knew that I was broke nine times out of ten, but they'd sit and chat about the club regardless. Some were happy with the place, and I was impressed with the general one-for-all mood the girls had. I suspected cat fights and lone guns galore. Others were pissed at the world, pissed at management, and thoroughly disgusted with the clientele on the whole. I can't blame them for being upset with customers.

After spending a solid two months 'researching' the club, I've seen my share of business suits and an equal share of hillbillies, dirt bags, and other assorted guys with no common etiquette to speak of. On a slow day, some men would sit at the rail (where you're supposed to tip, isn't that obvious?) passing hours without dropping so much as a penny on the stage. That'd harden me a bit, too. One of the things I like about Madam's is the pole proficiency factor. I've been to more than my share of strip clubs, I think we've established that. But I've never seen such a consistent talent with the pole acrobatics anywhere else. From half-gainers to death defying flips to slow yo-yo like slides, the house dancers are truly astonishing on the poles.

It's a New York state club, so they have to work that much harder for tips with less skin availability. And for every ten skin-flints (I don't accept any legal responsibility for that pun) there'd be one executive fat cat throwing money around like it was water. Most of the big shots get their kicks treating women like dirt and paying for it, since women in the real world simply won't put up with it. And then there were the everyday joes like me, who know their way around the club, tip as well as they can, and behave themselves most of the time.

Timmy's job as a DJ (it turns out) is one of the hardest jobs in the club. He has to be a ringmaster of sorts, spinning the songs that will prize dollars out of the crowd (dancers don't pick their sets), calming the gang out if they're playing the primadonna act, answering phone calls, announcing dancers, and basically doing his best to keep everyone happy at all times. All this time I thought the disc jockeys just threw the cds in and carnival barked a bit. I'd seen a few cat fights that he headed off at the pass, and a few ruffled feather boas smoothed out in the time I spent in the back. Since the owners of the club ran a few other places in the area the other DJs went on rotation, but Tim was my big hook up. He even bought some of the girls Christmas gifts when the holiday came around. It may be a partially sleazy job, but I came across a lot of genuinely decent people on the way. O.K., I'm lying. They paid me to say that. Kidding.

After surveying the basic schemata of the club, I got to interview the headliner for a given week, one Amber Waves. The headliners I've seen have been in films and/or magazines and they're somewhere in their late twenties/early thirties but holding it astoundingly well. Amber was very friendly, red-headed, and she had an incredible southern accent. The interview took two days, two ninety minute cassettes, and about thirty questions in change. For some portions of the question and answer sessions, we were in her personal dressing room. There were times throughout the course of my assigment at Madamoisselles when I could pull off acting like a consummate professional without a hitch. But sometimes (for instance, watching Amber walk around buck naked just as nature intended while she answered questions) that bedside manner fell away instantaneously, and I felt like a starry eyed fourth grader bringing in an apple for my teacher all over again.

The ebb and flow of the club is evident to anyone who goes to the same place (or works there) on a regular basis. When it was that special time of the month, when the visitor with claws and a psychosis the size of Ottowa came strolling into town, all the guys at work basically kept their heads low and tried to keep their mouths shut. I've worked at jobs where women were the ruling majority, but these girls were a whole different can of worms altogether. I have what you could call an artistic temperament; so did they. Once when I was in back, one of the girls came up to Tim and started screaming about losing her cigarettes. She left them at my table, and another girl happened to come up and scam them away without my noticing. We're talking Defcon 5 behavior here: employ nuclear weapons to take out necessary casualties.

The dancers, for the most part, were angels. It's a trend (I've learned) for the girls to fly off the handle, quit their jobs in a spectacularly vocal manner, and come back a week later. Some of them have quit or been fired upwards of 500 times per business quarter. With the amount of money involved, it's tough to stay away. And with the amount of shit they have to take from some drunken mooks, it's difficult sometimes to stay there. Love/hate. It reminds me of a shot-toast that Sunny, one of the girls had: Here's to leather, here's to lace, here's to men who give good face.

I asked around quite a bit, and most of the bouncers were either leg men or they enjoyed the aesthetic beauty of a woman's posterior. I'm partial to large breasts; it's my cross to bear in life. The breast issue is very polarized, though. Some men like them all (that'd be me). Other guys have an immunity to implants. I see no problem with them whatsoever. If you have a nice apartment, you buy a Van Gogh reprint. If you have a tremendous body, you get implants. It's more a matter of good business ethics. Implants equal cash. Which brings us (moving right along here) to the lovely and talented Ronni.

I have no idea why she chose that name as her dancing nom de plume. Veronica would be better, I think. Ronni and I spent a lot of shifts just talking about anything that popped into our heads. She was very down to earth, very no-bullshit. We hit it off. We were the same age, had the same cynical world view, and the same sense of humor. After a few weeks, we went on a date.

Dinner, drinks, the whole bit. It went very well. The physical existence of an alter ego is very, very appealing to me. I think we should all have two personalities just in case. One for public appearances, and one for private occasions. Or one for day and one for night. An extra face that isn't fake so much as it's a completely separate identity. Color me bipolar. I've dated girls who had more personalities than they did socks. At least Ronny was up front about hers. I knew what she did for a living, and I was fine with that. Ronny wasn't really a career dancer, but rather one of those girls who wanders through the clubs like a cool breeze, makes her money, and gets out. She had a daughter and schooling to raise funds for.

Many moons ago, I knew a guy who met his future wife at one of the clubs up in Canada. As soon as they started dating, it was suddenly wrong to do what she did for money. Why?! Immediately, he was telling her that all the guys who went up there were scum, and that he wouldn't have his girlfriend working there. Where did you meet her, you bonehead? I didn't want to be one of those guys. That's the main reason why clubs have a policy against dating the customers; it's terrible for business. Not only do you lose a client, but you lose a dancer.

We put these gorgeous creatures up on a pedestal higher than Lily Tomlin's height chair, and with good reason. Guys think that you have to be a special breed of alpha male in order to date a stripper. Not necessarily so. This is why I ventured to put so much time and effort into researching this piece. Dancers have ambiguous self esteems. The world sees them as stunning and untouchably gorgeous, but they normally don't. Some of them have been abused, and this is a way to regain control over the other sex. They take the stage and put men into the palm of their hand. They take your money and run. It's good therapy. Others date down-and-out losers with no job, no money, and no prospects. The guys wrap them around their fingers and treat them like dirt. So the girl gets a low self esteem. The job isn't perfect, and for as much as we'd love to believe it, neither are the girls. Everybody has issues. Isn't that what the '90s have taught us with their avalanche of political correctness?

I heard a story from Ronni about one of the headliners. A big name adult film star whose name I won't mention here. Back in the dressing room, a girl was telling her about a schlub she met in the club who was hitting on her. She said (and I quote), "He just looks like the type of guy who'd break your heart." If you look around a club, there aren't too many bronze Adonnis's there (except for the sculptures). Can you believe that? Any guy can date a dancer. But it takes time, effort, and an obscene amount of money (like any relationship). A slight caveat emptor, though. Not every guy can handle the lifestyle they lead. Jealous types need not apply. Only a choice few can keep the ball rolling. I was about to learn that.

After the dinner, a few days later, we had a fight. We'd made plans over the weekend. I stopped in to pick her up from work. She'd had a horrendous day. Was in a black, soul-less mood darker than anything I've ever seen this side of a grave. One of the dancers had an accident on-stage, and it scared the hell out of everybody. Not only that, but they were short-staffed, so the few dancers that did show up (trade mark winter weather) had to put on inordinately long sets on stage. Including Ronni. So I listened to her yell and bitch for about ten minutes. I was fine with that. Then she canceled our plans. Wanted to go home alone. I wasn't so fine with that. "I'm sorry you had a bad day," I said, "why don't you call me when you have a better one." And I stormed out, thoroughly pissed. To be continued...

I wasn't sure if I'd crossed the line of professionalism, or objective reporting, or any of that other stuff. I didn't care, either. I stayed away from the club for a few weeks because I didn't want her to think of me as the stalker type, nor did I want to see her if she didn't want to see me. We had one great date, so maybe it was best to leave it at that. I also felt like I needed a break. A solid month at a first rate strip club may sound like paradise to most people, but how much paradise can you handle? I didn't want to completely strip away my enjoyment of the experience. That's the forbidden apple of knowledge, dear reader. Once you take a bite, you can never go back. I still have a good time when I go, but I can see the man behind the green curtain, if you know what I mean.

When I came back a month later, the assignment was (for all intents and purposes) over with. Some days I'd come in for a follow-up. When I came through the door with friends, I'd tell one of the bouncers, "I'm just here for pleasure tonight. No business." In the same respect, I can never be an anonymous john at Madamoisselles again. I know all the girls, and vice versa. I know which ones are naughty, and which ones are really naughty. Which ones are out and out bitches to everybody. They're family to me now. When they have an anniversary or a holiday party, I go up and congratulate them on their success. When one of the girls lands something big, I give them a semi-decent tip and wish them well. If I want a generic experience, I can always go somewhere else. But when I go to Madam's now, I go there to be with friends. Perhaps the experience warped me even further in some way, but I like the lifestyle. I'm not cut out to be a 9-5 punch clock guy anyway. It just went a step further, is all.

If you pan around during a trip to a club, you can spot the addicts. Casualties of pornography have sort of a sad, vacant tint in their eyes. You could call it the million mile cleavage look. A lot of them either spend entire paychecks on a weekly basis in these sin salons, or sit and drink ice water while they get their fix. I enjoy my little adventures when I do go, but the fantasy (for all it's delicious temptations) is a pale substitute for reality. One look at the junkies will tell you that much. They have an air of failure and dysfunction thicker than the cigar and cigarette smoke in the clubs. It's as if they passed some point of no return with intimacy, whereby the caresses of women can no longer be earned (or awarded). Where every conversation, every touch is the result of a transaction.

There's a sampling of frequent tourists like myself, too, though. We're not that far removed from a functional world of female interactivity, but we enjoy the delights that strip clubs seem to offer (or the stepping stones that they lead to). Some of us follow different moral rules. I was Catholic half of my life, and I'm not ashamed in the least of telling people that I'm heading out to the clubs. The girls who work there are generally bisexual, and, more often than not, will do anything if a little fun's involved. Our moral line in the sand has shifted, moving back further to accommodate a lack in inhibitions. A world where head games and prudish behavior aren't involved. And what's wrong with that?

I've seen incredible dancing skills, theatrical sensibilities, and set lists that would give an older man a coronary on the spot. It doesn't take much to be a dancer, but it takes a certain sort of girl to stay in the business. You have to be a bit extroverted, a little wild, and pretty talented to make the big cash. It's not what you have so much as how you work it (no diggity). There are a lot of job hazards, but the same can be said of other high paying occupations. After going for so long (and so consistently that the bouncers at Mademoiselles normally don't even raise a hand to wave me past, opting for a head nod or a hand shake instead), I can spot the ones that are going to make it and the ones that aren't. The girls who have talent and the girls who are going through the motions. I have another friend named Scott used to work in the business, and we share the same feelings: it's a beautiful place to visit, but we wouldn't want to work there for the rest of our lives.

Too much paradise is still too much. I never want to become desensitized to women. I don't want to get to the point (on any rung of the adult entertainment field) where I have to have a small Sherman Tank in my ass before things get interesting in bed. Or where I'd need an entire cheerleading squad, instead of one special partner. Consensual sex is still a gift. I'd like to keep it that way. The tease is great, but I'd prefer a girlfriend any day of the week. If she happens to be a stripper, then I'll have the best of both worlds. There's a little pole dancer inside all of us, dying to get out, and a little priss, shy and coquettish at the same time. Combining the two is the trick. Once I can get that down, I want a <u>C-note</u> for my rail tip.

Having fun so that you don't have to,
Tom 'Jeremy' Waters

A Whole Bunch of CDs You Wouldn't Touch Without Surgical Gloves and a Mask

The older I get, the worse my musical tastes become. I have every Peter Cetera CD, 2 Ace of Base albums, Rick Astley's entire catalog, and even a few Paul McCartney winners from the mid-80s. It's not all that bad, though. Everybody has a few time-tested classics that mean a lot to them for certain reasons; disfiguring break-up with a loved one, one terrific summer that you'll never forget, or a concert that captured your generation, or your teenage years. I've got a literal *wall* of Cds (I'm very thorough), and these are the 10 that have been played to death, and will be played to death for years to come.

Elton John and Bernie Taupin's *Sleeping With The Past* (1989, MCA) is, in a word, a masterpiece. Sure, everyone loves and adores *Goodbye Yellow Brick Road*, but the man was at the top of his game! When *Sleeping* was recorded, both the lyricist and the musician were at the lowest point in their lives. Elton was bald, doing cubic miles of cocaine, and just plain depressed. Rock bottom. What's amazing is the music that comes out of this cathartic period. John and Taupin were always better at writing the depressing stuff, and they really shine on every track with this one.

Bjork: *Debut* (1993, Elektra). Perhaps the greatest dance album of all time, it still holds up. She was innocent and naive and pixie-esque, and we weren't annoyed with it yet. That, and she wasn't 'collaborating' her brains out with every DJ on the face of the planet whose name ended in a Y. Bjork's my girl. She could use me like a hypodermic needle and just cast me on the side of the road when she was done. You could loop 'Big Time Sensuality' and 'There's More To Life Than This' through my brain for the rest of my natural life and I still wouldn't be sick of them. Who were the Sugarcubes again? Never heard of 'em.

Uh-Oh by David Byrne (1992, Warner Bros.) is one of the ballsiest solo efforts I've ever heard. It was tough trying to decide which David Byrne/Talking heads album to go with, but this album is a solid mambo romp! The former lead singer of the 'Heads went completely off the deep end to do his own thing, and it shines on every track. For example, "Now I'm Your Mom" is a rock/salsa hybrid about a parent who's explaining their sex change to their child. Need I say more? This was the one that made me go out and scoop up everything else that Dave's done (even the freaky Brian Eno collaborations from the early '80s).

Terence Trent D'arby's Symphony or Damn (Columbia, 1993). You've never heard of it, have you? And no, it doesn't have 'Wishing Well' on it! Sure, he's a pompous man, but he's got reason to be. Terence Trent D'arby is the incarnation of James Brown, if indeed James Brown were dead. With the Tower of Power's horns in tow, this is a theme album that takes you from Motown to rock to Lennon-esque acoustic ballads to country and right back again. Who else could pull off a line like "You're sub plot world/is so cavalier/but you knew the tension inside the sweetness was so near/" without sounding like a cheeseball? Sex, religion, and ego are all one animal to Terence. He's got soul, and he's super bad.

The Beastie Boys got everyone's attention with *License To Ill*, but they really came into their own with the follow up album, *Paul's Boutique* (Capitol Records, 1989). In my opinion, this is the greatest rap album of all time. Not only do they drop the mad beats on these tracks, but they do it with a vicious sense of humor: "Like Sam The Butcher bringin' Alice the meat/like fred flintstone drivin' around with bald feet." Chock full of infectious rhymes, the only theme album that comes even close would be De La Soul's *Three Feet High and Rising*. After *Paul's,* they became a frat boy institution. It sounds like they were still having fun back then, instead of targeting the 16-25 male market first and foremost.

I used to be one of those people who couldn't stand Bob Dylan's voice. I made the common mistake of assuming that he sounded like *Blonde on Blonde* on all of his releases. Then I bought *Time Out Of Mind* (1997, Columbia). After thirty years, Bob had finally paid honorable homage to all of his folk heroes. Produced by Daniel Lanois (a mastermind who's furthered the careers of U2, Peter Gabriel, and Sarah McLaughlin), Mr. Zimmerman sounds raw, scratchy, and vital, and the lyrics explore a degree of loss and pain that only a lifetime of heartache could dredge up. His voice comes off with none of the whiny tricks that bother most non-fanatics. I currently own about twenty five Dylan albums. This one is the reason.

At the pinnacle of his video, radio, and all around global stardom, Michael Jackson's *Dangerous* (Epic, 1991) is perhaps the greatest pop album of all time. Say what you will, but he has the most melodic voice I've ever heard, and his sense for rhythm is impeccable. Sure, *Thriller* may be the greatest selling album of all time, but *Dangerous* really pumps out the jams. Mike set off a powderkeg in the business that led to a breed of stars for whom video images triumphed over anything, including talent. The fluid beauty (musically and visually) of "Remember The Time" is overwhelming; the avalanche of hype surrounding the world premiere of "Black or White" was inescapable. Ironically, he won the Nickelodeon Kid's Choice Awards that year. He performed "Heal The World" during the Superbowl half-time show. And he was still Mike the Humanitarian who loved all children, and not quite Mike the Accused Pedophile yet. "Will You Be There" (the theme song from *Free Willy*) went up the charts with a bullet. Michael Jordan starred in the video for "Jam". And renowned photographer Herb Ritts directed the video for "Keep It In The Closet" (with a very steamy Naomi Campbell). Pound for pound, it's an amazing album. And then the dirt surfaced. Mike's place in music history is secured. Will he ever reach the same level of stardom again? Probably not. At the time of writing this, he's had a finished studio album for a year now, but nobody wants to release it because executives think that he's tapped out as a performer. I'm glad we have this album to remember him by before he got too weird for words.

Us by Peter Gabriel (Geffen, 1992) let the healing begin before people even got obsessed with therapy. Admittedly, it's very touchy-feely in terms of introspection, but Pete still had hooks. I listened to "Steam" about seventy five times in a row when I first got the album. Using classic fables and core images from Western culture, the former lead singer of Genesis (and the only decent one, at that) tries to make sense of himself, a failed marriage, and relationships between the genders. Men are from Mars, and Peter Gabriel is from an entirely different galaxy of genius! That he got into a relationship with Sinead O'Connor after collaborating with her on the album whereby she almost committed suicide is besides the point. I like this one just a little bit better than *So*.

Imagine by John Lennon (EMI, 1971) has stood the test of time in my library. It was basically the only album I listened to when I was 17, and it's still getting some off-shelf mileage. What's great about Lennon's solo music is that he has three speeds: hurt, pissed, and in love. McCartney gets lyrically skewered in "How Do You Sleep?", John goofs around a bit to a country sound with "Crippled Inside", his trade mark dreamy vocals work their magic in "Jealous Guy", and the annoyance of dealing with insincerity shines on in "Give Me Some Truth". And, of course, there's the title track. It's a great song, 'nuff said.

Pop by U2 (Island Records, 1997) is incredible. To be honest, I never liked their folksy religious/political stuff from the '80s. I didn't even pay attention to them until they sold out completely, and then they actually started to sound interesting. *Pop* is a free-floating, spontaneous, schizophrenic blast of modern culture, more erratic in lyrical style than Charles Manson after ten pots of coffee. It's techno, it's rock, it's house, it's disco; it's nothing short of breath taking. "If Coke is a mystery/Michael Jackson History/If beauty is truth/and surgery/the fountain of youth/" For one album, this band was perfect.

We've all got central cores to our CD collections. Cornerstones of seismic importance, holding up the one-offs, whims, and bandwagon purchases. The ones that weigh out over the embarrassing phases, or the foolish choices. There were so many other favorites that I wanted to mention, but I just couldn't squeeze them in. If my archives were flooded and these ten albums were spared by some quirk, I'd be all right. These are the ones that matter. These are the ones that make the rest of the wall look good. That make me feel like the excitable fourth grader glued to his first radio listening to Casey Casolm like clock work every Sunday afternoon. Will Britney Spears be one of the new classics ten years from now? Will Beck have a double disc by then showcasing some other strange new musical mastery? We'll see, and let's hope so.

Tom "Grand Funk" Waters

SimAuthor

Growing up, I always thought that there was some hidden manner of breaking into writing; secret handshakes, special connections, or a short-cut that nobody was telling me about. I was (obviously) wrong. I would refuse to write a proper query letter because I thought it was stupid that I had to follow 'the man's' rules, that was one of the main things that held me back. I bullheadedly avoided researching the markets because I figured that my work was suitable for any and all of them. I'm not exactly at the top of the heap right now, but I'm starting to follow the few cordial paradigms of publishing, so I'm making some headway. And some friends ask for advice now. How do you go about it? What special rules are there? The special rules are that you have to abide by their rules. Aside from that, it's all about hard work, perseverance, and much more than your daily allowance of humble pie.

I liked to complain about how, once I was done writing the article, that should have been all the work that was required from me. That's just the beginning. You have to find out where your work can be used, and look even further to see what pays. If you don't have enough of a pedigree to get into paying markets, you learn to enjoy not making money, and relish in the fact that you got something published. There's no such thing as going from 0-

Esquire in most cases. The publishing world has a certain pecking order that you work your way up in. Start with papers, or journals, or reviews, and parlay that into smaller regional magazines, or specialty magazines and e-zines. I discovered magazines I've never even heard of that pay some pretty decent rates. After you get a few acceptances under your belt, you send a pitch or a proposal to a higher echelon. They're impressed with your professionalism. What you've learned along the way. And you get accepted. Hopefully.

The old wives' tale about wallpapering your room with rejections is completely true. Take pleasure in watching your work get ignored, shelved for months on ends, or ripped apart and shot down in flames in front of your terrified eyes. Form rejections always bothered me, because I knew in my heart of heart's that the editor either just read the first paragraph (hopefully) or didn't read any of it and let the secretary shoot it right back to my mail box. That's generally all editors have time to read so you need to send an intriguing pitch or hit one out of the ballpark in the first few lines. I've gotten some very pleasant rejections with constructive advice that it's taken me years to finally pay attention to. As much as it hurts me physically to say this, play by the rules.

Know who you're sending your work to and follow it up. Dear Sir(s) is the biggest, rudest, foulest phrase that you can send to a company. Write that and you're guaranteed not to hear back from them. Or, if you do, it won't be pretty. There are a lot of writer's market lists in print and online. Take the time to find out who the managing editor or the submissions editor is, and address your work to them. That's half the battle right there. If you've never dealt with the publication before, make sure that the work looks impeccable. Spell check it, single space it, and for god's sakes, type the thing out. Anyone who's surprised when they don't get a response from their cocktail napkin epic has a long way to go. Find out how long it generally takes to hear a response, and if you don't get one, follow it through! People respect perseverance. Not nagging, mind you, but determination. Call or fax if you can with a quick reminder. Or send another letter if it's something national just to check in on the piece. You'd be surprised with how often that works.

Take assignments and pitch ideas. Sure, the stuff that you write is the greatest that's ever been seen in the genre, but nobody cares. Which reminds me, always compare your work to something popular in the field that the recipient can relate to. It doesn't really matter what you write when it comes to assignments so much as how well of a personal spin you put on it. Assignments are like pop quizzes; little tests to see if you can jump through a hoop or two before you get what you want. Oftentimes, they pay. And it makes you limber creatively. I used to abhor the idea of assignments. Refused to take someone else's idea and run with it. But that's the way it goes, and it's a good way to stretch out and turn into the writing machine that you have to be if you're serious about your work.

Get as much feedback on your own work as you can possibly handle without bursting into tears. It'll toughen you up, and it's impossible to judge your own work in a non-biased fashion. In the same respect, take your advice with a few grains of salt. If it's coming from an editor, or a fellow writer, odds are that their ego is the size of Nebraska, and you're peeing on their territory. Take it with some perspective: sometimes they're trying to help you, and other times they're just getting a couple kicks in while you're at the bottom of the ladder. Distinguishing the two is pretty easy. You'll have to appease a lot of established self-esteems before getting to your own. Your work can always be better, and there will always be somebody out there who's better than you. Accept this and embrace it. If you don't want to improve upon what you're doing, then what's the point?

Stephen King didn't write 2,500 page novels when he was 22. He worked his way into it. Raymond Carver didn't write short stories that inspired open weeping until about fifteen years before his death. It takes some time to figure out what you're good at, and what will sell. Writers get better with age. They stretch out a bit and noodle around a tad more once they get some acceptance. You also have to suffer quite a bit and learn about the human condition before you can accurately report upon it. Love and then lose it. Try being completely financially destitute for a while. Let a few people die around you. All of these will do the trick. The world changes around you, and you change with it. Your vocabulary expands, and a rigid sense of creativity turns into a free floating entity that's as much an extension of yourself as your hair or your clothes.

Don't get into it for the money, because you're not going to see any of that for a while. If you want to write a few melancholic poems to keep in a shoe box and look at from time to time, that's fine. Or if you're happy to show a short story to friends and family for the rest of your life, that's fine too. But it's not about cash. It never should be. As far as freelancing goes, it's not the most lucrative business in the world when you start off. It'll take years, hell, even decades before you can quit your day job in most cases. Housewives make up about 80% of the buying market out there, so if you don't appeal to them, expect to wait awhile before your ship comes in.

If you do what you love, though, the money will follow. Keep at it! That's the most important thing I can pass on. Never stop writing, because it can only get better by virtue of practice. Read incessantly. Read whenever you have a free moment. I read somewhere that John Grisham never reads books and it sent me into a tizzy! Everything you absorb in the world will have a unique trickle-down effect on what you write, so absorb as much as you reasonably can! Study your field. Most writers are super-fans of the markets they work for, so follow suit.

Whenever someone asks me a generic writing question, I shoot this question back at them: What are you willing to sacrifice to make your biggest Dream come true? And if the answer isn't everything, you obviously don't want it badly enough. I've lost a lot along the way, and I haven't even made it that far. Friends, jobs, sleep, money, and my own peace of mind at times. But it's the greatest form of therapy around, and one of the oldest professions in the world. Everybody says that they want to write the Great American Novel after they get out of college, or when they retire. Why wait? Brett Easton Ellis wrote *Less Than Zero* in one weekend before he was a freshman in college. The book was published and praised when he was a sophomore. You can always make time for the things you love. Whenever life seems tough, I think about William Carlos Williams, one of the best conservative poets of the 20th century. William put in an insane amount of hours every week as a staff doctor at a hospital. After work, he'd spend time with his family and tuck the kids into bed. Once everything else in his life was attended to, he'd write poems while his family was sleeping. And then he'd get up and do it all over again. Most peoples lives aren't nearly as busy as his. If you truly want to go somewhere with your work, there's no better time than the present. So get cracking! Incessantly scribbling,

Tom "monte blanc" Waters

Competing With The Expresso Machine

I've been performing on stage for going on five months now, and I still get butterflies. Whether it's five minutes before I'm certain I'm going up, some slow, half-hour terror that drags through me while I'm waiting to take the stage, or simply a nagging anxiety that eats away at me while I'm reading, it's always there. And you know something? I'm beginning to like it. Weight lifters talk about the high they get from pain. How they can't stop working out until they're tendons are screaming and they're ready to collapse on the floor into a pile of sweat and muscle. You look forward to the fear. You grasp it and hang onto it for dear life. And then you kick it in the ass and send it running for mommy.

At the outset, I made every open mic in town for the sake of promoting a book in town. Now, I'll go up there for any damned thing. It doesn't always happen, but there's a rush you get that's better than anything. Almost better than writing for me, but not quite. When you show up somewhere, and everything feels perfect. The weather's just right, the crowd is up for something random, and they're receptive to what you have to say. The thrill comes in when they're rolling with laughter, or dead silent because they're paying attention to every....single.....word that you're saying. It's a dangerous thing. I'm taking a month off for my own good very shortly. Let's hope I can stick to it.

I still remember my first time like it was yesterday. It was a couple days after my birthday, and my friend Alicia asked me if I'd read a bit at a comedy showcase. She booked a sprinkling of local stand-up comedians and thought that I'd fit in nicely. Stand-up comedy is a big pet hobby of mine, so I was excited. I got to the place about two hours ahead of time and hung out near the bar to gauge the crowd. People started pouring in about an hour before the gig was set to go, and I was fine with that. She gave me some great advice, too. If you get heckled, give it back at the same level. She also warned that there were gonna be nights when the venue you played at was dead, or when nobody was listening and people would just talk over you.

It was 8 o'clock, and the brewery was packed! Al started off and the show was up and rolling. I was completely at ease. Then it dawned on me (an hour in) that the guy on stage now was the guy I'd be following. Oh boy. Oh dear. Every nerve in my body did the merengue. I was going to fail miserably. Nobody was going to laugh next to these pros! What the hell was I thinking? All my friends came up to see me and I was going to die a terrible death on stage! I bolted for the bar in the hopes of drowning the butterflies. After gulping down a double of scotch and three pints, they were docile, but still breathing. And then Al was giving me this ridiculously generous intro! Aaaaah! I stumbled onto the stage, set my tape recorder down, and ruffled through the book. Within five minutes, the room was howling. They liked me! I didn't suck! My friends heckled with impunity and I laughed them off rather than quipping back. Once my three bits were through, I walked off to a roar of applause. I was a very happy camper.

After that came the hard task of "paying your dues". This means that the regulars could care less about who you are because you're new, and that you have to play out enough to show them that you're not going away. You have to prove to the veterans that what you do is professional, enjoyable, and that you can bring a crowd in. Or at the very least, that you won't scare people off. Then they accept you. Paying your dues could take anywhere from four months to the rest of your natural life.

Keep in mind that when speaking about playing out, I'm referring to a very big grab bag here: open mics, coffee houses, comedy clubs, bookstores, poetry readings, etc. It's all pretty universal, though. What's ironic is that I don't even *drink* coffee! Never liked the stuff! I've got enough acquired tastes without taking on another one. The rest of the touring troubadours and proficient poets are the hardest crowd to win over. And show business, as they say, is murder. Until you see the same faces at twenty different spots, you're just some schmoe doing a guest spot. Once a person is done playing their set, or reading their thing, they'll get up and leave in the middle of your act. That used to bother me, having people get up and walk out. But in the same respect, I enjoyed it.

One thing I can't stand is apathy. I don't know how to deal with that. Total silence; how do you respond to it? If I've offended a person so much that they storm off in a huff, telling me what a bastard I am on the way out, that's fine! I love that! The business in question isn't exactly thrilled about it, but at least I got a response of some sort out of the person! Problem is, most folks wouldn't have the hubris to heckle me while I was up there, and the cowards waited until afterwards to get their licks in. Zinging some heckling idiot while you're onstage is fun if you can think fast on your feet. And a crowd that laughs, or claps, or hangs on what you're saying is great too, although a little scary. I never expect to do well, so when I do, it throws me.

And when a crowd is tough, they're really tough. At one point, I called an bar that I told a lot of people I was going to. Turns out they didn't do open mics anymore. They hadn't done open mics for over two years. That the paper got it wrong, and they normally did Karaoke on Tuesdays, but I was welcome to come up and do my thing. So I figured, "How much worse could I do than some drunken putz slurring his way through 'Love Shack'?" A lot worse. A friend drove out with me, and I decided to go with a trophy case crowd-pleaser. With a room full of forty people, Ron was the only guy listening. I was pissed. I stormed out saying that I was never coming back, and I never did.

You don't want to pull the primadonna act, though. It never goes over well. One of the things that helps is remembering that you can always do better, and that somewhere out there, there's somebody who's better than you are at what you do. You don't walk into a place acting like everything you touch is gold. That turns a lot of people off. On the flip side, though, doing anything onstage requires a lot of confidence, and if people can tell that you're confident, they'll pay attention for at least a little while. There's a very fine line between confidence and pretentiousness, and we all stumble over it at the beginning. If you're not humble, then you better learn how to fake it well.

One of the co-hosts at an open mic never got that, so I stopped going to that location. This guy acted as if it were some great travesty that record executives weren't knocking down his door to sign a twenty record deal. When he played the same two cover songs every single week with little variation. To top it all off, he'd introduce people with a facetiousness that I thought when on the endangered species list in 1986. You learn to put up with a lot of that, though. If it's not your show, go with the flow.

Paying your dues means taking shit from everyone. I played at a restaurant downtown near a big local college that pulled in three customers on a good night and the manager thought she was Colonel Tom Parker. The first time I went there she rattled off a list of rules and regulations, and then snapped at me when I inquired about when I was going on (since they didn't have a sign up list and her close friends were granted hour and a half sets when the standard was fifteen minutes). You just shake your head and take it like a man. Word gets around fast in a small town, and it turns out that none of the performers go there because everybody knows that the lady is a tramp.

I really lucked out one night. I played in the heart of the city at a bar, and bars are tough for me, because I do spoken word. If I don't go on early (before people are drunk), I'm a dead man, and usually, if I go on late, I don't have the attention span left to listen to myself. The weather was rotten but the room was filled with some convention. The guys had been drinking there since four that afternoon, and they were all slapping hi fives and dropping the f bomb like there was no tomorrow. I went up and did a time-tested bit about driving, and when I started ranting about construction workers, one of the clowns shouted out "I'm right here, mother*&^%er!". Unphased, I shot back, "You're the guy that waved me by with your little orange flag on the thruway today, right?" He didn't say anything after that. Tough crowd.

It's usually a good idea to have your act down pat, too. I tried things out for a while and after a bit, you can discern which things work aloud and which don't. A piece that's a half an hour just isn't going to fly unless you're in a bookstore setting. And you don't do sling jokes about cysts if you're playing out at a cancer ward. It just makes good sense. Know your crowd, I can't stress that enough. Feel them out and gauge before you even set foot near a microphone. My problem was, after doing the same piece thirty times,

I got sick of it, so I'd move on to dangerous territory, or something that I wanted to do. Or I'd start with a happy, fluffy bit and then BAM, hit right below the belt when the audience least expected. That's sort of fun, because once you get people warmed up, they're willing to swallow a bit more as opposed to accepting some putz who just walked on.It made me think about how unbearably sick Elton John must be with singing "Your Song" for the five billionth time in concert. Wouldn't that drive him over the edge? It's nice to find something new in a piece, or to put a different spin on it, but there's only so much spin you can apply before the act is about as polished as it's going to get. Doing the same thing a few times gives you the chance to work on delivery, and to give the big lines the respect and the pause they deserve.

And it's best to shoot for regularity. If you go to the same place every week, people keep coming back to see you. Fortunately, after driving all over hell's half acre, I lucked out and I've been offered to host my own open mic. This way I won't be stretching five dollars of gas to make it to Niagara Falls and back, stammering in front of a drunken crowd of suits, or suffering through an intermission in a Karaoke set. I guess that's the key, to find a home after a spell. Traveling from club to club and coffee house to coffee house like some mad lyrical gypsy is fun for awhile, but so's having free time and a life the rest of the week. I'm ready to settle down into a groove. It's back to square one, as I'll have to earn an audience that wants to come back week in, week out. I don't want to be one of the jerks that all the troubadours complain about on the road. I'm the sort of guy who likes his open mics to be a lot like his bowel movements: regular. The adventure has just begun.

would you like to see any naked pictures of your pet hamster, sir?,
Tom "improv" Waters

Star, Pound, Function Function, What's Your Junction?

At my old job, I just thought people were annoying. At my new job, I spend more time with each customer in a given situation, and I've come to this new conclusion: people are dumber than rocks. I started as a temp shortly before Christmas at the largest cell phone company in the cosmos (we'll call them Confusion Wireless so that I don't get sued), and the majority of the organisms that I dispense my 'customer care' to are not only too stupid to own a phone, but I'm amazed that they can put their own clothes on in the morning without burning the house down. Sometimes, I want to rip the phone away from a customer and say, "I'm sorry, but you're just too stupid to own this phone. I'm taking it away from you now." Granted, phone contracts and the actual programming of the phone can be difficult. Until I started there, I didn't know jack squat about portable service. I'm going on five months now, and I know more about the contraptions than people who've had service with the company for ten years. Which isn't saying much, believe me.

I don't even have one of the phones yet, as they don't really pay me enough to afford that luxury, and it's not exactly a crucial part of my life. I used to abhor cell phones, but it seemed like a case of starting with the right company at the right time. It's a nice enough job, but the pay leaves a lot to be desired. A little less than a year ago, three small companies got cannibalized by one gigantic corporation, so they've been cutting back since, and the small guy on the totem pole always gets screwed. I am that small guy. I'm making more money than my old job, or I would've gone crawling back, but not a king's ransom by any means. I'm still on a first name basis with the poverty level. The salesmen complain about how much they used to make at their jobs while playing with a row of gold rings on their hand at the same time. If I buy a hamburger for lunch, I'm spoiling myself. You figure it out. We manage to have fun with it, though.

I pinballed from store to store for a little while, racking up overtime and meeting new people, and finally, they placed me at a mall location. I've been working in malls for going on twelve years, and thought I'd escaped, but they pulled me back in! Our staff is cozy, quirky, and a lot more office-like than anything I've dealt with before. There's a water cooler, but nobody talks around it. Most of the gossip goes on right behind the door leading out to the sales floor. We print out five reams worth of reports in the morning and file them according to number. Then collate them. Then they get the three hole punch and get filed in a folder. After being faxed to ten different home offices. Then twenty pages of those reports are pulled back out and used for inventory purposes. And, eventually, they go back into another folder, or a mailbox. At the end of the day, all the documents get shredded. This is what's known as bureaucracy.

The phone's are really neat, and I'm still amazed at how far they've come in such a short amount of mass consumption. The majority of them are the size of a remote control, and they weigh a little bit more than a car air freshener. They keep getting smaller, too! One of the phones we carry is the same size as a large pack of gum; in a month, they're coming out with one that you need an electron telescope to see the numbers on. It's the size of five dust motes, side by side. Who wants a phone that small? I'd like something that I could use personally, but people always want the newest and coolest and smallest piece of technology that they can get their greedy hands on. So that they can go home, throw out the instruction booklet, and then call me to complain about how they don't know how to operate their cellular machine.

Customers complain about everything. We've been called criminals, a-holes, idiots, and a whole bunch of other words that I wouldn't be able to print anywhere. They throw a lot of tantrums. An old lady threw a phone into the garbage once after rediscovering that it cost almost two hundred dollars to break contract. People come in to sign up, buy the cheapest phone on the floor, and then complain when the service isn't top notch: "I got this phone for two bits and a cup of coffee and it's not working now! I want my money back!" They don't seem to understand that the word <u>contract</u> means 'legally binding document' and not 'happy-friend-agreement, which you can break at any time'. They complain about their bills and how they're being cheated when they go 3,000 minutes over their monthly plan. When we break the math down for these whiz bangs, they still fume. As I said, too stupid to own a phone. In the town that I work in, everyone uses the word "Youse". As in "Youse guys got any phones?" Certainly not for youse we don't. I wonder how some of the customers function in their everyday lives when they can't read, behave, or execute elementary math.

The salespeople all own the same phone. It's a black flip-phone, sort of a status symbol, really. Let me point out again that I'm not a salesperson. I'm 'customer care', which is a nice title that translates into 'bottom feeder'. I'd like to go into sales some day, though, as it looks very challenging, and you get rewarded for your trials and tribulations with commission! I've had a lot of retail jobs, but I've never had the opportunity to work on commission, and I think it'd be fun. You work with a quota. If you don't make your quota every month, you get fired! Doesn't that sound like fun? The one advantage of being hourly is that, towards the close of each month, when the rest of the staff is cleaning their guns, preparing shots of drainer fluid, and fondling nooses, I can relax and take comfort in the knowledge that I make the same amount of money either way. That amount being chickenfeed. A quick breakdown on the employees, though.

If you take a look at the coat rack in the back room, we all have black leather jackets. This is not part of the dress code, but merely some coincidence that spans the entire company. Are people who wear black leather jackets more likely to work for a cell phone company? Or are people who work for cell phone companies more likely to buy a black leather jacket?

I'll never know. It would be nice if someone conducted a study. Flying in the face of every sexual harassment suit in history, all the employees talk about is food, money, and sex. This is what our small talk revolves around. If it's not one of these topics, it's another, or it incorporates all three: "I got some from my girlfriend last night on top of the pot roast while I was checking the account balance on my platinum card." would be a good example.

The salespeople are in a league of their own. There are haggard old pros with a customer base that's more disciple-like in it's scope and size than anything else who've been selling products since they were young turks. There are young turks with a chip on their shoulder and the confidence of an entire basketball team who want to be CEO by the time they're thirty and retire at forty. And there are lots of attractive women who can flirt their way into selling ten phones in the span of five minutes because they know how to wink properly at a married prospect when his wife isn't looking. Lastly, there are new guys who don't know their ass from their elbow, dying to rocket out of training because they think they'll sell 3,000 percent over quota. I watch them all and take mental notes.

There is a corporate totem pole, and I'm at the very bottom of it. There are the managers, the assistant managers, those who go above and beyond their quota, the rest of the salespeople, the service technicians, the Inventory person, the UPS guy, the guy who brings the bank bags in the big armored truck, the person who professionally clean the rugs every four months, the guy who cleans the windows every six months, and then there's my position. I've been working for five months with this company as a temp and I still haven't gotten permanent placement. There's probably a very good reason for that, though. Well, I know the reason, actually.

After five years at a family owned company, one forgets the rules to big corporate culture. I was used to saying and doing whatever I pleased without having to abide stringently to five binders full of laws, by-laws, and their attachments. So it took awhile to break me in. A good four months out of the five. In one week, I (accidentally) did just about everything you could conceive of to get fired, and somehow escaped the clutches of the unemployment line. At the beginning of the week, I a)opened a coal-based toner cartridge over the inside of the fax machine, costing the company five hundred dollars. Shortly thereafter I b)showed up an hour and ten minutes late for my shift and then made a snide remark to my boss, thinking I was only ten minutes late. The next day I showed up on time, but, due to a (ahem) sleepover the night before, I was c) wearing sneakers. Filthy, ratty, mold-encrusted Converse Sneakers. The day after that I d)spent an hour and a half drawing an amusing caricature of one of my co-workers, who (in the picture) was saying "You're fired, bitch!" My boss really didn't take that well. I wasn't the one who tacked it up on the wall in the back room!

So I suppose it's a miracle that I still have a job with the company. After that, I made an effort to behave myself. There's a time and a place for certain behavior, and most of my behavior is best left outside of the work place. You really have to watch what you say, and to whom (omitting the word 'bitch' as often as possible). That was a month and a half ago. I must be doing something right, though, because word has it that I'll be going permanent soon. I've learned that a leopard can change his spots, but he has to attend to them one spot at a time. Throughout my job-hopping and temporary rotations, I've gone out of my way to work at stores with neat products and neat discounts, like music, movies, books, games, or toys. I thought that you needed to work around something fun in order to have fun. Not the case. And it gets less and less cool as you get older to brag about the nifty discount you get while everybody else has stock options and a 401K plan along with medical and dental benefits. You can have fun (to a certain extent) wherever you go. I look forward to whooping it up with my co-workers when I leave for work, now, rather than poring over stuff I don't have money for anyways. Hopefully I can go into sales sometime down the road, and get my stock options along with all the other happy benefits. One of those benefits being a portable phone.

not for disclosure outside of this essay,

Tom "six inch pedestal" Waters

The Sound-Head and The Fury

Aside from a brief stint with an evil, face-less multiplex corporation (and by brief I mean shorter than the lifespans of arthritic houseflies), I've been employed by the same theater for almost five years now. It's rather amusing to think that I've spent more time with this company than any other job, institution of learning, or teenage vietnamese brothel. I'm working right now, actually, if you can call it that. I finally stayed at a job long enough to ascend the ranks to a position of abusive and near absolute power! A few weeks ago I was put out to pasture (or stud, considering that there's a sizable university right across the street) at my employer's best movie house in the area. I think I'm gonna like it here. The clientel is well-behaved most of the time (except for howling yentas and bombastic freshman of indeterminate sexual preference), the staff is timed like a swiss clock, and I have a swank office with an electric typewriter. I felt sorry for the poor girl (the typewriter), having been used only for perfunctory chores like film schedules and my tyrannical memos. Plus I can't resist the tangible onamatapiea of writing something on a typewriter. But I'm long in the tooth, aren't I? Rambling away like this won't get the two of us anywhere. Let's start with the blind chance of it all.

In 1995, I'd spent four months unemployed. It was winter time, and unless you want to toil at the front lines of the pagan god of retail as a worker drone, there was really nothing to be found. I applied (and sat through) a training video and company synopsis for Wal-Mart, for God's sakes! That was truly my personal and professional rock bottom. And it certainly wasn't for lack of looking for jobs. I went back to a toy store I worked at (Pricks R Oui) to beseech them for a return tour of duty only to find that the new store manager (they go through general managers faster than the little tykes go through a can of Play-Doh-not a good sign) had read a published article that I wrote about my time there, and that his sense of humor was wildly disproportionate to his frame. Strike eight. Four months, friends. Four long, arduous, penniless months, and nothing sucks worse than being broke during the height of Kwanza.

I'd spent the majority of these months doing productive personal projects. For instance, I was very adept at laying on my back and glaring vacantly at whatever basketball game happened to be on the tube from my Davenport of solitude. Granted, it was a really good season to watch hoop, as this was the fourth year in a row that the Bulls swept the playoffs. Other resourceful chores: gaining so much weight that I could balance small vases aloft my girth, sleeping for thirteen hours at a stretch, waking up at the crack of 4p.m., and listening to the same Paul McCartney maxi-single while wallowing in self pity and disgust.

But anyway, one day I was taking a constitutional with my friend through the mall (friends at the time liked to get me outdoors and air me out a bit) when I saw a help wanted sign outside the cinema. I marched up the ramp dressed like a yuppie hobo and grabbed an application. A week later I had an interview with the neo-Nazi who was running the place. Two weeks later I was hired and suited up in my spangly bowtie and Payless black work shoes. The fickle anus of fate had descended upon me.

It's baffling how well the job suited me. In all these years, (aside from a traffic ticket), I've probably had to get out of bed before noon a dozen times. The feast-or-famine atmosphere of on again, off again rounds of shows going in was super conducive to my own bipolar pendulum of high tide and low tide. And free pop is always a plus in my estimation. Now I've always been a sieve for anything media, and, up until that point, I had never dabbled in film. After two jobs at music stores and one long stint with a bookstore, it was the next logical move. At the very least, it's helped to make me well-rounded in counter-culture cocktail conversation.

When I first arrived, I was a meat and potatoes man when it came to flicks. Action movies, the occassional drama, and my thirst for incessant Nicholson for starters, but the friends and colleagues I made in the business molded me into a lean, mean arthouse machine. Where I used to get my kicks from heavy dollops of special effects and painful onscreen carnage, I began to lean towards dialogue driven, shoestring budget, first time out directors who had a knack for well-lit, well-framed, painful onscreen carnage. I feel as if I've grown as a person. What suprises me is how the public (and I was guilty of this at one time as well), doesn't really pay attention to, or look for, works from certain directors (other than the brand-name schlock purveyors). And in any other medium, there is a prediliction to seek out that one musician, that certain best-selling author, or the specific breakfast cereal. When asked, the average douche bag (not you, of course), would be hard pressed to name twenty of the best directors in the last three years. We're all familiar with Spielberg, Kubrick, and recently, James Cameron (inward twitch of repulsion). This is all well and good, but I nearly wet my shorts whenever some chimp in line actually throws out a name like the Cohen brothers, Terry Gilliam, David Fincher, David Cronenberg, or Spike Jonze.

These are exciting cinematic times to be a part of, polarized as they are. While uninspired remakes and motivational pamphlet adaptations wither in the wake of indifferent summer masses, the scribes and the glitterati stay glued to the pulse of the arthouse, anxiously awaiting the next Pulp Fiction or the new Neil Labute or the fifth coming of John Travolta after he's bounced out of the sewer again. The main thing I anticipate is the painful scalding of Tom Hanks, some altruistic soul who will lock Joel Schumacher back in the closet (re-bricking a wall over him), and an end to the deliberate and diligent pussification of James Bond.

Note one prophetic sidebar: When I was five or six, cable became accessible and chic enough that our lower middle class household could afford it. Superchannels were trickling onto the tub, and we landed HBO, which is still my favorite movie channel. In addition to multiple viewings of Pete's Dragon and For Your Eyes Only (my first Bond flick, and the reason that I'm the only Roger Moore fan in the history of recorded time), they aired an avant short. In the short, a live strip of film slithers out of a man's bathtub and chases him around his apartment. The man, mortified, runs into another room and locks the door while the reel-snake giggles maniacally, then proceeds to slip under the door. After three minutes or so of this, the film ends up strangling the guy. Now, I'm sure this was supposed to be funny or quirky to those privy enough to catch it, but I was six years old! I have yet to pull the band-aid off of the psychological scars, and to this day I will not be alone in a room with film.

Day two since the beginning of this essay. I've been relegated back to my old haunt so that the general manager could go on a camping trip with a near-stranger in the hopes of scoring. So much history in these walls. If they could talk, they'd probably complain of prostate difficulties, old person stench, and sore stretch marks. This once magnificent palace of delights has faded to a tarnished and sad memory of it's former glory. After being appointed to a manager almost two years ago, I'd sometimes feel like a desolate king in a dilapitated castle closing at night, guarding over all of the ghosts who haunted it's insides before him. Other times, I'd feel like an utter and unschooled failure with a sub-rate job and sub-rate pay, on the fast track to being one of those full-time forty year olds you see at less than perfect jobs. The ones with the sad and vacant looks in their eyes.

We've changed a lot, this theater and I. People may no longer flock to see us, but we stand still and endure, watching the world transmogrify around us. I always tell friends that if you want to dissappear, the best thing to do is stay in one place. It rings true, trust me. If you could create a stop-motion camera that flashes once every four months instead of once every few seconds, you'd see the change. The Eastern Hills Mall Triplex, which opened in 1972, was once a two screen that opened it's doors at the same time the rest of the mall did. The carpets were a blinding burgandy, the parking lots were stuffed to the gills, and, as I'm so constantly reminded by the special super friends who stroll in as customers, pop corn was around half a cent. Things change.

When my company took over in 1991, buying out General Cinemas (a former leviathan in the industry), they decided that the most practical course of action was to let the place rot. C'est La Vie, right? Entropy marches on. Now, for the trickle of patrons that amble into the place, one is greeted with threadbare carpets patched with vinyl hobby tape in some spots, bathroom pipes that burp and spit and dribble with all the fury of an undigested foot-long cheese chili dog with extra onions, and a roof in the larger theater of the three that pisses rain in random segments onto the filmgoers below, who roost in seats that make scoliosis look like shiatsu back therapy by contrast. This is why there is a preponderance of soggy hunchbacks in the area. I've fared slightly better, as this castle was booming for three years before my birth in '75, not to mention the fact that few people are allowed to walk, sit, urinate, or spill food on me except for a chosen circle of friends. Since I started here, my average weight was None Of Your Business, billowing up to an embarrassing level of cinch straps for belts, down to being rail thin and super-fine, and now I'm sort of solid, but in the right places, thank you very much. I've gone from large satellite dish shaped owl glasses to slightly Aryan looking specs, long nappy ratty slicked-back ponytails to streamlined, high lighted young Republican locks, and the demeaning part-time uniform was swapped for slacks and a tie. From goatee to no goatee to a handlebar, Old West Saspirilla moustache (that was a confused time, that one) to a baby face that made me look like a fat 12 year old, then back to the classic Van Dyke. They call me The Manager Formerly Known As Tom out here. Ok, I told them to call me The Manager Formerly Known As Tom. Oof. This is embarassing. I'm actually the only person who calls myself The Manager Formerly Known As Tom.

This position has reaped one girlfriend (quite short lived; she listened to angry female folk music, lived in a trailer park with her mustachioed lesbian divorcee mom and was 17), one best friend who went on to other things long since, but was still my best friend until recently, after having certain indescretions with a certain ex-girlfriend, one or two sworn enemies of critics (rhymes with Biff Hymen), one very close friend, standup comedy aficianado and former boss, and one love lost. My boss teeters somewhere in the balance as a sort of gray area friend, ball buster, and sparring partner tri-yearly when we butt horns over something inconsequential. I helped him move out of his townhouse and into the home where he and his wife would live two years ago. He sold me a set of speakers for my home theater three X-mases passed. I was treated to a severely elegant dinner at an exclusive restaurant just last fall while we were on the road surveying the roving empire that is Dipson Theaters. Not quite a friendship, and not quite a professional working relationship. I'm constantly lauded for my writing talent, which comforts me.

He firmly believes (my boss, Mike Clement) that one should never spend time informally with subordinates as it tends to breed contradiction and insubordination in the ranks. I firmly believe that you can easily walk a tight rope between the two, and that when the chips are down you can truly depend on your confidants to come in for a shift or understand if you've done an unforgivably shit job on cleanup etc. We agree to disagree. And you're probably curious as to the love lost mentioned not six sentences ago, right? We'll sollipsistically swing back to that one somewhere down the line. Day three, by the way, and the hometown football team has ruined everyone's hopes again, so this place is a graveyard.

You can set your watch to a lot of the trends in volume with regard to days of the week, holidays, and other blind variables that the layperson doesn't take into account. Christmas, Easter, and Thanksgiving are all pretty slow. You get mostly Jehovah's Witnesses and divorcee families who don't know what the hell to do with their kids when they have them so they opt to go somewhere in public where they can sit in close quarters, and not talk. Along with a flock of smelly Canadians in Winnebagos gearing up for their inadequite and so-called 'Boxing Day' with felonious shopping excursions and poor film choices. I saw a man last Easter who had gray hair that appeared for all the world like a poodle was dry humping his scalp. One of the many advantages of management is that you can relegate the customer service to a peon while you walk around a corner to laugh your nuts off.

Trends, though. Anyone who shows up for a seven o'clock show on a Saturday and finds themselves baffled when there's a line around the block should be fitted in the ass for a super sized mudhole. A slight tip: If you don't want the back of your seat systematically kicked by some faux-gang-banging fourteen year old with an asinine visor, a forty year old with a cashmere scarf yammering away on a cell phone who doesn't know how to control his volume, a gaggle of teenage girls tittering away as if they're in the middle of a school bus, and the rest of the madding crowd that fills up an entire stadium and destroys the joy of watching a film in any conventional sense of the word, then you go to see a film on a Tuesday or Wednsday night. If you're so horned up about seeing something that you absolutely have to catch it as soon as it comes out, you go on opening Friday (unless school is out). Most of this is common sense, but I believe that a decent cross section of audiences crave being sardined in the thick of a sell out crowd. I've seen it. As with all the bell curves of the volume/business end dynamic, there are certain universal truths to clientele. A sociologist could write a five volume coffee table series on the topic.

Younger couples; the woman *always* pays for everything. I get it, but it makes me ill. Time and again, I'll see some slovenly goof stumble his way in with a stunning waif, and she pays for the full ride. Chivalry was reportedly filleted with a melon baller some time during the close of the seventies. With older couples, it's reversed. And even more lacking in subtlety. The women walk off to the bathroom, or as far away from their spouse as they can, while a line of men stand in mute defeat as they fork over the bones. Extended families are usually the size of a third world country. The father dumps the contents of his wallet onto the counter in resignation while the rugrats perform an impromptu off-Broadway production of Lord Of The Flies in the lobby.

What I really enjoy are the single moms who lasso and round up every prepubescent monster on the block, stuff them into their SUVs, and bring them to my theater. Children's movies are the absolute worst. The first weekend of my unchaperoned assistant management, I politely told a child who was yanking on the barrier ropes to stop that, please. The crispy headed, lesbian hair sporting hag corralling the herd barked in that he was only a child. One more perk of general management? You only have to be nice if you choose to. In the wake of that confrontation, we now have a seat cover at Eastern Hills that resembles a Caucasian boy. The barrier ropes befuddle those who have no problem figuring them out in a bank, stadium, or university setting. They always bust out of the ropes.

There's always a chucklehead who, in his own disorientation and hubris, thinks he knows a faster way out or that the bathrooms won't be at the end of the vinyl rainbow we provide. I take a profound pleasure in sitting in the office, or the projection booth, and reading while they scurry around like moths obstinately banging up against a light bulb, discovering that every single exit except for the big goddamned green sign at the end of the path we create is hermetically sealed for my own enjoyment. Outlawing ignorance, one dummy at a time.

Foibles, quirks, and skewed memories. An old woman, alone in a theater with her keeper, had the werewithal and complete lack of social convention to stand up in the middle of the showing, let loose her bowels, and leave the theater without telling anyone. She wasn't one for roughage, either. A downside to management, you ask? When a chore or task is so reprehensible or difficult that when no one else will do it, you're suddenly the lucky stiff that the rest of the line-up takes three steps back from simultaneously. On a very slow night, I caught the only couple in Air Force One committing an act on the carpet that's reserved for the bedroom. After a children's movie on a Sunday afternoon in mid-November, a father and son left an empty six pack of beer in the aisles. Now either the kid was an alcoholic circus midget and I didn't get a good enough look, or the father of the millenium strolled through our hallowed halls. Understandably, it was a live action Disney film (and *Song of the South* and *Mary Poppins* don't count, as they are half and half).

Continuity. It's best that I keep rolling along with the history of the place, my job positions in general, etc, before I get carried away with the anecdotes, eh? It's been a week since I've been fired, by the way, and two months since the inception of this essay. Alarmed? Don't be. Where were we on the timeline? Oh, assistant management! Back in '97, we were right on top. The theater was booming, but everyone knew it wouldn't last. Regal Cinemas, a gigantic startup chain that was nationwide, was spreading towards our town with a wave of four or five gigaplexs, and one of them was opening right....down...the street from us. The buzz was enormous, and one of the main reasons why myself and my friend got promoted was because our fair manager was leaving for greener pastures. The twelve screen beast was slated to open in mid November but, owing to lazy local union construction and other unforeseen difficulties, they didn't open until around Christmas time. Some employees jumped ship as soon as they heard about the other theater. They were the smart ones. Others thought they'd wait and see. And then there were Mike Bolis and myself, the two assistant managers. We were dazzled with a pay raise and posted to keep the place from falling down around our ears (literally and figuratively) in the quake of progress that rippled our way.

Once the other theater opened, the place turned into a graveyard. Everyone was dazzled with stadium seating, impeccable film presentation, and the looming enormity of twelve choices all wrapped into one gigantic spot. My employers had blue prints to expand that location into a ten or twelve-screen for three years before the other company staked a claim, and they let it go. They haggled, hemmed and hawed and blew the opportunity. Eastern Hills has had lucky hits, award-films and exclusives to the area that have drummed up some decent business since then, but it will never, ever have a sold out crowd again. The brand name loyalty that we were sure we'd cornered the market on had dissappeared like so much smoke filtering past a projector lens. To make matters worse, by March, we found out that the location was closing. Another out of town racket, a dollar fifty theater, had whisked into the mall and, unbeknownst to us, wooed the management into selling our lease. My boss didn't hear about it until the deed was done. And we didn't hear about it until the last possible second. Things were not looking good.

I went to go work in shipping and receiving at a superstore. Within three weeks, my boss called to tell me that by some loophole, the other company was backing out and we were moving back in. Come April, the theater was re-opened and re-christened as the Eastern Hills 'Art-House' theater. They didn't mention that the arthouse we'd be showing was a week away from hitting video stores, but people figured that out soon enough. The summer droned on to no business, bored employees, and the next big loss of faith I'd had in the job. By September, I had to make one of the hardest decisions of my young adult life.

Mike and myself had been promoted to assistant management, you remember that much, right? This brings to mind the story of Gilgamesh, where two identical brothers take two completely seperate paths in their lives who end up having a colossal falling out when they meet again. Mike and I were peas in a pod. In the beginning of the job, we found common bonds, tastes, and vices, becoming best friends quickly. And then, the promotion. I took the promotion very seriously. Almost too seriously, to the point where it seemed as if I had one of the Tensabarrier poles up my ass at all times. I would have dreams that I'd left a breaker on at work, or a cabinet unlocked. Mike took to the new position like any other job he'd had: half assed, half asleep, or half drunk. When he didn't show up late, he was wearing four day old clothes. When he wasn't wearing four day old clothes, he'd brought a bottle of whiskey in for work. And, like a good friend, I looked the other way and cleaned up the messes he'd made. He would spend entire shifts doing absolutely nothing (which, mind you, is going to be an ongoing theme), and it showed. For a solid year, there was no central manager. Mike and I traded off shifts, and our boss would stop in once a week or so and tell us what wasn't done. Mike took vacations, and I made up the difference. Mike made obnoxious comments to the customers, and I'd deal with the complaints. Mike showed up forty five minutes late with another concocted apology. He got away with it for awhile. Then it got worse.

In September, I came in for a shift and he'd told me that there'd been a 'mix-up', that apparently I'd written down the wrong closing ticket numbers on the sheets from the previous shift. That's how we kept track of sales, and, more importantly, what little money was coming into the theater. After double checking my daily sheets, the weekly sheets, and his numbers, there was a discrepency. A hundred and thirty dollar shortage, to be precise. There was no way in hell that it was my fault. The ticket numbers never lie. To further complicate things, Mike was waving money around the day before payday (when it was common knowledge that he generally spent his paychecks before the weekend was out). Since business was so slow, our boss started scheduling us to manage the place by ourselves during the week, so we had to do everything. This also left my co-assistant with the opportunity to get away with anything. I had a problem.

I was conflicted, big time. There was my loyalty to the theater that had employed me faithfully for so many years on one hand, and on the other, Mike, who'd been my friend through thick and thin, when no one else was around, even when I couldn't stand myself. I thought about it after work that night, and in the end, I wasn't going to get fired for something that I wasn't a party to. I had to go to the employers about it, or get dragged down with him once it got worse (which it would). And <u>fuck</u> him for putting me in that position. So the next day, I went to the owner's stepson with the paperwork and levelled with him. Supplied the facts and let him do the rest of it.

Sometimes, tickets get punched out of the machine and go missing, but this was a lot different. With two shows in one theater, there was no way that both numbers could get accidently punched up because one set of tickets wasn't even in the machine! This was no accident.

The problem with the upper management (aside from the fact that they're all related to each other) was that they never fire anyone for anything. That's why Mike was allowed to slack for nine straight months without any fear of repercussion. So they told me to sit tight and act as if nothing had happened until they could find a suitable replacement. Presumably, this wouldn't take that long. It took them almost three months. Three months that I worked with this person knowing that the axe would fall any week. Three more months of keeping an eye on him to make sure he didn't pull more felonies. And three months of guilt over having to do the right thing, even if it cost me my best friend.

Friendships are funny. We'd had one or two knock down, drag-out fights in the past, but I was certain that, if he figured it out (which I'm sure he did) that it would be the end of our bond. I spent four and five days a week hanging out with him because I knew things would change, or that we wouldn't speak again. And finally, one day, he came over to the house on my day off to tell me that they'd let him go. They never brought up the theft, but the owner's son said that he'd been goofing off too much and that he was sorry, but that was it. I had to put on a surprised face and help him drown his sorrows that night. I felt like a heel. Like a traitor. But the die was cast.

Meanwhile, at work, they'd brought in a guy from the Amherst to be an assistant manager. We were going to try the whole assistant management arrangement yet again with no acting head. His name was Tony. A really nice guy, but unfortunately, very accident prone. Within a month, he was driving me nuts. He'd call me five times a shift on my days off regarding his incidents. One day he locked his keys in the office, on another, he dumped half of a film on the floor. This guy had been with the company for a year, and he was pulling rookie mistakes. It'd be hilarious if I wasn't getting called every five minutes about these things.

So after calling my boss (again) about another one of his mishaps, he said "Congratulations. I'm promoting you to general manager." So the position (again) was placed on my shoulders. This is when I was introduced to the wonders of management. Like salary. Salary is a nice term which means that you can work seventy hours a week or forty hours a week and you get paid the same amount either way. I was expected to come in on my days off to check up on things. I had the opportunity to work ten and twelve days in a row. And I got more phone calls than ever about bland problems that could've been solved had the assistant in question spent five minutes to think through the problem. I really liked Tony, but they fired him for dumping *Shakespeare In Love* all over the floor, then calling my boss at four in the morning for advice on how to fix it.

Whoah! I forgot all about Bill! Bill was more of a miracle in the form of a former marine than an assistant manager. They shipped Bill over from the Amherst while I was having my problems with Tony and phased him into the place. Bill was cocky, mouthed off to short tempered customers often, and told our respective boss off more times than I can count. But he was the hardest worker and the best supporting manager I've ever had under my employ. Bill showed up early. Bill came in on days off. Bill didn't drink, smoke, or involve himself in anything that didn't involve hockey, work, or his girlfriend. Bill was incredible. The Anti-Mike, really. After Tony left, it was just the two of us managing the place. That'd set the clock at around, oh, early 1999.

I promised Bill that I'd get another assistant manager so that scheduling and overtime wouldn't be such a frequent issue, but something would always fall through. One kid came in for the job, worked one shift, and then never showed up again. Another kid, Nick, trained with me for an entire month and then flipped out, saying that he had to do all the work. So he quit. And what the hell was the other kid's name? I always forget it.....Kevin, I think. No, that's not it, either. Well whatever his name was, he worked for a few months, overslept for a shift, and then told my boss that he forgot to set his alarm, so he had to get fired. The third party never worked out, so for a good year or so, it was the two of us.

And speaking of firings, I lost my fear of executing those. Since Regal Cinemas was down the street, most teenagers (the meat of any minimum wage job) got a job there, and why wouldn't they? More free movies to watch, more prestige, and more opportunities to get a lot of hours in. So I had to take what I could get, and a lot of times, it wasn't much. The majority of my part-timers were 15-18 yr old girls who either didn't want to work a whole lot or went on vacation with their parents every other month. Guys generally didn't apply for some reason, and the ones that did either stole, showed up late often, or didn't know what the hell they were doing. I fired one of those clowns in front of a sold-out Saturday crowd. That was fun. Bill got to fire one or two for me too, until I got yelled at for not doing it myself.

So this brings us to Lindsay, whom I've written about at length in other things. Lindsay was 18 when I hired her, and she'd worked at a fast food joint before the job. I tended to schedule the people I had fun working with on my shifts, and we worked together a lot. I'm bouncing around a bit on the timeline here, but this was the second time (in the history of my employment there) that I had to put the job and the friendship in question. Lindsay was sweet. She was fun. And she flirted with anything that moved. I myself am anything that moves. She had a boyfriend for a very long time and then they broke up. After working with her for a year or so, we started hanging out together, and my role as a Manager started to slip away and our friendship became more important. More on that shortly.

I was still friends with Mike (even after he was fired) and then another girl got in the way. Melissa. Melissa got hired on as a manager at Amherst, and she came over to (presumably) train at Eastern Hills. Little did anyone know that Melissa was biding her time during a back ground check for a management resume with Regal Cinemas. Melissa was my type to a T. I was involved, though, so I didn't think about it. Then I wasn't involved anymore, and it made sense in my mind to hook her up with Mike so that she wouldn't be available when I was involved. That was stupid. So I made a play for her and she shot me down, then she got dumped, and we still worked together in all this melodrama. And then she left for Regal. More on that shortly.

It got to a point (well, the entire year of 1999) that I hated the job. It wasn't fun anymore. It wasn't cool to be 23 making poverty money to work 50 hours a week with no benefits at a job that you could basically train a monkey to do. I'd stopped going to college after getting promoting to assistant management in '98, and was beginning to think that I'd made a grave mistake. Writing wise, I'd had nothing published for a year. I had no girlfriends for quite a while. The job, better or worse, was my life. And it really sucked. Every day I shut the alarm off and dreaded having to go into a graveyard that didn't even get many customers. During the week it was pathetic. Some days we'd only pull in fifty dollars, literally, and about twelve customers. It was like jail time with a pop machine. Working alone Monday through Thursday, I'd go in with two books and a magazine, sell the tickets, start the movies, and then read for the majority of the shift, which was nice, but got boring after a while. And you can only make so many phone calls before that gets tired, too.

I was more a sole employee left to do all the work than a manager. Since I was there 90 percent of the time and the rest of the staff was there the other ten percent, I did the majority of the cleaning, restocking, mopping, paperwork, and inventory. Since I was disgusted with myself and my job, I'd go a few months and let the employees slack, doing all the work or not depending on my state of catatonia. I was a second rate manager at a second rate theater with a second rate life. Something had to change.

One of the perks that I introduced to the job (and one of the things that made the job bearable) were midnight screenings. On thursdays I made up the films for the following week, so.....since the job had turned me into a night owl, I'd invite some friends up and we'd watch the movie with the added bonus of being able to drink and smoke in the theaters. There have been quite a few notable screenings that spring to mind. "Fear and Loathing in Las Vegas", for one. We had about thirty people in the theater and all of them were smoking and drinking. It looked like a four alarm fire there was so much smoke. On a first date once, I took a girl to a private showing of "American Beauty" and the night ended very well. And during another ("Pi" if memory serves) the owner's stepson (who came back from college with a disposable degree and a cushy new job with the company) walked in half way through. That flipped me out. There were three of us in the theater and I had a cigarette in one hand and two beers resting on the floor in the aisle in plain site. The Clements were lazy though, so they never fired anyone if they didn't have to. Bryan took me aside and told me that I wasn't supposed to smoke in the theater, and that I should worry about people driving home and the legalities behind that. I felt like I was being scolded by a third grade substitute teacher. He was going through the motions, and after that, I implimented the eleven o'clock rule. Rarely, if ever, did my employers show up after eleven o'clock and therefore, we wouldn't screen any movies before said time.

Then we finally found a decent assistant manager. His name was Jon, and we'd gone to high school together. We were never really friends in the traditional sense, more acquaintence than anything, and he was a huge film buff, so I figured he'd stick around longer than previous applicants. He broke a few films going into the job and messed up one or two things, but he was basically a nice kid and he had great customer service. So then there were three, finally. Mike Clement didn't like Jon, but I fielded interference and tried to keep the two away from each other.

All of a sudden it was February of 2000, and I'd been working for the same rate of pay for over a year. I was told that benefits counted for a raise. Then I was promised a raise.....the previous November. After four months of being strung along, I was getting fed up. Bill, who'd threatened to quit ever since he came to work with me, was leaving for a military job. Plus the Lindsay thing. After spending the majority of Christmas break, I'd grown very fond of her, and didn't feel like we could work together anymore. I'd broken my personal work code of dating a subordinate, which soured the job even further for me. With a second job to attend to, I let her go and we stayed friends. We tangled a few times, but again, I've written about it in greater length and it's really not important to go into here. I'd kept in touch with

Melissa since her departure from Dipson, and she constantly bragged about what a great time she was having at Regal and how I should consider hopping on board. One day, in the middle of complaining about the raise issue, she said she'd ask her boss if he was hiring any new managers. I told her not to act on it yet.

Whelp, typical of Melissa's behavior, she asked her boss that day. The boss called me after the weekend and drilled me over the phone with a tantalizing offer: more pay, less responsibility. After listening to Mike Clement yell at me for an hour about how he couldn't afford to pay me more, his offer sounded enticing. I was invited to come check out the theater downtown, and went the following week.

Regal was gorgeous. They had a fleet of projectors, an entire infantry staff-wise, and twelve screens. I was psyched. Renny, the general manager, gave a convincing pitch. And Melissa said it was a fun place to work, and I'd be a pussy if I turned down the chance. So I slept on it, and decided to give it a shot. I gave a month's notice at the other job. Everything was set to go for March 1st.

My old staff was sad about the departure, but they understood. Jon, who seemed like he was starting to learn the ropes of the day to day operations, was very nervous and, although he knew why I was leaving, wished that I wouldn't. They were bringing back Michelle to manage the place. Michelle had worked at the theater on and off for more than seven years, and hated the place more than anything, but wanted the comfort of a steady paycheck. Mike Clement was understandably upset. He was losing (as he put it) "his best and most loyal employee". I told him that if this was going to be my chosen career that I had to move on, and that they had more opportunities for advancement. At first he was pissed because I wasn't leaving for that much more in terms of pay. By the end of the month, he was resigned about the issue, and nostalgic. I almost felt like crying on the last day. I spent the entire shift mulling around and remembering something special wherever I looked, and thought about how it would be the last time I swept out theater one, and the last time I checked the lefthand upstairs men's room. That night, Mike came in to collect my keys and we had to monkey around with a projector head after one of the films got out. We parted on good terms. It was the end of an era. So when and how did I come back, you wonder?

Regal was a complete nightmare. I'd been dropped into the biggest problem location in the area. Right from the first day I knew they'd sold me a lie. The staff was stealing the place blind. The inventory was off. And I was scheduled to work at 8 a.m. for the foreseeable future. After spending so much time rolling out of bed at noon and driving down the street, it was a shock to my system to have to get up at six or seven and then drive for a half an hour through downtown traffic in order to show up on time. Everybody complained about the place; the employees, the customers, and the managers, as well. Apparently, Renny (my new boss) had gone through a nasty break-up before Christmas (one of the busier times of the year) and subsequently went out of his tree for a month or so. During all that, he let the place run itself, which didn't work too well, and now that he was back on board and in charge of his senses, he had a colossal amount of theft and insubordination to deal with. That was where I came in.

After losing a few managers and dealing with a turnover rate that was larger than some fast food chains, I was going to complete the 8-manager staff that they'd gone so long without. Renny was a very nice guy, and if he wasn't, I wouldn't have considered the job. But in the big business of films, you have to be nasty, and everybody walked over him for a while there. He wanted me to specialize in maintenance repairs since the influx of customers over the year took a noticeable toll on the building. I knew absolutely nothing about maintenance. I figured somebody could show me the ropes, but nobody was offering. So I spent a morning or two wandering blindly around a hardware store looking for a caulking gun and then sealing up frayed areas of carpet in the movie-houses.

Add to this the complete fish-out-of-water shock of dealing with a weekend crowd at such a big complex and I just couldn't take it. I didn't want to adjust. I'd never dealt with so many people before, and it flipped me out. They had lines of customers twelve deep at the concession stands and three employees on a Saturday night. The movies went in and let out every ten minutes. There was always a situation that needed to be remedied immediately, and I had no clue what I was doing because nobody was training me so much as dumping me into a spot and telling me to go. And then we had our second staff meeting, where Renny said that the mounting loss prevention problem had to be nipped in the bud. Apparently, some of the company big wigs were coming in over the weekend to oversee this catastrophe and we were assured that we wouldn't have jobs if the situation continued. Wouldn't have jobs? Continued? But I just got there?

So I went home, thought it over, and decided that I'd made a grave mistake. I called Renny and told him that I couldn't stand to work another day, and that I was leaving and very sorry for getting into the mess that was Elmwood. He asked me to think it over. He asked if I was going to give two weeks notice. Why the hell would I give two week's notice for a job that I'd only worked a week at? It made no sense to me. I got up the next day, drove to work, and left my keys by the ticket booth. Melissa called about three hundred times that day, and I ignored the messages. I crawled into bed at ten in the morning and turned my back on life.

Mike Clement had a wonderful time crowing about how stupid I was to leave his fine local chain. I called him on the phone the following week begging for my job back, and he was smug and satisfied in his catbird seat. He had me right where he wanted me. I lied and said that I was still with Regal, but I was willing to quit at a moments notice because I couldn't stand it. So he said we could talk about it when he had the time. I was pissed, but there wasn't much I could do about it. I'd never left a job on such horrible terms, so after the Regal affair, I flew into a black depression whose only salvation seemed to lie in going back to the only thing I'd known for so long. So I spent three weeks holed up in my room trying to figure out what the hell to do, watching bad television, and smoking too many cigarettes. I met with Mike, and he said that I couldn't have the management position back because it was filled. He went on to tell me that he wouldn't be able to give me that many hours, and he wouldn't be able to pay me a whole lot because there were just so damned many people who wanted a management position at his theaters! I knew it was a crock of shit, but he had me. I went crawling back to the old job beaten and broken.

This is where I learned that you should never stay at a job for too long. This obviously wasn't what I wanted, but I was there again, wasn't I? I agreed to work at the Amherst in order to fill some shifts out there and eventually take over. Everyone was very understanding about my blunder, but I could tell that they were dissappointed in my failure. After bragging for a full month about how much better off I'd be, I'd returned with stories of corporate hell. And now I was really going through the motions. For the duration of my time left with the company, I sat in the office at the Amherst and listened to the clock chew up my life. I ordered food and gained weight on purpose. And I sat on a bench and watched the world go by.

It turned out that Jon was leaving to go make a movie locally, so that freed me up to jump back into a salary slot. Jon was one of the few people who made the job bearable, and he was doing what I'd hoped to do not two months prior. Michelle hated Eastern Hills, and did absolutely nothing in terms of cleaning, paperwork, or managing. Bryan, the stepson, didn't do a lick of work at the Amherst because he didn't have to. He was family, and it was understood between myself and the two assistants that we just cleaned up after him like so many managers had since he was born. Sure we were all lazy, but not nearly as lazy as the heirs to the throne. So I trudged through my depression, and they let me get away with it. It was obvious that I just wasn't in to the job anymore, that the place was on autopilot when I worked, and they looked the other way. I was turning into the other Mike who got fired, and it was making me sick.

Sometime in June, two important changes took place in the company. They bought out the multiplex downtown after Angelica backed out of their arthouse blunder in Buffalo, and Bernie Clement (the owner) had passed away after struggling with cancer for more than a year. I wouldn't necessarily say that I knew him that well, but I respected him. Here was a man who built up an empire and his offspring were turning it into shit. Bernie had a presence of power whenever he came in to visit. Employees would shiver and run off to clean something. Years ago, when he did work at the Amherst, I heard that he stashed a bottle of vodka in the office and would proceed to get blind stinking drunk on Sunday afternoons. Then he'd nap in the office for hours on end while the manager on duty went on with business as usual. But now he was gone; and Mike was at the helm.

Bryan (of course) was promoted to manage the newly dubbed Market Arcade Film and Arts Center downtown, which put me in charge of the Amherst. The Amherst was, and still is the hub of the arthouse scene in this town. I worked one or two shifts a week at Eastern Hills, and spent the rest of the time goofing off at the Amherst (which some old employees dubbed 'The Slumherst Theater'). At some point in the late summer or early fall, Melissa called me and asked if I could land her a job. She was too afraid to call Bryan directly because she left on horrid terms. And the Clements took her back, too. She started working at the Market Arcade along with Bryan.

For the first time in a life filled with bipolar disorder, I think I was clinically depressed. I spent the entire summer of 2000 partying like a rock star and going through the motions at work. To make matters worse, my car got stolen in late July, and Mike and Bryan gave me a hard time about getting the day off, which is ridiculous. Chris, one of the assistant managers at Amherst, became very resentful with my new position. I figured if so many people before me were allowed to do nothing for so long that I was well overdue.

Chris had a real job in the stock market. I wasn't sure exactly what he did, but he made a point during every shift to mention to everyone that he worked with about how he didn't need his job at the theater because he was so goddamned intelligent and profitable at the full time job. Chris had issues. He started to crack around October, when I was spending the majority of my time promoting, marketing, and tying up my first book. It was beginning to look like I wouldn't have to spend my life working in that hellhole, and that perhaps my dreams were worth taking a shot at. So I didn't clean much. One night, I stopped by to check on something and saw a note that he'd written to the other assistant. He'd referred to me simply as "asshole", so I turned on all the lights, wrote down all of the things that he didn't do, and then called Bryan to tell him that I wanted Chris gone.

We'd talked it over the next day and he liked Chris too much to see him leave. So I called Mike and discussed it with him. Mike was always big on respect, so he gave me complete authority to do whatever the hell I wanted in lieu of this total lack of said respect. I'd never enjoyed axing someone until I fired him. It took a half an hour to explain to him why he was a rotten human being, why I didn't want him anywhere near my theater anymore, and why I wouldn't tolerate him as a person, but it was well worth it. At one point during the firing, I told him to step outside. He asked why a bit sheepishly (because I was so worked up) and I told him that I needed a cigarette. Chris stormed out of the picture kicking, screaming, and psychotic, which was fine with me. Little did I know I'd be the next one out of the gate.

Mike and Bryan had agreed to ease up on me while I was getting the book off the ground, and then proceeded to do anything but. After numerous fights in person and on the phone, it became blindingly apparent to them that I just didn't care what they did. By the end of October and the beginning of November (during the inception of this very piece, actually), I was trying to get fired. Mike had gone on unemployment for six months after he was given his walking papers, and I figured that it would be a nice break. So I went and did everything short of stealing (because I refused to go *that* far) in order to get fired. It was a fun time.

I left entire theaters uncleaned after a weekend shift. I let the employees do whatever the hell they wanted. I spent entire shifts at the bar next door. And they still didn't fire me! They chose to yell at me rather than let me go. I'd been there too long. According to Jon, I was the golden boy who could do no wrong in the eyes of the Clements. It was amusing to think that I couldn't get canned after putting so much effort into it! And finally, things escalated.

One monday afternoon, Mike was yelling at me on the phone for about a half hour and I'd had it. I called around and within five minutes I had three solid job prospects, so I called Mike back with another month's notice. I assumed that it would take that long for them to replace me. I was wrong. Bryan came in that night looking so red that I though his head would pop off from the internal pressure. I worked the following day, and then spent my day off getting some things with the book taken care of.

When Thursday rolled around, I stopped in to grab my check. Bryan was there, and he informed me that all of my shifts were taken care of, and that all he needed were my keys. It threw me a bit, but it figured. After all these years, they weren't about to let me leave on good terms. Not this time. It was an unfortunately stunted end to the longest standing job I've ever held. In some manner of power play, they'd promoted a kid who started as a general employee a month prior. With the intention of screwing me as much as they could on the way out, they were placing a novice in the hands of their most important location. Again, it figured. With this company, that sort of logic was typical. So I set things in place with the next job and decided to take the next three weeks off.

And now the essay itself comes into the story, now that we're at the end of this monster. The following Monday, I'd printed the first three pages in a newsletter, and noted the shoddy terms by which I was cheated out of a proper passing. Jon (out of either a sense of retarded and misguided loyalty or lack of thought) had printed up the email and showed the first portion of this piece to him. He didn't take the blunt honesty well. In fact, he called me that day to yell at me, and I hung up on him. I wasn't his grunt anymore, so why the hell would I sit and listen to him scream and holler? He called back and left a nasty message on the machine, so I called and laid into him. That was the last time we talked, and it was five months ago.

I haven't set foot in any of the theaters since I left. Jobs are weird like that. You can spend such a large chunk of your life living and breathing your day to day tasks but in the aftermath, it's like the residue from a dream. I could probably still thread up a film and start it in less than three minutes, or clean out a crowded theater alone in less than five, but I haven't tried. And now that I'm not there, movies aren't that important to me. Yesterday was the first time I went to see a movie at a theater since leaving, and it felt....different. Like I was just another ignorant filmgoer again.

It felt good. I didn't have to spend every five minutes idly wondering if every thing was getting done outside the movie, and I didn't weigh the pros and cons of the competition. I went alone, and sat in back, away from everyone. Sure I look for things in a film that most people could care less about, like lighting and cut-tos and different cinematography techniques, but........the magic was back. I felt like a six year old kid watching the Muppet Movie again, and I went through that fifteen minute post film high that makes the rest of the world seem bursting with possibilities. It's what makes people want to go to the movies all the time, I suppose, and I missed that feeling for so long I don't remember when I last felt it. I'm so goddamned jaded about so many things and it's nice to have a little vestige of innocence in my life.

A lot of people have moved on to bigger and better things since they left the Eastern Hills theater. I still keep in touch with Dave, one of my old bosses, and we go out drinking. He manages an 18 screen Regal out in Rochester so he's still living the life. The last time we met up he was going on about a store Oscar party. I don't even know when the Oscars are on this year. Peter, another one of my old bosses, is now the district manager for Regal in Atlanta, Georgia, and Austin, one of my old employees, is one of the top three guns at the Regal down the street from Eastern Hills. Jon is the general manager at my old stomping ground now, and I'm glad he's there. It's nice to know that somebody who I trained and approved of is keeping the tradition going. Melissa, in her trademark flightiness, had a job with Troma films in NYC and was flying back and forth, but we've lost touch. I haven't talked to Mike Bolis since our falling out. The theaters (and myself) go on even after the symbiosis has drifted off.

And what the hell have I learned after five years? Whelp, I know which movies are going to be terrible and which ones will be incredible just from the trailers, the pedigrees, and the posters, so I don't waste my time with teen slasher flicks or bubbly romantic comedies. My doorman sense is still so keen that I can tell when a film will be over in two minutes having never seen it before. It bothers the hell out of my friends. And I know that the business itself, the movie business, has gone corporate and gotten larger than it ever was. I read somewhere that the Academy Awards have replaced the Superbowl in terms of popularity. I was twenty when I started and in that time, films have gotten bigger in every sense of the word. The box office grosses. The special effects. And the theaters themselves. On my end of it, it's turned into a leaner and meaner industry, and I don't know why some people choose to stay on and make it a career. It appeals to the dreamers. We get hooked. But I like having my weekends off occassionally. And it's nice to spend the holidays with my family rather than guarding my post. I've talked to 80-year-old customers who reminisce about their time working at the matinees in the fifties, and I'll be one of those geezers soon enough down the road. The experience touches you, and stays with you. I'm glad that I spent so much time as another cog in the wheels of pop culture, just like a sprocket grinding away mindlessly in one of those monstrous projectors. I had a purpose, and I did it well most of the time.

more epic than even Tom Hanks (occassionally),
Tom "juju" Waters

Occupationally Impaired

People just aren't designed for free time. I've been unemployed for a week now, and I'm starting to get weird. Everyone talks about what they'd do if they had more idle time, or vacation time in a week. Well here I am on the other side of the coin telling you that you'd do nothing. For all the stress and anxiety they provide, jobs are a good way to devour the better part of your week. They make the remaining time in your weekly calendar valuable. I've had seven straight days of unlimited free time, and it's too much. There's only so much you can do when you have nothing to do. What with the economy taking a nose dive, you just might be joining me, so here are some helpful hints on making the day go by with no schedule of any kind.

Find a reason to get the hell out of the house. It doesn't even matter what that reason is, but it will keep you from getting more eccentric than you've already become. Work provides a much needed social aspect, so it's good to compensate by getting out in the world. Interact with complete strangers by swearing at them in traffic, cornering them in stores for idle conversation, or sharing woes in the unemployment line. If worse comes to worse, mall walk. Hopefully it won't come to that, though. I'll turn a five minute outside project or errand into the hub of my day. Returning a film to the video store evolves into a ten step process. All of a sudden, the thought of driving around aimlessly for three hours is appealing. Picking film up from the drug store turns into the adventure of a lifetime! Although it's a practical solution to the dilemma, going out on job interviews should be avoided. It tends to shatter any efforts at utter denial and brings out issues of shame and failure. Save it for another day when you're not so busy doing stuff.

Create a schedule of activities. It provides the feeling that you're a responsible adult with important things to do. Here's my schedule: Fourteen hours of sleep (one must be sufficiently rested), one hour of leisure reading (so that you can keep up with people who have jobs), three hours of mindless television (to occupy the idle mind), one hour of bath time for necessary hygiene and contemplation, two hours of shiftless internet browsing, two cumulative hours of snacks and meals to keep the strength up, and one hour of video games. It's amazing how you can pass the time without accomplishing anything useful!

Drinking, eating, and smoking are great ways to pass the time, and who doesn't feel a sense of pride after making an 'action item' out of ten beers? Habits and activities that were once regulated can be indulged and abused. Open a bottle of whiskey during "Good Morning, America" sometime. Feels good, doesn't it? Nothing can stop you! You've got nowhere to go, so why not misbehave? The workaday world may be accomplished, but can any one of them finish a jumbo sized bag of potato chips during a Three Stooges marathon? Exactly. When was the last time Johnny Punch-Clock bragged about smoking four packs of cigarettes in an hour? Aside from the money, the benefits, and the prestige, people with jobs are the real losers.

Adjust your budget. This is the painful part. If you've got a date at a classy restaurant, suggest an informal evening at a hot dog stand. Rather than flying to the Bahamas for a week off you might want to think about driving to the zoo. And instead of buying a new wardrobe it's probably time to consider boning up on your sewing skills. The problem is that once you get accustomed to making a certain amount of money you grow accustomed to spending a certain amount of money. So it's a bit painful to downsize you current spending trends. Currently, I'm trying to stretch twenty dollars for the next three weeks. I'm sure I'll be selling my kidneys for gas money in a few more days.

And stay positive! Having no prospects of any kind isn't necessarily a bad thing. All the free time tends to make one stoic. Test drive the bankrupt notion that money doesn't buy happiness, and turn a blind eye to a world obsessed with consumerism. Okay, I'm lying. Not having a job sucks, but you might as well make the best of it. It's like walking around all day with one of your shoes untied. You're well aware that something's wrong, but you don't want to think about it. You pretend not to notice the shoe, even though it's driving you nuts. You tell yourself you're not going to bow down to the shoe and continue unthwarted. And eventually, the shoe is all you can think about, so you bend down and tie it. I need to get a job desperately. It's tough to feel a purpose in life, or even that you can perform a duty that's valued, without somewhere to clock in, a paycheck to abuse, or co-workers to whoop it up with. I've worked since I was 14. I'm not the sort that takes vacations unless they're forced. I'll be back to work soon enough. I'll just have to watch eight hours of television on my day off.

dying my collars blue,
Tom "drone" Waters

Disembodied Anecdotal
Tiddlywinks

-a collaboration for the sake of one-

Everything we are about to tell you is true. Maybe we have over embellished a little or added a few things for the sake of entertaining ourselves, but it's all true. This is how we perceive things and this is our reality. Tom and I have a tendency to one-up the other, so keep that in mind. It's not competitive in nature, but merely instinct.

Most of my horrifying experiences have been due to my own stupidity. At a high school party my senior year a few friends and I decided to take the party elsewhere, so four of us ended up at the school baseball diamond. They had recently installed new backstops that resembled a huge three dimensional version of Pac Man's upper jaw in mid-chomp and so we decided that the ample space on top would be a great place to drink a few beers. Climbing the chain-link monstrosity was no easy feat with a six pack in hand, but once up there I felt like King of the Mountain. As the last two guys were making it up towards the top I had to move to make some more room. My pants had snagged the fence and left me dangling fifteen feet over the homeplate. The three seconds I was suspended there were spent in total fright and in a futile attempt to get my friends to stop laughing long enough to give me a hand. My pants finally gave out and I managed a good slide into home base. Luckily, it had rained and I had a soft, muddy landing. I don't really remember how I explained my condition to my parents, who were waiting for me when I got home, but that would be another story all together.

Kids do a lot of stupid, cruel things when they're young, and I was fairly tame most of the time in grammar school, choosing to wise-crack my way out of most tight spots rather than mixing it up during recess. I even remember crying my way out of getting beat up by the school bully in the fourth grade (and I realize that I'm forfeiting whatever sense of pride you may have had for me before reading this, but it worked). That's not what this story's about, though. When I was in the fourth grade, after seeing the James Bond movie "For Your Eyes Only" and reading "Harriet The Spy", I decided that I would become a spy. I had a little kit with plastic handcuffs and two dollar binoculars, and a stack of cue cards with finger-prints and profiles on all my class mates. I wasn't very good at being inconspicuous, but most of my neighbors would let me go on about my covert business anyway, as I was harmless lying on my stomach behind a bush. Eventually, after talking our way into this girl's house and 'borrowing' her journal, a rift rose up in an otherwise happy gang of grammar school espionage entrepreneurs, and we became two groups of two spies in a dead heat to terrorize the other. My next door neighbor (who later went on to turn gay, which is another horrifying sentient thought that I'd rather not dissect in the same blurb) and I represented one gang of spies, and the tom-boy girl and the neighbor kitty corner to me represented the other. I armed myself in the coarse of a week with a pair of Fisher Price walkie talkies, and I talked my father into making a chain-link whip fashioned onto a wooden dollie (I was a smooth talker back then, no?). So one day these two chased us down and cornered us in my next-door neighbor's garage, and in a fit of rage I blasted out of there and ran the boy into his yard, where I proceeded to beat him unmercifully with the chain whip until his mom came out of the house, hysterically psychotic and ready to hang me from a telephone pole. Luckily, I made it back to my own home, where I proceeded to call the kid that I just bludgeoned and apologized. I'm going to hell.

For five years I worked as a lifeguard at a country club in the summertime. Everyday, the clubhouse would issue one golf cart for running members up to the tennis courts because the members were too lazy to walk up there themselves. Anyway, the pool is at the bottom of a steep hill and one morning I discovered that if you gunned it down the hill there was a grassy area in which you could spin the cart around in if you slammed on the breaks. On good days, when there was still dew on the grass, you could coax the cart into a 720 degree spin. One day, the pool manager's little son asked if he could join us in our little pre-opening activity. He gunned it and went flying down the hill but didn't realize the concept of hitting the breaks. He overshot the grassy area and proceeded into murky mire where the cart started sinking. Fortunately, the kid was all right but the cart was sunk up to the roof in mud. There was no way we could get that thing out of there so we covered it up with leaves and one of the other guards snuck up and grabbed another cart without being noticed. We got off scot free and I never found out what happened to the cart itself. Needless to say, that was my last summer working at the pool.

Most of my summers as a child were spent at our cottage in Rushford tearing around with friends that I only got to see two or three months out of the year, if that. Since there wasn't too much to do, we'd find things to do, like climbing mountains, swimming from sun up to sun down, and (our favorite) taking a row boat or a canoe out into the middle of the channel, sinking it, and then dragging it to the shore. One of the kids across the way, Willie, was a real butterball. He was always bashing himself up and getting scraped and bitten ad nauseum. Let's just say that he didn't have to go looking for trouble from the elements, and that he wore nose plugs pretty frequently, and still ended up crying about how his ears were plugged. Allergy-boy. One year, when my bigger brother had gotten a fair sized Honda motorcycle, he let us take a few test drives. I rode around, shifted gears, nothing special. Willie hopped on and did something wrong, because he went tearing up the road wailing his fat head off. We ran after him trying impotently to stop whatever random disaster Willie'd willed upon himself at 35 mph to see a car coming down the road at him. In the child's equivalent of shell shock, Willie threw his hands into the air (while still on the bike) and autopiloted himself right into the swamp, where the bike stalled. By the time we got there, he'd worked himself into a good cry thrashing around with the tadpole spores.

My friend Read and I were partners in crime throughout most of high school and whenever we got together after that. We met at the beginning of our sophomore year right after he moved here from Memphis. On my sixteenth birthday, Read was determined to take me out on the town and show me a good time. For two sixteen-year olds, we didn't do too badly. We finagled our way into a few bars and saw a few bands. Read, doing it up right, bought me a few drinks until I had a slightly mongoloid expression on my face. Anyway, a common practice of ours was to to finish up the night by playing a few games of pool at the Hippodrome. The Hippodrome is really no place for two young white kids to be at 1:00 in the morning. In fact, Read almost got his head taken off by some huge black guy with a pool cue after we cleaned out his pockets. Hey, he challenged us! But that is another story. On this particular night it was my turn to have a brush with death. We were accosted by a gentleman who so eloquently said to us, "You honkies better hand over your money or I am going to kick your ass!" I turned to Read and offhandedly said, "I really prefer to be a cracker." The gentleman didn't care for this comment and grabbed for me. Well, he picked the wrong moment to do that, because right then the liquor I had consumed didn't feel like being there anymore. I puked all over him! To me, it was the funniest thing in the whole world. I couldn't stop laughing. Read was just standing there in total amazement. And the other guy, well, his attention was now on his brand new Nike's (which I had coated with a mixture of whiskey and bile. It took puking on him a second time to finally get him to go away.

Speaking of big, burly, tough guys, there was this guy Greg I used to know, a two hundred and fifty five pound gorilla with the brain of a sloth (and that was before he got into doing drugs!). There are a few boys you come across in your existence who are born bad seeds, work as hard as they can at being worse, and will die bad seeds under bad circumstances. Greg is, and always will be, a bad seed, and it's best to give these people a wide berth because they're like karmic lightning rods. Well during the summer of my sophomore year I think it was, this kid was stringing my money along for a bag of pot over the coarse of a week. I'd raised and allocated funds from friends, family, and somehow, he couldn't seem to locate the herb. "Next time" he'd say. One day, determined to get the money or the devil's weed from him, I walked across town with my friend Sutton to talk to him at the basketball court. This was also around the same time that this kid Greg had impregnated a girl four or five years younger than him, so he was hanging out near her house. We tailed Greg and got back around his neighborhood (even farther across town), walking since his license had been revoked that week (again). We hung outside the convenience store smoking cigarettes while he made phone calls and faces telling us that it wasn't going to happen, he'd tried his best, so sorry. We told him politely (and I do mean politely, 'cause me and my friend Sutton are pussycats) to keep calling his connections. It was getting dark out, and we were still trying to hook up, as it were. Greg said to wait a while for his one friend to call back, and he wanted to start something with me, mock-wrestling and trying to scare/get a rise out me. While I'm not a scrapper, acute psychotic tendencies and a relatively drug free, healthy body outweigh an overweight sack of amotivational sludge like Greg, so when he tried to pull a headlock on me, I simply lifted him of the ground and flipped him onto the ground, ass over teakettle. We got our pot shortly after that (with additional monies, Sutton's school clothes' money from his mother), having to walk out into the boonies to this shack in a field that might as well have been made of cardboard, and Greg talked us into smoking some of it with him. By then it was morning, and with no ride home, Sutton and I had to walk about ten miles home as the summer sun rose to beat down on our sleep deprived bodies. I crashed out at his house, and by the time I woke up, Sutton had managed to call all of his friends over and smoke the whole bag without me. And you know what? I don't miss that scene one bit. Wanna know something else? Since the time that this anecdote happened, Greg has been stabbed repeatedly, in and out of jail, and has more warrants than boy scout ribbons. Some things never change.

In eighth grade there was a kid who would do whatever anyone else told him to do. Most of the guys used to terrorize him and yet he always used to come back for more. It was a daily occurrence to find a pair of his Fruit of the Loom's that somebody had just torn off him laying in the middle of the hallway. A group of us bet him one day that he couldn't eat a whole box of Choco-Lax without going to the bathroom for the entire school day. Well, he ate the whole box, and by the middle of first period his face was flushed and he was sweating bullets. We all nervously laughed because we could only imagine how hard it was for him not to shit himself. The teacher asked if he was all right and he said everything was fine. As the period was coming to an end a nervous look came across his face. It was the look of someone who knows everyone is looking at him and he knows something bad is about to happen. Well, as determined as he was to keep his sphincter tight, he bolted up and screamed, "I really have to take a shit, Mr. Dahl!" He ran out of the room and unfortunately didn't make it to his planned destination. We let him keep the money that he owed us.

Throughout my entire elementary and high school education, I was never one for gym. Off the top of my head, the three-legged race was about the only thing in that class that I was good at. I can't think of one time in twelve years that I hit a baseball, one time that I wasn't in the last fifth percentile to wheeze past the finish line, or one solitary occasion where I didn't duck and cover at the blow of a whistle during dodge ball. Therefore, I had to get by on charm with my classmates and instructors. Cracking jokes and making fun of my bony girl arms was one way to take the heat off of my total lack of muscle tone and coordination. Well, it's tough to pick a dividing line in taste when you're drunk with the power of being a clown. One February, when swimming classes were over (one class that I did enjoy, since that meant that I didn't have to take a shower for the rest of the day), we got stuck with a co-ed activity, or rather, a number of activities. And it's one thing to have guys who hit warp speed when they came to puberty beating you in a sport, but another altogether to have a five foot girl lambasted with acne who's just totally spanking you in badmitton. Which just happened to be one of the activities. So when we all came in to main gymnasium, the lady instructor had us do our laps, pull off a few jumping jacks, and then she hit us with it (since we still hadn't received word from the governor) "You're all going to split up and either play a tournament in ping pong, or a few rounds of badmitton." Springing quickly with a comeback, I shouted "Ms. Printup, that sucks hard!" The entire gym roared with the laughter of my peers, washing over. Most of the teachers got a few chuckles out of my witty candor. Not her. "Gimme four laps, Waters, and I better not hear another word outta you!" Pitifully, this is one of the one achievements that my graduating class remembers whenever I run into them.

Believe it or not, but everyone always thought of me as the nice little boy. I was clean cut, I was in the chorus, I got good grades, and I didn't do anything bad. Don't get me wrong, I was nice to everybody. I just didn't get caught doing anything incriminating. That all ended my sophomore year. I went on a school trip to Montreal with the chorus and came home with a week long suspension. While having lunch, we realized just how easy it was to purchase alcohol there. That same evening, we were allowed to go out on our own for a few hours and check out the town. Being curious teenage boys, we had to find out if it was that easy everywhere. Our curfew was midnight and it was only 10, so a few of us figured we might as well try and put our theory to the test. Our plan worked fine for a while. We went from bar to bar and discovered the finest in Quebecois entertainment. From a Weird Al Yankovick cover band to this fine French tart who could do unusual things with your beer bottle. Like I said, the plan was going fine until we realized that it was nearly 3:00 in the morning! Staggering into the lobby, we were greeted with menacing glares from the nearly catatonic chaperones who had been waiting up for us. We were suspended immediately upon arriving back at school and our little tale was circulated while we were gone. The next two years were spent being chastised by teachers on how I shouldn't drink. The funny thing was that I never really drank after that, and I found out that as long as they were so sure that I was drinking, that left room for me to get away with other things.

It's been said that I butted heads with a few of my teachers. I got a 50 one marking period for refusing to memorize a sonnet from Hamlet (for personal beliefs), a very upset and stern talking to in my creative writing class (for writing a story wherein I, or rather, the incredibly similar character in the story, mows down his writing teacher with a submachine gun), was asked by a teacher who didn't even have me as a student if I was retarded when I was caught smoking in the bathroom, and then there was Mrs. Light. I'd had her for English class my first two years of high school and I escaped her b.s. and the influx of worksheets to Honors English after that. Thought I'd escaped her. For some really asinine reason, I joined a course elective in travel literature. Taught by none other than. She was that special breed of bible-thumping teacher who is just so secure in her beliefs that she can't help force-feeding them to her class. My senior year was not a good year for this kind of pairing, as I was beginning to assert my independence and my own writing. Towards the end of the school year, every class would turn into a one on one cage match, with her on one end, trying to shame me into paying attention and behaving, and our hero on the other end, trying to think of the most crude, offensive comment to set her off in front of the class. Most of the time it was a dead tie (well, she was in charge of the grades), but we had a group field trip to her cabin somewhere around the finger lakes in May. I didn't even want to go. They drove to my apartment and dragged me out of bed. So we went to this shack out in the boonies, canoeing, the amish, whatever, and that night, she's giving another one of her writing sermons to the class in front of a bonfire. I get a phone call from my girlfriend, one of the only people I could depend on at the time, and she comes into the cabin to chew me out. Apparently, listening to everyone's stupid journal entries about the day was more important. That was it for me. It was time to split or get off the pot, so to speak. Five miles away from school and town and home, I took off in a huff. Went deep into the woods across the highway and hunkered down, waiting. People started searching around and I just watched, smoked, and looked at my watch. After a few hours, and after everyone went to bed, I crept back to the cottage and slept in the minivan so that no one would know what hour in the middle of the night I returned. And so that my teacher would have more trouble sleeping. She kind of let me do my own thing after that incident.

Relentless Logic

Author's Note- I'm a little bit nostalgic, and by chance I came upon an old vignette that I wrote at 17 during a writing workshop. To give reason to this blatant addition of filler, I shall say that this gives some perspective on how far I've come, if at all, in terms of style, humor, and content. Plus it will show you how terribly unpolished I was some seven scant years ago. Blathering aside, the piece is essentially verbatim, other than a few cosmetic corrections.~

My dad took me to the hospital so that I could witness a beautiful thing. A miracle that most only witness once or twice in a lifetime. I saw my mom behind a glass window, sweating and clearly in pain. My father paced back and forth across the corridor, furiously smoking a gouda cheese and talking to himself nervously. The doctor, a sober-looking fellow with a shock of gray hair, came in and put on his sterilized rubber gloves. He made many serious faces and had a habit of carrying on his medical consultations with a sock puppet made out of sheer panty hose and two cherry tomatoes. My mom laid down on her stomach and the good doctor stretched her nostrils into the stirrups. Father and I looked on with a mixture of fear and awe. The hairs in her nose quivered and her nostrils dilated to about twenty five inches per chamber. I saw the doctor mouth the word "mallet" to his assistant/panty hose puppet beyond the observation glass and an assistant, well used to their work ethic, took a rubber mallet out of a surgical cabinet. Mother was exuding great gobs of sweat. The doctor took a few warm up swings and then, once the puppet had a firm grip, brought the mallet down on her head. A little boy rocketed out of her right nostril, and then, thirty seconds later, a twin girl jettisoned out of the left. Dad, overcome by the moment, moved his face away from the camcorder, and swabbed a tear away.

'Ars Longas, Vita Brevis'
(Art is long, life is short)

Time is certainly relative. And rarely is it portrayed with such individuality and dimension as it is in popular fiction. In letters the passage of time is allowed to take shape, to push and tug at the central characters, to swoop and volley in the periphery of the tale unfolding before the reader. In turn, its perception is a functional gauge for the wisdom and scope of a given author. Omnipresent and cathartic but silkenly subtle, no story could conceivably move onward without a sense of flow. What I will attempt to prove, touching down on a number of popular works or popular authors, is that an author's grasp of, in Martin Amis's words, "Time's Arrow", is just as crucial to a narrative as the narrator him/her/itself. And what better way to travel through such an undertaking than chronologically?

The rogues and romantics of O.Henry's short stories (1904-1910) flutter rapidly to their conclusions. In what might be his most well-known tale, "Gift Of The Magi", the reader has barely met the love-sick couple before we find that they've given up their most prized-possessions in order to get thoughtful yet tragic gifts for each other. In "The Last Leaf", an old painter jeopardizes his own health by painting a leaf on a tree in the cold dead of night in order to buoy the spirits of an ailing girl convinced that she'll pass away after the all the leaves on a tree have fallen. The beauty of the short story form, as the author illustrates, is that one event, or one action, can shape a person's life irreversibly.

The blind romantic obstinacy of Jason Gatz, better known as *The Great Gatsby*(1925), would be curiously lacking in its entirety without his total contempt for time. A self-made man for the sake of his only unattainable prize, Daisy Buchanan, Gatsby ignores the progression of the world and furthers his fortune to win her heart at any cost. During a crucial chapter where Gatsby is reintroduced to Daisy in Nick Carraway's household, he even goes so far as to knock a clock from the mantle. Whether out of anxiety for the moment or pure opposition to a force that married Daisy off and took her away from him is unsure. Yet the clock is the central antagonist in the novel, side-tracking Gatsby from capturing the love of the one person who loved him before he became a hiccup between myth and mogul in the '20s Long Island jet set. That Fitzgerald agonized over the perfection of the finished version of the novel has been documented. Yet the author's alcoholic indifference or lack of temporal structure in his own life seems to have bled over into the star of one of his most critically lauded works. Certainly not a mistake of motive in the character, but a pleasing contrast nonetheless.

A traid of subconscious squalls assault the senses in confusing and revelatory prose in William Faulkner's *The Sound And The Fury*(1929). The cognitive mechanism is laid bare before the reader to dissect and ingest at the speed of light. Benjamin, Quentin, and Jason Compson are respectively tortured, maddened, and infuriated by the infinite quagmire of their thoughts. The beauty of Faulkner's attempt, or accomplishment in the writing is his ability to capture, however irrelevant to the reader, the nonsensical navigation of universal daydreaming. Benjamin, the disabled Compson son, is trapped in a world of overwhelming sadness and mute terror at the loss and familial excommunication of his sister Caddy, sleepwalking through life at the attentions of the household servants and inspiring a deep empathy and pity in the reader. Quentin, the college matriculated son, is slowly held prisoner by his own guilt at the act of incest he's committed with his sister, lost and aimless in judgment and in the walkabout he embarks on in his portion of the novel. And Jason is caught up in a whirlwind of materialism, dwelling on the fortune he could have if he hadn't stayed on to support the extended family that remains in the aftermath. Faulkner's prose soars where lesser professionals like Burroughs and Kerouac have drifted off into substance-induced gibberish.

Mick Kelly, the lovable firecracker at the, well, the heart of Carson Mculler's *The Heart Is A Lonely Hunter* (1940) has all the intensity and impatience of a child with a big imagination and limitless youth. Before her inadvertent deflowering and subsequent descension into adulthood, she mocks and stretches time, trying her best to get as many things done at once, her exuberance and her emotions propelling her through her waking days. McCullers does an excellent job of capturing the ants-in-the-pants exuberance of children in Mick Kelly- their hopefulness, their contagious energy, and their immediacy. Oddly juxtaposed in the book by his strange affection for Mick, Biff Brannon, the proprietor of the diner, catalogues his days, nights and newspapers behind the cash register of his restaurant, watching the world chug along with emphatic patience, coming out of his thoughts only when a human oddity passes his field of vision. Brannon's despair at the loss of his wife does well to balance the emotional tone of the book.

And in the universe of yarns maintained and serviced by Flannery O'connor (1946-71), the South is portrayed mainly in two subspecies: the old, forgotten clock watchers, and the spinsterly busybodies. Old Dudley, a man tricked into moving up north to live with his daughter in "The Geranium" passes the hours staring across the street at a plant to find it ruined one day, while Mrs. Turpin, the central focus of "Revelation" cannot sit still in a doctor's waiting room without indulging in a flurry of gossip that incites an attack from a woman's daughter. A little of the down-home, southern drawling, good-Christian mentality in O'connor's stories is enough to last a lifetime.

Time truly crawls in the small but oddly magical town of Macondo in Gabriel Garcia Marquez's award-winning *One Hundred Years Of Solitude* (1967). It follows the incest, ingenuity, madness and war that visit the Buendia family throughout their time in the village. Whether intentional or not, the similarity of the family names (the men are either named Jose,

Auereliano, or Arcadio) leads one to believe that genealogy is proportionate with fate. Time is a stubborn successor in this novel, breaking hearts and ending wars simply by outlasting them. What agitated me about the prose was the repeated use of the word solitude, whether it was appropriate or not: "Colonel Auereliano Buendia scratched for many hours trying to break the hard shell of his solitude." Perhaps something was lost in the translation.

The works in Donald Barthelme's *Sixty Stories* (1981) defy all laws of prose as well as time. Many of the tales read like a textbook for attention deficit disorder. The narrator from "The Falling Dog" bounces from one absurd thought to the next: "I noticed that he was an Irish Setter, rust-colored. He noticed that I was a Welsh sculptor, buff-colored (no, really, what does he notice? how does he think?). I reflected that he was probably a nice dog from a good home (bourgeois dog) but with certain unfortunate habits like jumping on people from high windows (rationalization: he is a member of the television generation and thus-)" The key to Barthelme's humor lies in the cockeyed chronology of the tales.

John Irving's breathing panoramas have a charming ability to sprint and halt without damaging the stories. *The Cider House Rules* (1985) is surely no exception. Homer Wells, the endearing Everyman orphan at the book's heart, plods from adolescence, flash forwarding to young adulthood, and finally blurring from the observable eye into the accepted fate of his sudden middle age. One of Irving's many gifts for writing is his penchant for portraying the aging process as it truly feels to most of us. We're given a breathing sense for life's stops, starts, transformative tragedies and affectionate triumphs. Homer's chronology is near-perfect in it's punctuation, as he grows from a conscientious member of the orphanage to willing apprentice to Dr. Larch, his father figure, a force of change in the lives and hearts of the Ocean View Orchard, a misplaced lover and atypical father, and finally, another person entirely as he accepts his fate as a doctor, abortionist, and successor to Larch. Reading the book, one feels as if they have just witnessed the span of someone's existence passing before them. At the close of a paragraph, we are blessed with, "What is hardest to accept about the passage of time is that the people who once mattered most to us are wrapped up in parenthesis." To write such a line shows insight, but to slip such a line unsuspecting into the general framework of the story is a sign of true talent.

Thomas Pynchon's meter is nearly as inept and uninspired as his prose in *Vineland* (1990), a muddy literary attempt at action and political existentialism that comes off like a mobile built by an amputee. The book follows Zoyd Wheeler, an aging hippie, as he and his daughter are forced on the run by federal forces and they are in turn forced to face their past and come to grips with Zoyd's former wife and Prairie (the daughter's) mother. It isn't quite fair to say that the book follows Zoyd, though, as the main character completely disappears from the story for the better part of the book. Flashbacks are poorly pasted together with starched opinions about the government and sad attempts at universal correlations about the love generation, while loose plot ends and retarded sexuality limp throughout. The end of one chapter has this to bruise the reader's mind: "his erect penis had become the joystick with which, hurttling into the future, she would keep trying to steer among the hazards and obstacles, the swooping monsters and alien projectiles of each game she would come, year by year, to stand before, once again out long after curfew, calls home forgotten, supply of coins dwindling, leaning over the bright display among the back aisles of a forbidden arcade." This is one instance of a metaphor being almost as painful as the desperate stab for humanity that follows it. Someone once said that writers became boring once they received critical praise, and Pynchon is the poster boy squared for such a rule. Previous novels may have been ground breaking and visionary, but after reading *Vineland*, I would sooner reach for a rabid porcupine.

One's sense of how events pass in the course of a story can deeply affect the intensity with which its received by the reader, and in turn, an author's background can have a strong impact on how they portray time on the page. Substance abuse, regionalism, individual era, attention to detail, and humanity are all variables to the pace and voice of a story, and with a superb story, the synchronicity is seamless and magnificent. Ironically, through an author's mastery of the minute on a printed page, such as Fitzgerald and Faulkner, he can obtain something almost beyond the scope of imagination: literary immortality.

The Sting Of Local Satire
-by Ken Barnes

I was scheduled to meet the writer at one of his favorite haunts, a strip bar in Cheektowaga. "Damn this is tacky," I thought to myself. It wasn't Salvatore's Gardens tacky, but it was close. I pulled past the white stucco and neon green facade and parked in the middle of nowhere.

The Bills had won and the natives were celebrating, stuffing not only singles, but fivers in the G-strings of some beauty school drop out. Tom was nowhere to be found.

I ordered a beer and tried to camouflage myself, combing my hair into what could be mistaken for a mullet. After ordering a $4.50 Labatt Blue, I watched the floor show. The aforementioned beauty school drop out was swinging upside down on a pole, for a crowd of three. A large Indian woman sat in the corner. Where the hell was Tom? He was dating one of the entertainers, and said that he'd be parked up front "cheering her on," which I thought was a nice sentiment at the time.

After finishing the last 50 cents of my beer, I continued to sip at it, trying to ward off the waitress, who was around every 30 seconds. "You look like a savage!"said a woman out of nowhere, who was now circling me and touching my shoulders. Where's Tom? Is this his girlfriend? I turned around. "Huh?" She was still touching me. "Your hair. I love your hair. Do you wanna go in the back room with me?" In shock, I ignored her. "Do you know Tom Waters? He's dating one of the dancers, and I'm supposed to meet him here."

She started to think. I could tell by the smoke. "Oh yeah, he was thrown out for swinging on the pole!" Apparently, such behavior is against the rules. When I got home, I e-mailed Tom some questions, and received the following:

At 530 pages, I assume your book has lots of pictures? Only two, sadly. A cartoon that somebody drew of me as a pompous ass. It's the most realistic portrayal, photographed or otherwise, that anyone's ever done. The other picture is my first publicity photo. It's a black and white shot of my ugly mug, and it looks like I'm howling at the viewer from a padded room. I figured that I'd land the family vote with that one, Ken.

Who is your biggest influence as a writer? That's a toughie, that one. I can't really give you any one answer, so I'll give you five or six. Andy Rooney was the reason that I started writing essays in the ninth grade. A lot of contemporary fiction authors have had a lasting influence on my prose as well, like Brett Easton Ellis, Jay McInerney, Nicholson Baker, and Douglas Copeland. I don't like to name names, because the pretentiousness factor is off the Richter Scales. I'll always love Clive Barker's books, and for the last month or so, I've been reading graphic novels like The Sandman, Kingdom Come, Mr. Punch, Batman: The Long Halloween, and I read The Watchmen for the first time. That just blew me away. I don't really have time lately to read anything that isn't accompanied by pictures. Everything I read, everything I see on tv, every video game I play, and ever cd that I listen to trickles down into my work. I like to listen to Elton John or Bob Dylan when

I'm actually writing, though, as it soothes me.

Word is you have a few psycho-sexual dysfunctions. Would you care to elaborate? Well, I do enjoy sodomizing teams of ferrets, but who doesn't, really? Perhaps dating five women at once is a failing, but if that's wrong, then I don't wanna be right! What's beautiful about being locally quasi-famous is that all of a sudden my attractiveness got re-upped. I got to have sex with an ex-best friend's one and only true girlfriend. They hadn't dated for a year, and I got the scoop on every despicable habit and sexual dysfunction he ever had. Plus she was incredible in the sack. I'm considering going down his entire list of dream girls in the area, and then going down on them. Can I say that? Other than that, I can't think of any other dysfunctions. Oh, I'm a marathon man. I can't manage to goof with someone in less than two hours, and I prefer five to seven.

Who is your favorite all time writer, and why? That'd be a tie between Brett Easton Ellis and Clive Barker. Brett has the highest rereading value of any author in my library, and Clive just keeps getting better. What I love about Clive Barker, or any other British author, for that matter, is that they can write a murder mystery well. And after that, the same author will say to himself, "I think I'll write a children's book now. Or a suspense novel. Or a comedy. Or a tragedy. Or a pop-up book about Princess Diana's innards." They are probably the most multi-faceted people, author-wise, that I've ever read. And Clive is a genius. His scope and his prose just keep getting better. Lord of Illusions aside, that is. That movie sucked.

Is it true that you will only date women 55 and older? No sir! 8-80, she's my lady. If there's a heartbeat and two working appendages, I'm all up in that mug. I prefer the toothless variety, but you can get that sort of action with trailer trash, too. And it helps to have a peg leg, for any of you fine mahogany women out there who are reading this.

Give me your personal synopsis of Soup To Nuts. For some reason, the expression isn't as popular as it was forty years ago, but so's I don't have to explain it to each individual person, it means "Everything but the kitchen sink." It's a 530 page beast of a book that's mostly humor, mostly essays and lightly peppered with some projects, poems, correspondence, and one or two short stories. The humor is pretty universal stuff, like getting a tooth pulled, or going on the internet, or going out to clubs, or hunting and driving and dating and going to school and all the things that normal people do. The stuff that isn't universal is local, and there's a goodly amount of that. Plus I stuffed thirty empty pages in the middle for filler, because I figured nobody would make it that far, and if they did, I'd be out of town with their money by then. Just kidding.

No, you're not, you're right. Any turn ons/turn offs? Long walks on the beach, back hair, unibrows, Hungarians. No, not really. I like fiesty women. Someone who can hold their own in an argument, and somebody who's cynical, but not embittered for life. I'm very big on noses, too. I like little button noses on a girl, I think that's the cutest thing. And freckles. Or redheads. It doesn't hurt to have a decent sized chest, either. I like individuality in women, and independence. Blondes are dead last on my list, because they think they're God's gift to the world. I like short petite girls or buxom amazon women. Mousy haired, intellectual women. Gorgeous, vacuous college chicks. There's not too many things about women that don't turn me on, to tell you the truth. I love women. You're getting me excited here, Ken. I may have to call in my harem.

-Tom has yet to be clinically diagnosed, but he's definitely funny. Not unlike that substance abusing uncle of yours who, (after a few) starts expelling his twisted, hard-leaned, but most of all, scathingly accurate views on the world he inhabits, Waters has a style and wit possessed only by great writers and the clinically insane. *Soup To Nuts* takes you through the inner workings of a hysterical and frightening mind.

Appendixitis

The way I felt for you, the time we spent together, your body of work, and *you* yourself, my darling, are a footnote[1]

---

1)We spent three weeks together. Well, physically. All told, I knew you for four weeks, and I was impressed. You had a beautiful figure, a picturesque face, boundless libido, and an intelligence that betrayed your maturity (or lack of it). Your pretentious reading voice and condescending poetry were amusing to me. It attracted and appalled me, because until I met you, I never believed in disclosing the intimate details of my relationships with other people. That seems to be the only thing you write about, your little 'fictions'. Self-important monologues about your sexual misadventures disguised as legitimate writing. I thought you'd make a suitable companion (maybe a power couple); we could type together, take turns in free hand (but God knows there was some of that), and share all of our favorite authors (you with your structured Nabakov and me with my meticulous and perverted Nicholson Baker). How was I to know that the 21 pages of prose that you ran into the ground were the sum total of your creativity? Writing never was your calling, was it? Just another phase to meet interesting people whose names you could drop in the company of friends in the hopes of making yourself look more important. Name droppers always did bother the shit out of me. I just ignored it during the first blush of our romance. Can you classify a 3-week stint, though? Break it into segments and analyze it? I'd like to think so. Yes. Let's start with your propositioning me via email after that reading. How fitting that our relationship began and ended inside of a word processing program. Maybe we were just better on paper. You were in a relationship for a year with this clown that you glommed onto at work and wondered if I wanted to have sex? It was forward, I'll give you that. I respected your honesty. You cheated on the first man you gave it to with me, and left him and his engagement ring in a heartbeat. 20 is a bit late to surrender a flower, but then again, who am I to say? It set a few warning bells off when we got involved. You were in college, you had a late start, and you wanted to whore things up a bit; see as many men as you possibly could at once. I told you after you broke up with him that you could take as much time to recover/cope as you desired, and you dismissed the idea, jumping head first into us. It was a wonderful first week. We couldn't get enough of each other. Sleep and work were the only variables to interrupt that sprawling week of getting to know you. You were almost as good in bed as you perceived yourself to be, too. But I remember that your ex had a thing for pillows, so I suppose (next to that competition), that anybody would look like

Cleopatra. I dropped every friend, speaking engagement, and obligation I had just to see you, and you did the same. Not that you actually <u>do</u> much. Sure, you've got three pretty jobs with pretty pay and pretty hours, but they add up to about 15 hours in, don't they? And but of course there was the overblown beauty school that you were attending your last semester at. You slept with your (married) English Professor, so you didn't really need to attend every class. He was married, if I remember. I got to meet your friends and do the things you wanted to do. I got to watch you sing Karaoke at a dive bar and shake your tits at the crowd, blowing kisses at the drunks. I didn't mind, I thought it was cute. Always in need of an audience, darling. Daddy was a musician, so I guess that's how he raised you. I'd venture that you blew your way into radio so you could be sort of a musical person yourself. There are a lot of barnacles in circles of creativity (who have none), like for example Sandra Bernhard, Bette Midler, Traci Lords, or Ethan Hawke. They do a lot of things, but they don't seem to *do* much of anything. Rather, they have a lot of projects, but none of them have any substance. Mostly women. Is that a coincidence? Should I cite that? Your friends all played up to your behavior; they allowed you to be the Karaoke superstar you know you are at all times, whether we were at your house, out having coffee, or anywhere else. You hung on me like I was a set of monkey bars on a playground whenever we went out, as if I was going to float away on you. I was happy for a while there, and I just may have. And you liked to talk. Especially afterwards. You could blather on about yourself indefinitely. There were times, in conversation, when I noticed that it didn't matter if I was responding to what you were saying, or even listening. That's pretty amusing in retrospect. You were like that space shuttle launch you were so high and mighty about going to for your job: loudly blustering away on a set course. "I met James Cameron", you dropped over the phone. Good for you, baby! Maybe if you meet enough famous people, you just might evolve into someone who.......meets famous people! Is that what you saw me as? "I met Lenny Kravitz", is what you told my best friend within five minutes of meeting her. Is that why your rhyme schemes are either terrible and trite, or nonexistent? I wish we had Christmas to spend together. I could buy you a rhyming dictionary. Do you up your popularity when you float about the in crowd, babe? Then we went out for your Big Birthday Night, so you could have and do everything your heart desired. Actually, that's how you always wanted things, wasn't it? We talked about your ex-boyfriend over lamb chops, and how much better your friends liked me rather than him. I didn't think I needed an approval rate up until that point. Most people who have lived one or two dozen years know enough not to babble about ex-lovers during a romantic dinner out, but I guess you were too into your own unique, womanly, quirky creative flux, weren't you? That's one of the two thousand annoying things about you that I overlooked. I thought (pompously) that you might become a better writer, that I'd get to be a better writer as a result of our pairing. I was wrong. I'm just a bit more cynical. I was an idiot for getting involved with someone five years younger than me. Call it a character flaw, if you know what that is. Go look it up between your dark room work, your radio dj spots, your hectic one-speaking engagement every 2 months schedule. Whoops! I forgot. You slept with the co-host at one of the open mics. For the sake of teaching him a lesson, right? And you despise your friend Erica for doing the same things you do, for latching onto local 'talent'. Forget going through the looking glass, try looking at the looking glass, gorgeous. The second week, though. I went out for drinks with someone and you were certain that I'd behave myself. I did. I'm a one-woman man, for the most part, and you're a one woman-woman. As for guys, though, well, you really couldn't care about fidelity. You're too busy lying to everyone in a five mile radius to 'fess up for even something so inconsequential as where you went after school. I was nervous about cheating after hearing your torrid stories, but I trusted you. I didn't want to be one of those controlling boyfriends who show up on your doorstep if you don't call them back instantaneously. I tried really hard with you. Tried not to do all of the things that usually destroy a good starting relationship scenario. And it still didn't work. But it's not my fault. You're wrecked in the head. I could tell at your family birthday party, when I noticed, coincidentially, that every woman in the family had a big mouth and nothing interesting to say with it. And a short fuse. I was hoping you were the recessive gene. Wrong again. You're the dominant one. Aside from your violent fantasies that I refused to play along with in bed. I may be experimental, but even I'll only go so far. Maybe it's a dj thing. I don't know and really couldn't care. Such nice parents and you still turned out the way you did. I know Catholic girls end up being the biggest freaks to walk the earth, so I'm sure it's got something to do with that. Maybe it's one of those high school remniscent popularity things that I never quite got, where you wish you were one of the cheerleaders, or the main star during the school play. I like figuring lovers out. I can't believe I bought a Britney Spears CD because of you, you bitch! And speaking of love, who drops the L-bomb after two weeks with anyone? You told me you loved me, and it made me a bit nervous. You also told me some time before that, bragging really, about how well you lied to your parents and your friends on a regular basis because it was easier than having to face a momentary conflict, but you didn't really say it in such a way. Honesty was a big stumbling block for you. You were too busy being fabulous to let me see the really vicious side of you until you couldn't hold her back anymore. It was nice for a day or three after you told me you loved me. Displaced emotions, perhaps? I went along with it, though, even though I didn't feel it. And then when I put up some resistance, didn't give you everything under the sun for one split second, and it was over. The moment I emailed and complained about your inconsistencies, your capacity to make plans and break them at the last minute, you tweaked. Went from lady to bitch in about 2.5 seconds. And I just figured, if that's the way she's going to act during our first fight, then it might as well be the last, too. You were proud of all the guys you ruined in your wake. It's not going to happen with me. I've had better, and I've had worse, and three weeks just isn't enough time in to inflict any damage. I'm over you after three days, princess. You're a ghost of a memory. Like dead radio air. The really poetic (or so we're told) pause between stanzas in a beat poem. Or the haze in the background from a grainy black and white photograph. It does take a severe effort to pen your libidinous tell-alls, though. I was always better at foot notes.

The Stigmata of Exorcist 3

Ask someone what their favorite horror film (note that I said horror film, not scary movie) is, and odds are about 3 billion to one that they'll say anything but *The Exorcist 3*. A lot of people haven't even seen it. In the wake of all the special edition hoopla from the first film (as well as the terrible taste that the second film leaves in your mouth), let me explain why the third time is an absolute charm.

From a psychological level, the first movie does nothing for me. When I was ten years old, the edited-for-tv version scared the bejesus out of me. I couldn't sleep that night, and I almost horked up some pea soup of my own. But I'm not twelve anymore. That whole defamation of innocence ploy just doesn't affect me. It's been done. Granted, the first film was very well executed, but every trilogy has a strong point and a weak link in the chain. The Exorcist was neither. It was just there.

The second film was a classic, textbook reason why sequels shouldn't be made. It was a shameless knock off that was rotten for so many reasons that the mind stammers trying to name them all. For space constraints, I won't even attempt to. Let's just say that a year's supply of locusts are not necessarily all of the elements you need to terrify people. The second film didn't follow any of the books written in this series, so it was essentially worthless. This is why it's not your fault if you haven't seen the last installment of the series. You didn't know (after a decade) that the third one, ironically, would be the most chilling and supernatural portrayal of the MacNeal exorcism case studies. How could you know?

I rented it when I was 16, and after watching it for the first time, I couldn't leave the house to sneak a cigarette. There is a world of difference between a good spook and a movie that frightens the living shit out of you. *Exorcist 3* does just that. I was Catholic for half of my life, so that helped. William Peter Blatty (the author of the books and a former Jesuit Priest) directed *3*, and he knows how to flash all the iconography; the opening, bleeding eyes of Christ on the cross, a stream of blood running out onto the floor from a confessional box, a solemn statue of a saint transforming into a grinning, diabolical sinner in one stroke of lightning, Rosary beads cascading down into a complete vacuum of darkness, and the peeling, burning skin of a priest who's fused to a ceiling during the thoroughly vicious end game. I'm teasing. Perhaps you want the plot.

Exorcist 3 was released in 1990. Brad Douriff (One Flew Over The Cuckoo's Nest, Child's Play, X-files) plays the part of The Gemini Killer, a malicious spirit who cut a deal with Satan and came back from the dead in the body of Damien Karras, the self-same priest who sacrificed his life for that possessed kid in the first movie, and subsequently took a spill down a flight of stairs. George C. Scott (Patton, Dr. Strangelove) plays Lieutenant Bill Kinderman, the detective who worked the case of the MacNeal brat, who somehow gets dragged right back into all of the old and ugly business. A rash of bizarre killings are taking place in Georgetown, Washington, and he's on the case.

A small boy is crucified with a pair of rowing oars, with gold ingots driven into his eyes and his face painted up like a clown. A priest is murdered. Then another one. The modus operandi leads Bill to believe that the Gemini Killer is back in action. Only one problem: the Gemini Killer's been dead for 20 years. After investigating the murder of his close comrade Father Joseph Dyer (cute last name) in a hospital, Kinderman stumbles past the cell of a lunatic who bears more than a passing resemblance to Damien Karras. The asylum doctor commits suicide in his office, and Kinderman examines the inmate.

About an hour into the film, we get into eye candy. Half of the film takes place inside the asylum cell with Kinderman and the Gemini Killer. Their conversations make up some of the greatest horror dialogue I've ever come across (and I've seen my share, believe me). Brad Dourif came into his own with this movie. His maniacal eyes glisten during the gloating psychotic rants he delivers directly to the camera. He portrays the pure embodiment of evil and mischievous homicidal tendencies. The fact that all of the monologues are delivered inside of a straight jacket makes his performance that much more difficult, and that much more amazing in spite of it. Watching the scenes time and again, I wonder how the film would go over as a stage play with the limited surroundings. That's the test of any good dialogue, I suppose.

George C. Scott certainly pulls his own weight, as well. A cynical, emphysemic lieutenant who was under the impression that he'd seen everything, his final climactic speech comes across swimmingly as he's pinned against the asylum wall, asked to give a dissertation on unbelief: "I believe in death, I believe in murder. I believe in ugliness, and corruption, and every crawling putrid stink, you son of a bitch!" It's a shame that one of his last great performances went unrewarded.

After rereading Blatty's novels (*The Exorcist* and *Legion*), one comes to the conclusion that , like any test of faith, the books and the films are meant to 1)scare the hell out of you, 2)raise questions concerning faith and theology and 3) strengthen our own beliefs and attitudes toward a greater power (or, as Kinderman puts it, "some cosmic Billy Burke, traipsing about the universe). The *Exorcist 3* passes with flying colors. The fright-core in these movies is the unmitigated proof that demonic possession is a real occurrence, and that maybe exorcisms are one of the only supernatural miracles that take place these days. I certainly can't think of a phenomenon more persistent or dazzling in it's intensity. Stigmata can be disproven. The appearance of Jesus in someone's potato salad in Nebraska can be chalked up as a hoax. But the fact that the Catholic church has a chapter dealing with the Rites of Exorcism, that they're still practiced around the world today cannot. William Peter Blatty is a genius. His directorial debut (as well as his books and screenplays) with Exorcist 3 is proof enough. I'm a dark believer.

fallen from grace,
Tom Waters

gem

fiery black widow
deliciously spinning her
silken seductions

auburn optimist
emerald-eyed girl (candid)
cherish precious youth

like a natural
force, your sweetness diffuses
any acidic mood

confessional night
trading wounds and other stray
milestones, communing

moments overpowered
by what a rare,wonderful
person you are

shannon she told me
conjures unattainable
beauty with her strength

diatribes deftly
delivered impulsively
our soliloquies

dodging diamond
operating under more
than men's surfaces

word universes
she's simply captivating
sharing histories

endearing, quirky
certainly, she wasn't born
yesterday; blushing

my heart doesn't
always do what my mind tells
it to...stoic truths

cloaked in a keyboard
a somewhat candid candor
anonymity....

~BURST~

id ego superego, psychosomatic, melodramatic, autocratic, democratic, dynamic/static, overemphatic, neurologic, heuristic, hierarchic, a priori, empirical, emphatical, hysterical, clerical, subconscious, collective unconscious, detached conscience, salient presence, federal, state, judicial, official, statute, astute, polygamous polyglottal philanthropy, catastrophe, entropy, sympathy, enforcing, horsing, desensitize, prioritize, maximize, downsize, curly, larry, moe, commercial arthouse, honest politician, competent statician, revealing magician, safe nuclear fission, industrial commercial technocratic, bureaucratic capitalist, communist, divine right, second sight, buddhist, monogamist, misogynist, androgynous, generation economic trading gap, misanthropic philosophic multimedia mogul, f-stop focal point, fast food burger joints, retail wholesale mandate merchandising, sentimental retro advertising, postal, union, brotherhood masons, red falcon bald eagle public relations, pop rock soft techno, visa discover am ex art deco, impressionist, surrealist, realist, optimist, pessimist, make-a-wish, photosynthesis one stop shops, abortion medicare less '50s sock hops, hula twist mambo tango, luxury conversion van harley angles, fiction non-, auto and bio, prenuptial autopsy, assault and battery, information overload, sensory deprivation, hackers encode, floppy hard-drive zip disc cosmos, ion, dendrite, neuronatomic rings of saturn, nasa, nascar, nra, bantam, harper, doubleday, lethargic dramaturgical method, symptomatic synaptic firing, evolution cannibal hard-wiring, black whole alternate parallel realms, fashion glamor, luster cluster galaxies, silicone, silicon, dvd fantasies, ambivalent, ambiguous, arbitrary rule, centimeter decimeter millimeter fools, legislate, participate, make your fate, hydroelectric, nickel cadmium eclectic heat lightning, homeowner, fire, theft, life's trampoline kiting, hetero bi transexual, threeway triangle ineffectual, divorce remorse and nuclear extended, piston, battery, solar powered, polar bear clubs and scattered showers, old folk's home, great unknown, hospital church school and bones, construction destruction implosion erosion, fiber optic psychic advice at the touch of a tone, this house is not a home, flight path thruway docking bay, continental peninsula sinkhole, orange rose and superbowl, nba cia nbc, free associated calliope, tai kwon kung fu akido defense, eastern western german fence, the great wall of mao, confucius tao, terroristic narcissistic mystic iced tea, snapple lipton fluid aristocracies, mad cow epidemic hiv halitosis scare, new york times, usa today, breakfast table fare, victorian lazy boy easy straight height chairs, 8 track back track potato sack slack, vhs beta 8 millimeter glock sawed off black market heaters, nabisco general dystrophy, meningitis, arthritis, archetype, prototype, superhype, icon siphon embezzle mettle, elementary, secondary, md., phd. manufacture, vivisection, birth protection, elemental, monumental, accidental, maxillofacial rhinoplasty, liposucted dynasty, republic privatized personalized checks, lock stock barrel savings and loan, infrastruced compacted concave -in monsoon, broadway 3-act play, feline canine serpentine shoe shine wrinkle in time, vaudeville nashville tennessee still, psychotropic, anesthetic, inhibitor pills, think global act natural, fuzzy factual boundaries, combusting sociologies...

gray

dreaming and daylight caving in
juggling virtues with cardinal sins

outposts with no dividing lines
goals with no providing fines

eyelid backdrops or just before dusk
the hairpin difference between curse and luck

like shooting clay pigeons
before the trigger twitch
like remembering to scratch
where one never had an itch

semicolons, these;
that punctuate our breaths
thoughtful pauses, tiny deaths

some misguided directions
that lend to the rest of a map

a sun drunk contented kitten
beaming while curling to nap

dead air crackling on a mute tv
stop light reflections and executive keys

smoke colored glass, these undefined eras
a tiny smudge in a house of mirrors

one wonders whence
and when they might come
or when they'll depart
once the tracks are laid down

a weathervane without a brain
a windmill without a gust
from the four corners.......

the distance between a and b
is up to you or me

honor and its intentions
                    like so many paper swans
pushed by the elements from one end of the pond to another

forgotten and novel, shiftless and brittle from a blind sun
        the swans take a life of their own

love
(or it's many disguises)
a famished and ugly duckling

not sure whom to trust anymore, snapping and running
smart enough for suspicion

passion is the child who collapses after a day on the playground
dizzy with every fresh adventure
sleeping sometimes forever

greed like a poisonous thorn
slipping softly through sun drenched open fields
overgrown and undetected

and trails of neglect
ghosts of ambition
faded and lost in the undergrowth

the whisper of the river
constant and diligent
calming and tempestuous
wearing away

time makes fools of us all
                -eventually.

wind-fall

the love you occupy
champions the moon, the stars, and the clouds of a black night
(slipping past like thieves in velvet)
each day a different fascination
each month, my spangled obsession
perennial beauty, dazzling goddess
suffering diamond, smile amiss
craters and flecks of insufferable helplessness
falling endlessly without cease every time i meet your gaze
passing in the darkness
fleeting through the uncertain days
stripping me raw with your voice
my only infallable vice
my heart is
plagued
with memories of you(s)
a thousand different windy days
a million romantic rainbow hues
consoling, confiding, torturing, deriding
the source of my pain
the answer to my prayers
totem to all i've suffered
bane to what peace i may find
first start sweet heart
varsity focus
young adult mirror sage
voice of reason and random impulse precipice
everything i want
the best of which i should never tamper with
what love i contain
could very well be you
or a sideways glance at an indifferent
yellow disc
gliding through the sky
constant and distant, perfect and full of imperfections
fertile yet cold
wonderful, horrible, and fantastic
my heart the sum of our conflicts
compelling,
magnetic

activity

——>>> ====*I love you so much*
i can barely [contain] it
a neural impulse
chain lightning
                kinetic whiplash
rippling from an adolescent
point of origin
and racing under the
                        skin
running point
reaching the ground
        off........
    lifting
then
before the
            (thought)
                    of it arrives
a blaze of cobalt
            shedding skin
                        flourish of
electric ecstasy
            whenever
you're-with-me
every day
every minute;
and with each sacred   ~breath~
a lifetime   of   happiness

in a different hug

a smile that shames the heavens

and each clock-stopping, heart-tugging kiss=>>
————————————————————Kismet
a rose is just a rose

crumbling, fading
struggling to hold strong

dried and tired
slumping toward the sunlight for guidance
doomed to inevitable circumstance

saturday night specials & sunday drivers
steadied scales & readied stingers

pastel expectations, willing invitations
stop-clock tempers & shower singing

a rose is withered

battered by elements
pulsing velvet and drained of a certain flush
awkward thorns, stunted trophy
simply for the purpose of
fleeting atrophy

neglect like a tulip
in the back of a flower box
despairing of hydrangeas
springing up wild and
punch-drunk
chrysanthemum sadness
heavy with the weight

lily of the valley
white
    and oh so sick
        of this conflict of fate   ((((((faith

a rose is eternal

gone but not forever
peeking through the darkness
seeking out a second spring
in it's step
reaching towards the impossible
pushing above
to the inevitable

blonde obsession

catastrophically
jubilant; my loftiest
aspiration-you

bruises & baggage
both, inextricably drawn
afterthought of choice

Was it moments or months since we met? It would be easier to tally ballroom angels on a push pin, as clocks are a quirk when i'm with you. A lifetime of all of the reasonable happiness I could ever *pray* for flashes before my eyes every time they dance with yours, and second hands fade away like rumpled childhood hand-me-downs. The grandfather clocks and pocket watches of the workaday world never stood a chance next to you. No one stood a chance. I've spent the tail of a century on your adoration, and for once, fortune has turned up her lips to smile upon us. Once upon a time is all I'll ever need in this charmed territory between dream, fantasy, and reality, as well as all I'd wish for, just as you're the reason I'm grateful, the justification for the flickering myth of Soulmates, and EveryGirl, Everything i will ever want. How foolish to think that my heart could pick up the beat after a decade and a half when you stop metronomes dead in their tracks. We merged in a time

(out)

of time, when want became law and emotions could no longer abide. Whenever we curl up in each others arms i want to burrow into your skin and evaporate, my soul soaring around chuckling and sighing inside of you when you need me the most. I see a stranger coming out of the mirror after every visitation with you, and i can tell we'll all get along famously. You demolished whatever i thought love once was the instant we kissed, and showed me what a rare and fragile and impossible creature it really is. i *adore* you for the child you were, *worship* you for the woman you are, and *love* you dearly and uncontrollably for who you'll become, whoever she is. In the moment we've locked ourselves away in, this romantic loop i adamantly object to leaving. No storybook fairytale equals the shimmering reflection the two of us cast across a calm and moonlit pond, and i wouldn't choose one even if it did. *i love you* more than my first and last breath, Jennifer. 11/26/99

trinket

(secretive)
smirking
seductive young girl
dark &
frowning
puzzling pearl
eyes of compassion
lips like obsession
such
blind-sided, wayward
fierce infatuation

little night puzzle
endlessly wonders
bittersweet looks

full of inverted chance
& envied hope
your passive silence
filling my ears
mulling the world over
until it
soothes you

a polished black charm

                           in a whirlwind

of noise
     twinkling
magical
     smiling
     ~poise.~

critical

a gorgeous delusion
i hope
never fades

amazing compulsion
devouring my senses

wholesome provocation   masochistic sweetness
a deja vu
making me
            wonder
                        if indeed
i've ever known
-insatiable
-infatuated
endeared to you

blue smoke in a shaft of sun
woven clothe over unsteady hands
of this i am certain:
nothing's worth fighting for
anymore   ....that can't be lost
maybe love
        inspires
fear
wishing you were
(here next to me)   (mine)
praying that i can   .
            keep a cosmos at bay
+ hibernate
      behind your eyelids
i don't care anymore
-for trivialities
-ships that go bump
            in tired clubs
in the night
it took a jolt
to a dull temporal lobe
a sudden flash*
mystical moment

stretched by the course of you   to see
what a fool
i am

sweetheart
            &
                    sociopath
schoolgirl   or   savage force
whatever i've done
whomever i've claimed
or tried
denied being
has been forgotten

selfish to be so happy
selfless to
        fuse with you
entirely
a shock
connecting so soon
red pulses   of monogomy
the more i discover
                about you
-the faster i plummet
-the less i know
and the less it matters
tomorrow's become extinct
other lovers
                a poor example
just to share

-that second-
                ....spanning between us.................
some foreign landscape
that never existed
the microcosm we created
i would pawn my soul
a million times
before hesitating;
-whatever you do to me

is
willing,
wonderful misery

miracle girl
with her heart stitched in lace
mood ring bangs
and teenage malaise
bittersweet tears
on a nest of pillows
hopeful ideals
in a storm of derision
lighting up a room
with her subtle grace
aching to nuzzle
my lips to her lidded face
a woman inside a child
a laugh
billowed in sorrow
dreaming of her hold
holding
                              her;
intangible siren
captive joy
kind like
an
autumn gust
cradling leaves in it's wake
a gorgeous amalgam
a foregone conclusion
gazing escape
lying solution
elegantly
wishing for catastrophe
as soon as we met
i was lost and taken

with
you
will always be a part of me.

reverie

A weary shapeshifter
looking for a form
a person that would please you
some chiseled man forlorn
perhaps you aren't right for me
and maybe i'm all wrong
though in this tide of catastrophe
emotions just follow along
ages so close
laughter like a cure
lord only knows
the reasoning behind this pair
compassion
compulsion
and whispered rejections
fusion
friction
compounded affections
what a fix
to fret
over someone whom you've
gathered no matter
of fine details
organic affinity
such a foriegn ideal
forgoing logic
and baffling me
brittle emotions
and sweet beyond others
telling admissions

and sometimes
your smile
all that matters
lithe and feline
soft and sorely missed
to see you again
erases
all traces
of scars long past

a hidden smile
some blooming affections
snaking through the skies
a jeweled doll
in lavenders and fickle passions
adorned like a thousand brides
a somber girl
under paper lanterns
aloft on a cloud of pillows
a brilliant soul
with a hope that burns
immune to being callous
a dazzling gaze
like a millions suns
yet impossible to look away
a sweet siren
and a soothing song
and i swear off a steady shore
forever

Marzipan

You ask me once why i can't commit to someone else when the answer is as plain as day. i told you that i was in love with you and perhaps that didn't make a mark, maybe it's a word like a little sponge candy that's too often about and rarely needed, seldom meant, seldom weighted, scarcely sincere. When i was foolish and brash i'd throw it about and see where it went, fall into it at the drop of a hat and hope that it swept me into deeper things, but perhaps my feelings find me arthritic these days, or maybe it's you that moves me this way, at any rate, i'm paralyzed with this feeling for you, and couldn't be more honest by saying that i won't give all of myself because like it or not i belong to you.......i love you, and it hurts and it heals me and scares me and wakes me from a numb little orbit where control meant so much and an apprehension to pain outweighed a chance to melt into someone else and i can't even remember the last time an intensity of feeling blinded every rational and cursed response from leading me towards

-contentment-

that i could spend days by your side is lost on you. That a sweet laugh or some accidental contact is more than i could ever repay is beyond you. Proclamations of sacrifices misinterpreted, let me put things another way: anything i could do to capture, no, earn your desire i would gladly pursue. i've been cushioned away from feeling for so long that i confused jealousy with pain, possessiveness with union, and force with fate. Maybe it's been an age or two, but i'm hard pressed to imagine anyone i'd gladly spend every waking moment with, any woman i can be myself with, someone so blindingly stunning, so down to earth, so fun and foolish, a comfort to laze about and read the comics on a sunday afternoon with, astoundingly sensual with a heart that belies her size, and tears that finish me. i no longer worry where we go together in this storm; my happiness for a time hinges only in being with you.

~Erosion~

In measures of sadness
We're all of us immortal
    centuries of pain
carving themselves
    into crow's feet
burrowed into our eyes
from a trail
    of tears
Through blooming
brooding
solitudes
the notion of eternity
comes off as a
sentence
rather than a gift
    loves lost or
stolen away
precious friendships
borne away with the wind
this is why children
cannot affect
    a frown
with the ease
    of an old pro
keepsakes, these
wrinkles
calendars of
sorrow
etched through some
shopworn
skin
My guess is forever
is something like
    a sob
        staved off~

linoleum lust (for s)

Time **&** torpid use

    zeal(!)
        or
                stalwart guile

nefarious
                am-al-gam

    # cunning

taut   tawdry

    languish   in   her

vapid   s p a c e   **&**   torment

almost   after   when

come   mean   soon

you

    are
        every

(onyx)

tuft   **&**   **din**

through(out)

        cat-erwaul

Queen City Checkers

red & black,
black & red,
jealous rage
the peace of bed.

back from the brink,
rebounded demise,
burgeoning fame,
in this local disguise.

color blind
as the
tokens bite back,
betraying my confidence
hollering
hack

far too busy
for all your
petty slights
& fool's
penny tragedies.

fiends of friends,
beginning or end,
serendipity finds the
author crouched,

lying in wait for anything   *random*

Defeat
inspiring your melancholy,
watching the children,
chugging along,
in their misanthropic calliopes.

painted into a corner,
& don't you make a charming,
black sheathed mourner,

at the gravesite
of your own ambitions.
Victory
in the oddest squares,
but doesn't this arrive
in more than pairs (?)

Thanks for the false accolades,
drowned in a sea of
your near sighted
admonitions.

Once upon a teen,
you spared me your
bitter
affectations,
and I'll king your ass,
basking in this honest
elation.

god forbid that i spot
your next move,
because success
is four steps away,
and i've got nothing to prove.

10/19/00

~Valerie

sweetly smiling like a cheshire cat;
sharing a dirty joke with herself
and no one else
{imagine that}
~She's
drawing me in
with those vast and
brilliant brown eyes
two seducing galaxies
twinkling with compassion & lies
~Her
hands are investigating
my back or my arms or my cheek bones
soft, quiet, slender fingers
setting off revelatory charges
hugging, caressing, they dance and linger
~Val
laughing, lighting up a room
singing, mugging, barely out of tune
howling, hollering, bantering, sauntering
barely wishing to be alone
~A girl
a lady, a woman, a dream
whispered up through memory
surreal/appeal, enticing or friendly
captive in mind, but briefly
~Seven
poems & seven nights
7 kisses & seven sights
seven wishes that just came true
in the seven seconds that i met you
seven times you came to me
my dear and treasured
Valerie~

tell me
it won't work

in sheer black
& spaghetti straps
whisper
it's impossible
while we're snug together
lying down
swear
that you and me
could never be an item
while waves of your hair
(the color of crayon orange)
break against my cheek
and claim
that you're unsuitable
for any kind
of involvement
between a volley of liquid kisses
claim me with
powder-blue eyes
shame me
in my arms
save me
in conversations that never want to end
tell me it won't work

& i'll tell you
in a life full of miracles
taken for granted
in a world of surprises
often forgotten
i hope
that you're wrong.